T0319789

Smart Transport Networks

NECTAR SERIES ON TRANSPORTATION AND COMMUNICATIONS NETWORKS RESEARCH

Series Editor: Aura Reggiani, *Professor of Economic Policy, University of Bologna, Italy*

NECTAR (Network on European Communications and Transport Activities Research) is an international scientific, interdisciplinary association with a network culture. Its primary objective is to foster research collaboration and the exchange of information between experts in the fields of transport, communication and mobility.

NECTAR members study the behaviour of individuals, groups and governments within a spatial framework. They bring a wide variety of perspectives to analyse the challenges facing transport and communication, and the impact these challenges have on society at all levels of spatial aggregation.

This series acts as a companion to, and an expansion of, activities of NECTAR. The volumes in the series are broad in their scope with the intention of disseminating some of the work of the association. The contributions come from all parts of the world and the range of topics covered is extensive, reflecting the breadth and continuously changing nature of issues that confront researchers and practitioners involved in spatial and transport analysis.

Titles in the series include:

Smart Transport Networks

Market Structure, Sustainability and Decision Making

Edited by

Thomas Vanoutrive

University of Antwerp, Belgium

and

Ann Verhetsel

University of Antwerp, Belgium

NECTAR SERIES ON TRANSPORTATION AND
COMMUNICATIONS NETWORKS RESEARCH

Edward Elgar

Cheltenham, UK • Northampton, MA, USA

Published by
Edward Elgar Publishing Limited
The Lypiatts
15 Lansdown Road
Cheltenham
Glos GL50 2JA
UK

Edward Elgar Publishing, Inc.
William Pratt House
9 Dewey Court
Northampton
Massachusetts 01060
USA

A catalogue record for this book
is available from the British Library

Library of Congress Control Number: 2013936186

This book is available electronically in the ElgarOnline.com
Economics Subject Collection, E-ISBN 978 1 78254 833 1

ISBN 978 1 78254 832 4

Typeset by Servis Filmsetting Ltd, Stockport, Cheshire
Printed and bound in Great Britain by T.J. International Ltd, Padstow

Contents

v

Contributors

Brien Benson, Center for Transportation and Economic Development, School of Public Policy, George Mason University, USA.

Kenneth Button, Center for Transportation, Policy, Operations, and Logistics, School of Public Policy, George Mason University, USA.

Gamze Dane, Urban Planning Group, Eindhoven University of Technology, The Netherlands.

Juan Carlos García-Palomares, Departamento de Geografía Humana, Universidad Complutense de Madrid, Spain.

Harry Geerlings, Erasmus University Rotterdam; Erasmus Smart Port Rotterdam, The Netherlands.

Regine Gerike, Institute for Transport Studies, University of Natural Resources and Life Sciences Vienna, Austria.

Javier Gutiérrez, Departamento de Geografía Humana, Universidad Complutense de Madrid, Spain.

Friederike Hülsmann, Chair of Traffic Engineering and Control, Technische Universität München, Germany.

Fedele Iannone, Department of Economics and Quantitative Methods (DIEM), Faculty of Economics, University of Genoa, Italy.

Mona Kashiha, Department of Geography and Earth Sciences, University of North Carolina at Charlotte, USA.

Benjamin Kickhöfer, Transport Systems Planning and Transport Telematics, Technische Universität Berlin, Germany.

Bart Kuipers, Erasmus University Rotterdam; Erasmus Smart Port Rotterdam, The Netherlands.

Cathy Macharis, MOSI-T and MOBI, Vrije Universiteit Brussel, Belgium.

Juan Carlos Martín, Departamento de Análisis Económico Aplicado, Universidad de Las Palmas de Gran Canaria, Canary Islands.

Hilde Meersman, Department of Transport and Regional Economics, University of Antwerp, Belgium.

Kai Nagel, Transport Systems Planning and Transport Telematics, Technische Universität Berlin, Germany.

Peter Nijkamp, Department of Spatial Economics, Vrije Universiteit Amsterdam, The Netherlands.

Piet Rietveld, Department of Spatial Economics, VU University Amsterdam, The Netherlands.

Concepción Román, Departamento de Análisis Económico Aplicado, Universidad de Las Palmas de Gran Canaria, Canary Islands.

Christa Sys, Department of Transport and Regional Economics, University of Antwerp, Belgium.

Jean-Claude Thill, Department of Geography and Earth Sciences, University of North Carolina at Charlotte, USA.

Harry J.P. Timmermans, Urban Planning Group, Eindhoven University of Technology, The Netherlands.

Eddy Van de Voorde, Department of Transport and Regional Economics, University of Antwerp, Belgium.

Thierry Vanelslander, Department of Transport and Regional Economics, University of Antwerp, Belgium.

Thomas Vanoutrive, Department of Transport and Regional Economics, University of Antwerp, Belgium.

Ann Verhetsel, Department of Transport and Regional Economics, University of Antwerp, Belgium.

Dujuan Yang, Urban Planning Group, Eindhoven University of Technology, The Netherlands.

Preface

This book stems from the 2011 NECTAR conference in Antwerp, Belgium. NECTAR is the Network on European Communications and Transport Activities Research. Within this research network different thematic workshops are organised every year and NECTAR organises a major conference every two years. In May 2011 the Department of Transport and Regional Economics (TPR) of the University of Antwerp (Belgium) hosted this conference. We were delighted with the presence of so many transport scholars and with the quality of their presentations. It was a logical decision to remember this conference by means of a book. The NECTAR series offers a well-established framework to publish a selection of interesting work presented at this conference. From a conference with nearly 100 presentations to a book with 11 chapters (plus the introduction) requires several selection rounds and lots of reviewing and refereeing. Throughout the process we received assistance from a wide range of people. First, there are those who form the backbone of the NECTAR network and enabled our department to organise the event. The series editor of the NECTAR series also contributed to this work. Second, we are grateful to the authors who sent their work to us and reviewed chapters of the other authors. In the refereeing process we were also assisted by other scholars whose contribution is not visible in the book. Special thanks goes to Michel Beuthe, Olaf Jonkeren, Jos van Ommeren, Marjan Beelen and Erik Verhoef.

1. Classifying transport studies using three dimensions of society: market structure, sustainability and decision making

Thomas Vanoutrive and Ann Verhetsel

1.1 INTRODUCTION

This introductory chapter is structured around a small content analysis of the chapters in this volume. In line with the title of this volume, three dimensions will be used to classify these texts, (i) market structure, (ii) sustainability and (iii) decision making. Market structure refers to the allocation mechanisms at work. (Environmental) sustainability covers the characteristics of the physical environment, the availability of natural resources and the effects of transport activities (for example, pollution). Lastly, decision making refers to transport policy, that is, the conscious attempts to change the transport system. Since the interactions between these three aspects are many, our classification tool does not subdivide the chapters into three categories, but positions the texts relative to the three aforementioned dimensions.

Some readers will detect traces of the 'triple bottom line' People Planet Profit (People Planet Prosperity; P3) or similar sustainable development slogans. However, we shall argue that the three concepts are deliberately chosen and that our triptych does not necessarily reflect what is understood under P3. A first thing to note is that the three dimensions of transport are qualitatively different. Market structure, environmental sustainability and policy making are different things which cannot be added up or measured using the same scale. Second, one may argue that 'people' should be included in our title, and that it can be summarised as Planet Profit Politics. The reason for this is that the three dimensions are three entry points to describe society and the role of transport therein. Hence, society (People) is situated in the middle of the heuristic and employing three major aspects of society allows us to make an overview of transport

in a general manner. Making of 'people' a distinct category would position society outside the economic system and separate it from the physical
world, which is an unrealistic simplification.

1.2 THE THREE DIMENSIONS: MARKET STRUCTURE, SUSTAINABILITY AND DECISION MAKING

As indicated above, market structure refers to the economy, which is 'a
set of human activities and institutions linked together in the production,
distribution, exchange and consumption of goods and services' (Daniels,
2008, p.294). Transport plays different roles in this system. On the one
hand, transport is a service which can be consumed just like many other
services. On the other, transporting people and goods is a necessary step in
the production and distribution of goods and services. The way transport
is organised and carried out, be it mainly market based or with high levels
of government intervention, is key to understand the role of transport in
society. Policy makers who want to intervene benefit from insight into,
and knowledge of, the forces at work in the transport system. The distribution of power among players in transport markets, the economic relations between different regions, and the vertical and horizontal integration
of firms that offer transport services, must be taken into account when
developing transport policies. This does not mean that market forces are
natural phenomena, they are to a large extent socially constructed, but one
should be aware of the processes that shape the economy. Market structure in its broadest sense also encompasses social equity and exclusion,
issues which are often overlooked in discussions on sustainable (transport)
development (Boschmann and Kwan, 2008).

A too narrow focus on economic activities might, however, result in the
(conceptual) disconnection of economic activities from their materialistic
environmental basis (Gendron, 2003). By using the term (environmental)
sustainability, we include how society makes use of the natural environment. Our environment imposes constraints on human activities and
physical and biological processes influence transport-related decisions
(and vice versa). Uncertain natural environment-related factors that are
relevant for transport include peak oil and constraints on other natural
resources, climate change and health-related aspects (Robèrt, 2009). These
aspects confirm that nature is not external to society and that we must take
into account our social organisation in discussions of the relation between
transport and the environment (Braun, 2006). Both the 'real' physical
processes as well as the socially and politically imposed limits, emission

caps and thresholds are relevant. Furthermore, concepts such as 'carrying capacity' depend on the type of social organisation and have a moral dimension too (Höhler, 2004). In summary, the word 'sustainability' in our title refers to how human beings make use of the natural environment, which interacts with the two other dimensions, policy making and market structure.

A third entry point to study transport is decision making. Policy making has the (analytical) advantage in that it encompasses a wide range of topics and conflicts. Given the broad spectrum of policy domains with a transport dimension, several authors argue in favour of policy integration, notably between land use and transport, and the development of policy packages (Marshall and Banister, 2000; Hull, 2005; Banister, 2008). However, it is not an easy task to resolve contradictions between policy goals as Fol et al. (2007) show in their analysis of programmes that subsidise access to a car for poor households in light of sustainable mobility policies. Furthermore, the task of transport planners is not made easier by the increasing complexity of governance structures with responsibilities dispersed over a multitude of government layers and semi-public and informal institutions (Marsden and Rye, 2010). Sustainability policies in general are also criticised for their often symbolic (Happaerts, 2012) and perhaps non-democratic character (Felli, 2005). The case of cycling fundamentalism shows that sustainable transport programmes can display fundamentalist tendencies (Cupples and Ridley, 2008). Despite the good intentions of most sustainable mobility policies and the ambition to involve the people (Banister, 2008), sustainable transport policies can become elitist and technocratic in nature (Baeten, 2000). Transport policy making is, of course, not restricted to sustainable mobility, but the 'sustainable transport' case shows the complexities of decision making in dealing with a myriad of objectives and interests.

In the discussion above, we presented a basic heuristic which makes use of three entry points to approach our study object, transport. In the remainder of this text, we shall structure the content of this book along the three dimensions, market structure, sustainability and decision making. The first three contributions (after this introductory chapter) are written by established NECTAR scholars.[1] These chapters address the three different – although interrelated – dimensions. Eddy Van de Voorde[2] and co-authors, in Chapter 2, discuss the topic of port competition and they convince us that nothing remains the same. Piet Rietveld, in Chapter 3, presents an interesting view on climate change and draws attention to the fact that there is something besides mitigation, that is, adaptation. It is thus not the 1,000th paper on sustainability and climate change but it offers a fresh perspective which contains inspiration for further research and debate. Ken Button and co-author, in Chapter 4, focus on decision making, in particular on the issue of biased forecasts in transport policy making. In his characteristic up-front style, Button not only criticises current forecasting practices, but also searches for ways of getting better information into our (technical) transport planning and policy implementation.

1.3   A SMALL CONTENT ANALYSIS

We analysed the content of the present volume to reveal the relations between the three first leading chapters (on market structure, sustainability and decision making) and the remaining chapters. Note that this is an exploratory analysis which only gives a rough indication of how to classify the chapters. Our content analysis is based on a small text mining exercise which examines the words and terms used by the authors. We selected a list of terms associated with the three themes and counted the number of times each chapter uses the respective term. Table 1.1 gives an overview

Table 1.1   List of terms used in the content analysis of the chapters

Market structure	Sustainability	Decision making
competition, competitiveness	sustainable	political, politics
market	environment(al)	policy
demand	pollution	decision
supply	climate	society
cost	weather	public
price	renewable	tax
enterprise	resource	institutional
labour	greenhouse gas	programme
capital	emissions	administration
performance	energy	agency
ROI (return on investment)	–	social
turnover	–	private, privatisation
efficiency	–	regulation
company	–	bureaucrats
undertaking	–	government
business	–	authority
merger	–	federal
takeover	–	planner
client	–	consultation
customer	–	accountability
profit	–	–

of the words that were employed in the analysis. Note that, although we analyse word counts, we do not quantify 'market structure', 'sustainability' or 'policy making' itself.

We excluded the acknowledgements, reference lists and footnotes from the analysis and checked whether our search method was sensitive to related words (for example, when searching for the term 'company', the word 'accompanying' must be excluded). For obvious reasons, the introduction was excluded from the analysis (it could only be written after the analysis). We opted to present the results of this analysis in a graphical way and Chapter 10 brought inspiration. Since we have three variables (market structure, sustainability and decision making) we can plot the data in a triangle as presented in Chapter 10. In fact we measured the balance between the three themes. However, since chapters differ in length and fewer search terms are used for some themes (sustainability) than for others, we standardised our measurements and applied three different methods. Note that the only goal of this analysis is to compare the chapters in a relative manner. Since the three dimensions used are not equivalent, no absolute meaning can be given to the results.

A first standardisation method starts with the transformation of the counts into percentages. For example, Chapter 4 contains 226 times a term present in Table 1.1. In this sample of 226 words, 71.2 per cent are decision-making-related terms, 3.5 per cent sustainability-related words and the remaining 25.2 per cent refer to market structure. In the total sample the 'market structure' category is overrepresented. Therefore, the second method standardised the results so that each category had the same share, and in a final step these results were again standardised per author in order to depict the figures in a triangle. This method decreases the overrepresentation of the 'market structure' category. The third method recoded the counts in the raw data. Observations with a value of 0 or 1 kept their value but values of 2 or more were recoded to 3 in order to control for extreme values. Indeed, some chapters use the same term more than 50 times. The counts were then treated the same way as in the second method.

1.4 RESULTS AND CONCLUSIONS

Figure 1.1 shows the results of the content analysis. It confirms that the three first leading chapters each covered a distinct topic. Nevertheless, the authors also employed vocabulary from the two other categories.

Chapters which are positioned in the top of the triangle (Figure 1.1) focus on market structure. Four of these contributions discuss maritime

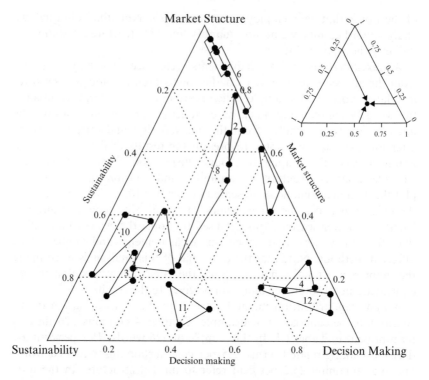

Figure 1.1   Content analysis of the chapters in this volume

and port-related topics, mainly the transport of containers. Van de
Voorde discusses, together with Meersman and Vanelslander, the debated
concept of port competition (Chapter 2), Kashiha and Thill contribute to
the trade and port literature by revealing which goods are shipped from
Europe to the US and via which ports different types of commodities are
shipped (Chapter 5). Sys investigates the market structure of the container liner shipping industry using the persistence of profits framework
(Chapter 6). Iannone's analysis focuses on the hinterland connections
of container ports rather than the maritime ones (Chapter 8). Finally,
García-Palomares, Gutiérrez, Martín and Román show that market structure matters not only for containers but also for passenger transport. They
selected an interesting case to discuss the competition between high-speed
rail and air transport (Chapter 7).

    The more to the left a chapter is depicted in Figure 1.1, the more it
contains sustainability vocabulary. Unsurprisingly Rietveld's ideas on
climate change can be found here (Chapter 3). Kickhöfer, Hülsmann,
Gerike and Nagel show how rising car user costs might influence air

pollutant emissions by its effect on travel demand (Chapter 9). Yang, Dane and Timmermans present an appropriate methodology to model responses (energy-saving adaptation) of consumers to environmental policies (Chapter 10). Geerlings and Kuipers make the bridge to decision making in their work on the management of sustainable mobility which is framed in the transition management literature (Chapter 11).

The two chapters in the bottom-right of the triangle (Figure 1.1) dare to critically discuss decision making. Button and co-author Benson discuss the contentious subject of forecasting and its role in transport policy making (Chapter 4). Last but not least, Macharis and Nijkamp illustrate how the viewpoints of different stakeholders can be taken into account when evaluating transport plans and projects (Chapter 12).

Can we draw conclusions from this small content analysis? Evidently, statistically sound conclusions cannot be drawn, but we believe that it is no coincidence that conferences in port cities have more presentations on port- and maritime-related topics by scholars who themselves are often based in a port city (a fact observed by Pallis et al., 2010). Furthermore, we suppose that sustainability is more widely studied in the Netherlands and Germany. Finally, it can hardly be accidental that authors of chapters on decision making have their base in capital cities. Although one might criticise these preliminary conclusions and the rudimentary character of the content analysis, it offers, nevertheless, a good overview of what you can find in this book. Our heuristic proved to be a useful tool to explore a varied set of contributions.

NOTES

1. These three chapters are based on the keynote speeches given at the 2011 NECTAR Conference (Antwerp, Belgium).
2. Colleagues from abroad were so positive in their evaluation of Van de Voorde's keynote speeches given on the other side of the ocean that his fellow department members encouraged him to give a lecture in his own institute. The resulting lecture was both informative and accessible.

REFERENCES

Baeten, G., 2000. 'The tragedy of the highway: empowerment, disempowerment and the politics of sustainability: discourses and practices', *European Planning Studies* **8**, 69–86.

Banister, D., 2008. 'The sustainable mobility paradigm', *Transport Policy* **15**, 73–80.

Boschmann, E.E. and Kwan, M-P., 2008. 'Toward socially sustainable urban transportation: progress and potentials', *International Journal of Sustainable Transportation* **2**, 138–57.

Braun, B., 2006. 'Towards a new earth and a new humanity: nature, ontology, politics', in: Castree, N. and Gregory, D. (eds), *David Harvey: A Critical Reader*, Oxford and Malden, MA: Blackwell, pp. 191–222.

Cupples, J. and Ridley, E., 2008. 'Towards a heterogeneous environmental responsibility: sustainability and cycling fundamentalism', *Area* **40**, 254–64.

Daniels, P., 2008. 'Geographies of the economy', in: Daniels, P., Bradshaw, M., Shaw, D. and Sidaway, J. (eds), *An Introduction to Human Geography: Issues for the 21st Century* (3rd edn), London: Prentice-Hall, pp. 293–314.

Felli, R., 2005. 'Développement durable et participation: la démocratie introuvable', *Belgeo* **4**, 425–34.

Fol, S., Dupuy, G. and Coutard, O., 2007. 'Transport policy and the car divide in the UK, the US and France: beyond the environmental debate', *International Journal of Urban and Regional Research* **31**, 802–18.

Gendron, C., 2003. 'Business, economy, and the environment: toward a new development paradigm', *Business & Society* **42**, 485–95.

Happaerts, S., 2012. 'Sustainable development and subnational governments: going beyond symbolic politics?', *Environmental Development* **4**, 2–17.

Höhler, S., 2004. '"Carrying capacity" – the moral economy of the "Coming Spaceship Earth"', paper presented at the 4S & EASST Meeting, Paris, 25–28 August.

Hull, A., 2005. 'Integrated transport planning in the UK: from concept to reality', *Journal of Transport Geography* **13**, 318–28.

Marsden, G. and Rye, T., 2010. 'The governance of transport and climate change', *Journal of Transport Geography* **18**, 669–78.

Marshall, S. and Banister, D., 2000. 'Travel reduction strategies: intentions and outcomes', *Transportation Research Part A* **34**, 321–38.

Pallis, A.A., Vitsounis, T.K. and De Langen, P.W., 2010. 'Port economics, policy and management: review of an emerging research field', *Transport Reviews* **30**, 115–61.

Robèrt, M., 2009. 'A model for climate target-oriented planning and monitoring of corporate travel', *International Journal of Sustainable Transportation* **3**, 1–17.

2. Nothing remains the same! Port competition revisited

Hilde Meersman, Eddy Van de Voorde and Thierry Vanelslander

2.1 INTRODUCTION

Science evolves quickly, and transport economics is certainly no exception, as its rapid development over the past decades has shown (Blauwens et al., 2010). Within the field of transport economics, port competition remains an important topic of study (for example, Van de Voorde and Vanelslander, 2010; Ersini et al., 2011; Gaur et al., 2011; Veldman et al., 2011). The amount of research attention it attracts is due to its socio-economic significance: depending on the competitive strength of a port, throughput volumes can be enormous and the impact in terms of industrial investment and employment quite substantial.

Moreover the field of port economics itself has also evolved considerably. In the past, the literature has tended to treat ports as rather homogeneous entities. A good example of this 'old' approach is found in Verhoeff (1981), where ports are considered to compete with one another at different operational levels: within the national territory for goods and investments in additional infrastructure; within the port cluster (that is, a group of ports in each other's vicinity with common geographical characteristics) for a shared hinterland; and within the port range (that is, ports located along the same coastline or largely overlapping hinterlands) for investment and traffic, especially from areas where the spheres of influence of different ranges overlap.

There is no denying, though, that this perspective has become somewhat outmoded. The concept of port competition needs rethinking, for two reasons. First and foremost, it has become increasingly apparent that ports are far from homogeneous entities. In fact they are so strikingly heterogeneous and complex in nature – characterised as they are by a multitude of market players and interrelationships – that a more disaggregated approach than has hitherto been taken clearly imposes itself. For that matter, the competitive struggle is not restricted to ports; in fact it unfolds primarily between producers and service providers who either are located in those ports or rely on them for their business. What is more, in recent years there has been an unmistakable evolution from competition between individual ports to competition between logistics chains. In order to be successful, ports must belong to a successful chain, otherwise they risk being competed out of the market (Meersman and Van de Voorde, 2010).[1]

This chain-based thinking implies a different kind of approach, whereby due account is taken of the various levels of competition, both horizontally and vertically. Each of the actors involved has different goals and a unique set of tools to reach them. One such goal is profit maximisation; another might be attracting the largest possible goods flow. However, port players operate in a dynamic environment, where ever-greater movements of capital have recently led to altered ownership structures.[2] This has been in evidence in the consolidation trend among terminal operating companies (TOCs), whereby the local and national stevedores of the past have increasingly been taken over by international groups. This inevitably raises the question of whether the profits generated by such groups are reinvested locally or channelled to other regions.[3]

Hence, the competitive strength of a port depends not only on its own infrastructure and organisation, but also on a variety of external market forces. The purpose of the present contribution is to explore the nature of port competition and how it has evolved over time. This requires insight into the nature of seaports and, even more so, into the decision processes of all the players involved. Where does the power of decision lie in relation to the choice of route and/or port, shipping company, terminal operator or hinterland mode? Which factors influence these decisions? How do such decisions affect decision making by other players? And which decisions by which actors determine the competitive position of the port in question? Is there a sequence to be discerned in decision making or are certain decisions made quasi-simultaneously? Each of these questions must essentially be considered in the context of individual undertakings before aggregation at a higher level of analysis.

This chapter is structured as follows. The next section defines the notion of a seaport within a logistics chain context. Section 2.3 identifies factors that are relevant to port selection and hence to port competition, and it applies them to a number of ports in the Hamburg–Le Havre range. Section 2.4 considers a number of scenarios of likely and possible developments in port competition. The final section summarises the main findings of this contribution. The focus is on container operations, although many of the conclusions also apply to other commodity types.

2.2   THE PORT AS AN INTEGRAL LINK IN THE LOGISTICS CHAIN

There has been some debate in the literature recently about the most appropriate definition of a seaport. Traditionally, seaports are regarded as gateways for transferring cargo and passengers between vessel and shore. However, this definition is too restrictive, for the sphere of influence of a port extends well beyond its own perimeter, towards both the hinterland and the open sea. This means that large seaports essentially require three elements: maritime access (that is, a suitable coastal location or access channel, as well as sufficient draught), goods-handling capacity,[4] and distributive capacity, including adequate connections with the hinterland.

The port product may be regarded as a chain of interlinking functions, while the port as a whole is in turn a link in the overall logistics chain (Suykens and Van de Voorde, 1998). Hence it is important to attain analytical insight into the roles of the various enterprises that are directly or indirectly involved in port activities.

Port activities are not just about a port authority and terminal operating companies (Coppens et al., 2007). In today's marketplace, many other players and decision makers operate within ports, and indeed within the maritime sector as a whole. These other actors may be roughly divided into two groups: port users and service providers. First and foremost among the port users are the shipping companies. Also belonging to this group are the shippers and industrial enterprises that are established within the port perimeter and have land in concession. The service providers form quite a heterogeneous group: pilots, towage services, agents, forwarders, ship repairers, suppliers of foodstuffs and spare parts, waste reception facilities, bunkerers and maritime insurance companies. Stevedores, who are increasingly evolving into TOCs, constitute a special case. They provide services (for example, transhipment, storage, stripping and stuffing) to shipping companies and shippers, for which they are effectively remunerated. Figure 2.1 represents the principal relationships between the various actors in the logistics chain.[5] It speaks for itself that the importance of these mutual relationships may vary from port to port. Moreover, the relative significance of each of the actors and their relationships may change in the course of time.

As this overview of port players shows, ports are highly heterogeneous environments, involving a diverse set of actors. Hitherto, a clear understanding of the relative importance and the negotiating and market power of each of these actors has been lacking, primarily because of inadequate insight into the nature of their relationships, mutual financial

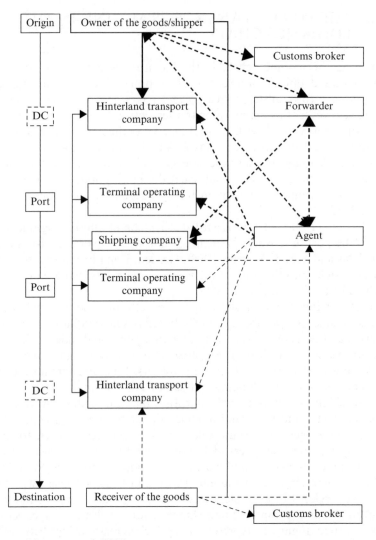

Source: Meersman et al. (2010).

Figure 2.1   The maritime logistics chain and relationships among partners

participations, and, as the case may be, forms of management control. Coppens et al. (2007) have recently shed some new light on these matters.

Figure 2.1 suggests that ports, as economic entities, have evolved considerably. They have become heterogeneous structures, a cluster of different undertakings that contribute to varying degrees to the success of a given port and, at the same time, are directly or indirectly affected by evolutions in the strategic position of that port as well as elements exogenous to the port perimeter. Each decision by an influential port player and/or service provider within the supply chain will set in motion a causal nexus. This can give rise to potential bottlenecks earlier in the chain, which may not be immediately visible, but which ultimately can seriously compromise the competitive status of the port as a whole.

2.3   THE NATURE OF PORT COMPETITION

The nature of port competition has evolved in recent decades from rivalry between (homogeneous) ports to a competitive struggle between supply chains. Back in the 1980s, Verhoeff (1981) distinguished between four levels of port competition: competition between port undertakings; competition between ports; competition between port clusters; and competition between ranges.

The factors influencing competition may vary from level to level. The competitive strength of individual undertakings within a port is determined mainly by the factors of production (labour, capital, technology and energy). Competition between ports, port clusters and port ranges on the other hand is also affected by regional factors, such as the geographical location, the available infrastructure, the degree of industrialisation, government policy, the standard of performance of the port (measured in terms of proxy variables, such as the number and frequency of liner services, and the cost of transhipment, storage and hinterland transportation).

However, this traditional way of seeing port competition has been superseded. It has made way for a viewpoint based on competition between supply chains, in which seaports, and seaport undertakings, are merely links. As the most important consideration is the overall cost of the supply chain, it is inevitable that the most significant factors alongside throughput volumes are the industrial and commercial functions (including warehousing and distribution of goods) and hinterland transportation.

Choosing an appropriate port of call is an interactive and simultaneous process, governed largely by the principles of supply and demand. Demand for port throughput, that is, the choice of port, is a function of a number of well-defined variables: the goods flows (compare the derived nature of transport demand); the distribution between merchant haulage and carrier haulage;[6] the generalised cost associated with the supply chain to which the prospective port of call belongs, including the rates charged by any given port.

Supply is determined by a combination of players who together define the port of call as a product. Each player contributes to the generalised cost of the supply chain. The balance obviously depends largely on supply and demand, and additionally on factors such as third-party cargo, which can ensure that there is sufficient volume to make a port call.

This section further deals with a number of characteristics of supply and demand in port transportation, which are at the same time elements of port competition. Subsection 3.1 will thereby provide generic results, which are applicable to any port globally, whereas the subsequent subsections make applications to the North-European port context.

2.3.1 Decision Making within the Supply Chain

It is crucially important to understand which actors within the supply chain take which decision(s). Additionally, insight is required into which decisions are taken autonomously and which are taken in consequence of or with due consideration to previous decisions, often at a different level. It is thereby important to start from the current supply chain-based organisation of international distribution, with container shipping companies being structured in networks with loops and a limited number of fixed calls per loop and continent. Other actors, such as terminal operators, have developed similar networks. Among ports, so far, similar types of networks do not exist. The public character of most port authorities may be a contributory factor to that.

On the basis of an extensive literature study[7] and own surveys, Aronietis et al. (2010) have drawn up the following list of factors directly or indirectly influencing the selection of a port: out-of-pocket cost; location; port operations' quality and reputation; speed/time; infrastructure and facilities availability; efficiency; frequency of sailings; port information system; hinterland; and congestion. The selection of a transport solution, including mode and operator (for example, a shipping company), is an important decision for the goods owner or the shipper, with or without the involvement of a forwarder. Shipping companies are often also involved in the specification of the supply chain. They often decide through which port the goods are to be shipped. This choice for a port of call depends first and foremost on the availability of cargo, which will in turn depend largely on the geographical location and the size of the hinterland. The latter factor is determined in part by the presence of competing ports. Two further decisions, namely the choice of TOC and the subsequent choice for a hinterland mode and operator, are a direct function of the choice of port. Conversely, the available hinterland options are likely to influence the selection of a port, as obviously once a port has been selected one is limited to the modes and operators on offer. Out-of-pocket expenses are usually the most important consideration in this respect, alongside other aspects, all of which are translatable into monetary units as part of the generalised costs.

To verify the information from their literature study, Aronietis et al. conducted interviews with the executive managers of 35 relevant actors, including shipping companies, terminal operators, logistics groups and European Logistics Centres (ELCs). Among these undertakings were 11 shipping companies that, together, represented 45.7 per cent of the global container shipping fleet. The interviews took place over a two-month period in early 2009.

The relative importance of different port selection criteria was determined on the basis of a list that was presented to the interviewees. They were asked to rank the criteria and to comment on them. In so far as the shipping companies were concerned, the main considerations – in order of importance – were out-of-pocket cost, quality of hinterland transport connections, capacity, reliability, seaport location (coastal versus inland), and the cargo basis. Factors that were considered less important included flexibility, quality of customer service, location within the port (if behind locks), door-to-door shipping time and frequency of feedering. The least important consideration was deemed to be risk of loss or damage.

The shipping companies pointed out that a decision to call at a given port also depends crucially on the availability of cargo to and from that port, which is in turn codetermined by its geographical location and the hinterland it serves. Furthermore, shipping companies tend to favour inland seaports, as this cuts supply-chain costs.

In the evaluation of inland transport services or hinterland transport modes, out-of-pocket cost was deemed by far the most important factor. Other considerations were reliability, frequency of service, flexibility, overall door-to-door shipping time and quality of service. Environmental impact considerations and risk of loss or damage were felt to be of minor importance.

The transport mode or combination of transport modes used tended to depend on the destination served, the value of the goods involved, time restrictions and out-of-pocket cost. The environmental impact of the modes appears to have gained in significance as a decision factor, primarily in consequence of government policies in respect of the internalisation of external costs.

2.3.2 Assessment of Five Ports

The respondents were also asked to assess five ports for a given set of port selection criteria. The response scale ranged from 1 (very poor) to 5 (very

Table 2.1   Scores of selected ports on principal selection variables

	Felixstowe	Zeebrugge	Antwerp	Hamburg	Le Havre
Out-of-pocket cost	3.2 (2–4)	4.0 (3–5)	4.4 (3–5)	3.4 (3–4)	3.1 (1–4)
Hinterland connections	3.4 (3–4)	3.3 (2–4)	4.5 (4–5)	4.4 (4–5)	3.6 (2–4)
Port capacity	2.7 (1–4)	4.3 (3–5)	4.6 (4–5)	3.7 (2–5)	4.4 (4–5)
Reliability	3.0 (2–4)	4.3 (4–5)	4.5 (4–5)	4.1 (3–5)	2.4 (2–4)
Port location	3.2 (2–4)	3.4 (2–4)	4.2 (3–5)	4.4 (3–5)	3.8 (2–5)
Cargo basis	3.4 (1–4)	3.1 (2–5)	4.4 (3–5)	4.2 (3–5)	3.3 (2–4)
Flexibility	3.0 (2–5)	4.0 (3–5)	4.5 (4–5)	3.8 (2–5)	2.4 (1–3)
Customer service	3.5 (3–5)	3.8 (3–5)	4.2 (3–5)	3.9 (3–5)	3.1 (2–5)
Frequency	2.7 (1–4)	2.9 (2–4)	3.4 (2–5)	4.8 (4–5)	2.6 (1–4)
Risk of loss or damage	4.0 (2–5)	4.4 (4–5)	4.8 (4–5)	4.6 (4–5)	4.3 (2–5)
Customs services	3.6 (2–5)	3.4 (3–4)	3.0 (2–4)	3.9 (3–5)	2.9 (2–4)

Source: Aronietis et al. (2010).

good). The set of seaports was deliberately composed of diverse ports in terms of size as well as origin and destination of the goods flows involved, in order to attain as wide a coverage as possible.

For most criteria, Antwerp scored the highest among the five ports (Table 2.1).[8] The greatest degree of diversity was recorded in relation to the most important criterion, that is, out-of-pocket cost. Le Havre was deemed to perform poorly in terms of reliability and flexibility, due to a state of social instability and frequent industrial disputes. A number of shipping companies even indicated that this had been among the most important considerations in their decision to discontinue calling at Le Havre. Inadequacy of hinterland connections was specified as a concern for Felixstowe, Zeebrugge and Le Havre. Throughput capacity at Felixstowe was also assessed as problematic.

2.3.3   Assessment of Capacity Interventions

The shipping companies were also asked to assess planned or current infrastructure improvement works in the five ports under consideration. Hinterland connection capacity turns out to be the second most important port call decision factor, whereas port capacity itself is the third most important factor. The investment projects considered are given in Table 2.2.

On the whole, the investment projects were assessed positively, but the

Table 2.2 Principal infrastructure investment projects in the five selected ports

Port	Investment projects
Felixstowe	Improved rail connectivity
Zeebrugge	Increased quay length at various terminals + new terminal (3 million extra TEU); new lock; development of a logistics zone; new marshalling yard
Antwerp	Completion of Deurganck dock (3 million extra TEU); new intermodal terminal; deepening of the Scheldt river
Hamburg	Terminal extension: 10 million extra TEU by 2010
Le Havre	Logistics zone and multimodal platform for rail and inland navigation (capacity of 4.2 million TEU)

Source: Port authorities.

respondents did make certain comments or suggestions. The development of better rail connections at Felixstowe was assessed favourably, considering the problematic nature of current connectivity. Zeebrugge was praised for the planned lengthening of the quays, the development of a logistics zone and the rail infrastructure improvement work. A number of shipping companies indicated that they were considering Zeebrugge as an operational hub for future activities.

In so far as Antwerp was concerned, the respondents found the plan to deepen the Scheldt to be crucially important. These works have since been concluded. Hamburg's plans to extend terminals were also assessed positively, as the port's capacity was found to be inadequate. The respondents also indicated that Hamburg needs to dredge its access channel, in order that the port could receive new, larger generations of vessels. With regard to Le Havre, hinterland connectivity was singled out as a focal area for future investment. It was felt that railway and inland navigation connections with Paris needed improving. The promotion of inland navigation to Strasbourg was also deemed relevant. The proposed improvements were assessed positively. Mention was made of the fact that Le Havre has no maritime capacity problems.

2.3.4 Assessment of Hinterland Transport Modes

The respondents from shipping companies were asked to assess the expected future quality of hinterland transport modes, given the current state and the expected policy developments and investment plans. Table 2.3 summarises their responses, which are overall evaluations starting from

Table 2.3   Assessment of hinterland transport modes

	Road	Rail	Intermodal (incl. SSS and inland navigation)
Reliability	3.90	3.56	4.40
Flexibility	4.64	2.44	3.50
Risk of loss or damage	3.50	3.67	3.80
Frequency	4.70	3.44	3.75
Out-of-pocket cost	3.40	3.33	4.30
Total door-to-door shipping time	4.09	3.28	3.50
Customer service	4.10	2.67	3.70
Environmental impact	1.90	4.00	3.90

Note: SSS = short sea shipping.

Source: Aronietis et al. (2010).

Table 2.4   Weighted average port scores

Port	Weighted average score
Antwerp	4.35
Hamburg	4.02
Zeebrugge	3.73
Le Havre	3.26
Felixstowe	3.14

Source: Aronietis et al. (2010).

the range ports considered.[9] Somewhat surprisingly, expectations for intermodal transport were higher than those for either road haulage or rail freight, particularly in terms of out-of-pocket cost and reliability.

The common perception of a low future out-of-pocket cost and good quality of service in the case of rail freight and a poor environmental impact of road haulage was confirmed in the interviews.

2.3.5   Relationship between Port Size and Performance

The generalised scores of the various seaports on the port selection criteria can be related to port size. Previously, Table 2.1 reported the scores of the seaports on each of the selected criteria. Table 2.4 takes due account of the relative importance of the various criteria, as revealed during the interviews, so that the scores it gives are effectively weighted average scores.

Source: Aronietis et al. (2010).

Figure 2.2   Comparison of port performances

These scores can in turn be used to compare the competitive strength of the five ports. Figure 2.2 shows that the ports of Antwerp and Hamburg achieve the highest scores. Zeebrugge obtains an average score, while Le Havre and Felixstowe score lower.

The comparison of port performances indicates that the ports with a larger turnover value are assessed most positively by the shipping companies interviewed. It is also apparent that a good score on the criteria considered is no guarantee for a larger market share: the latter is true for Zeebrugge as compared to Felixstowe and Le Havre.

Although the above results provide an important indication, it should also be noted that what they reflect is essentially a form of stated preference. Obviously, the port-related out-of-pocket cost is an important consideration, but what is its weight in the total supply chain? Time management is clearly also crucial, but to what extent is there a trade-off with out-of-pocket cost? There is an urgent need for a quantification – within a logistics chain perspective – of all of these decision variables. Individual decision variables have already been analysed for separate actors in the scattered literature (see, for example, Ben-Akiva et al., 2010; Tavasszy and Combes, 2010). At that point, it will be possible to take explicit account of the specific business strategy for each actor, irrespective of whether it is founded on generalised cost minimisation, maximisation of market share, or profit maximisation. Ultimately, then, the decision process can be reduced to a single variable, that is, the generalised cost, whereby due account must also be taken of the time cost and the value of time, and, as the case may be, external costs. This may serve as a starting point for further research.

2.4   COMPETITION-AFFECTING VARIABLES

Port competition is an extremely dynamic phenomenon. The competitive process, including the choice of port, is constantly subject to exogenously and endogenously induced changes. Each of these changes may affect the behaviour of the various actors involved. As these effects need not run parallel, they can moreover also impact on the competitive balance (Meersman and Van de Voorde, 2010).

A good example in this respect is a productivity increase at a given maritime terminal. As ports are links in the supply chain, it does not always make sense to consider terminal or port productivity as an isolated factor. Resolving a bottleneck in one link may, after all, simply move the problem to another link in the chain. In other words, a productivity increase in one section of the logistics chain may drive up cost elsewhere in the supply process (Valleri and Van de Voorde, 1996, p. 127). Increasing the capacity of ships, for example, will not only spread the cost of sailing over more containers, but also necessitate greater throughput capacity and hence require more extensive terminal facilities. Otherwise, the bottleneck will simply be transferred from the maritime route to the port and/or hinterland leg of the transport chain.

The various port actors manage one or several links in the logistics process. The fact that stevedores, shipping companies and port authorities tend to apply different definitions of port productivity is attributable to the specificity of the inputs and outputs in their leg of the supply process. However, it is not always possible to unequivocally ascertain for each actor their precise input and output status, since one must inevitably take into account company-specific factors. A terminal operator may, for example, serve different shipping companies, while a shipping company may call at different terminals in a single port.

2.4.1   Trends in the Development of the Principal Port Actors

It is important to gain and maintain insight into the most significant potential future developments in the industry, as well as their likely impacts on each of the players operating in the maritime supply chain. The following synthesis of the existing situation may serve as a starting point in this respect.

First and foremost, there is the changing context of the world economy, with growth in international trade and hence in maritime commerce, and characterised by an international redistribution of labour and capital, and an integration and globalisation of the markets. The world economy continues to be the motor of the maritime sector (Meersman and Van de Voorde, 2010; Meersman, 2009).

Shipping companies are strategically important clients of ports. On the one hand they attract traffic and industrial activity to the port, while on the other they are attracted by such industrial activity. Freight passes through the ports, after which drayage may be taken care of either by the ocean carrier (that is, 'carrier haulage') or the shipper (that is, 'merchant haulage'). The market has also witnessed substantial scale increases on the part of shipping companies in recent times. This has been achieved primarily through horizontal cooperation and/or mergers and take-overs. Additionally, shipping companies have set their sights on terminal operators and inland transport services, as operations are increasingly approached from the perspective of complex logistics chains, whereby each link must contribute to the constant optimisation of the chain as a whole. This has altered the competitive balance in the market, as shipping companies have gained in power through their overall control of logistics chains. Table 2.5 provides an overview of the degree of vertical integration initiated by the top-20 shipping companies. Crosses (x) indicate the presence of integration.

We have also witnessed important structural evolutions within ports. Traditional stevedoring firms have evolved towards more-complex TOCs, more often than not because a shortage of working capital has necessitated mergers, takeovers and externally financed expansion projects. In some cases, the external capital has been provided by shipping companies (Pauwels et al., 2007).

2.4.2 Possible Future Scenarios

Given the rapid evolution of the port and maritime industry, the question arises which scenarios may unfold in the future. Will long-term economic growth persist? And, if so, will it continue to translate into growing demand for maritime transport, or will future economic growth manifest itself primarily in services and not so much in industrial production? Will the aforementioned evolution towards scale increases based on horizontal and vertical mergers continue to manifest itself? And what are the likely

Table 2.5   Vertical integration by container shipping companies

Rank	Operator	TOC	Hinterland transport operator	Hinterland terminal operator
1	Maersk	APM Terminals	X	X
2	MSC	X	X	–
3	CMA-CGM	Terminal Link	X	–
4	Evergreen	X	–	–
5	Hapag Lloyd	–	–	–
6	APL	X	X	–
7	CSAV	–	–	–
8	Cosco	Cosco Pacific	–	–
9	Hanjin	X	X	–
10	China Shipping	X	–	–
11	MOL	X	–	–
12	NYK	X	X	–
13	Hamburg Süd	–	X	–
14	OOCL	X	X	–
15	K-Line	X	–	–
16	ZIM	–	–	–
17	Yang Ming	X	X	–
18	Hyundai	X	–	–
19	PIL	–	–	–
20	UASC	–	–	–

Source: Drewry Shipping Consultants (2010) + shipping company websites.

consequences in terms of vessel size, especially in the container business? What timeframe are shipping companies looking at in their quest for even closer cooperation? What strategies are market players other than the shipping companies likely to pursue[10] (Meersman and Van de Voorde, 2010)?

Each of the above questions is crucially important to the sector and its players, yet all are shrouded in uncertainty. One may reasonably assume that each market player will try to anticipate likely strategic moves by other players (Besanko et al., 2007). Container shipping companies are a case in point: although they tend to complain about relatively low freight rates as a consequence of overcapacity, they also tend to continue to invest heavily in even more capacity,[11] as Table 2.6 illustrates. The underlying strategy of these shipping companies is clear to see: in response to already low freight rates, they are attempting to deploy additional capacity at a lower operational cost per slot. Moreover, they consider a mixed fleet as a means of spreading risks. Additional cost control can be achieved through mergers and takeovers, and the capacity reduction this would entail.

Table 2.6   Capacity increase by shipping companies, May 2011
(TEU = thousands of TEU)

No.	Parent/main	Operated ships	Fleet TEU	Order ships	Book TEU
1	Maersk Line	600	2,258	55	441
2	MSC	465	1,966	53	561
3	CMA-CGM	389	1,264	23	208
4	Evergreen	165	612	20	176
5	Coscon	142	590	36	297
6	Hapag-Lloyd	135	588	10	131
7	APL	146	588	22	204
8	CSAV	148	574	12	99
9	Hanjin	110	517	15	155
10	China Shipping	142	489	14	122
11	MOL	97	411	10	57
12	OOCL	88	409	13	141
13	NYK	101	402	2	9
14	Hamburg Süd	117	383	24	150
15	Yang Ming	84	338	16	102
16	K Line	78	329	8	59
17	ZIM	98	329	14	156
18	Hyundai	60	303	5	65
19	PIL	135	255	22	68
20	UASC	58	237	8	105
21	Wan Hai	90	194	14	38
22	HDS Lines	24	89	0	0
23	TS Lines	44	87	0	0
24	Sea Consortium	54	60	0	0
25	MISC	23	59	1	9
Total Top 25		3,593	13,329	456	3,743
World liner fleet		5,978	15,277	613	4,125
Share Top 25 (%)		60	87	74	91

Note: 1,000 TEU, analysis based on data sourced from AXSAlphaliner.

Source: Dynamar (2011).

Strategic and financial considerations by the holdings that control the shipping companies will keep capacity further in check, through strategic alliances, new partnerships, and the rerouting of vessels.[12] These evolutions may/will give rise to changes in direct port calls. Moreover, this may also imply shifts in freight volumes to be transported to and from the hinterland. On the other hand, it is perfectly conceivable that a port may compensate largely or even wholly for a drop in direct port calls through larger cargo volumes per ship and additional (maritime and other) feeder services.

There is little doubt what impact the above developments will have on the maritime logistics chain in its entirety. In the short to medium term, these kinds of rationalisations are bound to result in a radical reorganisation of services. New alliances will be forged, within which further mergers and takeovers will occur.

A concentration movement has also been observed among terminals, in an evolution prompted in part by a need for ever-greater growth capital and the inability of the original, often locally based, owners to raise such huge sums. This concentration movement, coupled with new market entries by players such as PSA, HPH and DP World, has also created a buffer against a potential verticalisation drive initiated by the shipping companies.

Such a market development obviously has certain consequences. For example, the prospect of even further concentration among terminal operators poses an economic threat to shipping companies, as reduced competition may lead to lower productivity growth, longer vessel-handling times and, perhaps most importantly of all, higher rates. This last evolution is primarily a consequence of the fact that shipping companies no longer have a choice between any number of rival terminal operators, but are increasingly dependent upon large players who operate in different locations and are therefore able to negotiate longer-term package deals for services in those different ports.

One may assume with a high degree of certainty that shipping companies will not be prepared to (continue to) undergo this evolution. As their relative market power is at stake, it seems logical that they should put greater effort into acquiring so-called 'dedicated terminals', be it under joint ventures with locally based terminal operators or otherwise. Table 2.7 shows the extent and the acceleration of this phenomenon. But this evolution need not be detrimental to the port authorities' cause, as it will at least make shipping companies less footloose, in the sense that a long-term relationship is forged that makes them less likely to relocate (Heaver et al., 2001). However, in the short term, such dedicated terminals may lead to lower utilisation rates of available capacity.

With regard to the land-side activities, it is important that the economic benefits shipping companies seek (and often achieve) through far-reaching scale increases and the corresponding cost reduction must not be wasted through time and cost bottlenecks on the quay, in the terminal or during connecting inland transport.

Clearly, each of the possible developments considered above will impact

Table 2.7   Involvement of container shipping companies in TOCs: scope and development

Operator	TOC ranking 2009	Total number of entities	New entities in 2009
Maersk	2	65	12
MSC	6	24	5
CMA-CGM	10	21	10
Evergreen	8	11	5
APL	15	11	2
Cosco	5	14	4
Hanjin	11	19	5
China Shipping	–	13	3
MOL	20	10	2
NYK	12	18	1
OOCL	17	4	–
Yang Ming	18	8	2
Hyundai	22	7	3

Source: Own processing of data from Drewry Shipping Consultants (2010).

on crucial decision variables, such as cost, price, and supply and demand. As the various players are not affected in the same way, their strategies will vary accordingly. This explains the highly dynamic nature of the maritime supply chain and associated consequences in terms of port competition.

2.5   CONCLUSION

Port competition is attracting ever-greater attention from an economic, a social political and a business perspective. This is due not only to the substantial social and economic significance of seaports within a regional and national context, but also to the fact that their short-, medium- and long-term future is shrouded in uncertainty. Moreover, ports are clearly highly heterogeneous and complex environments, characterised by a multitude of market players and interconnections. Competition unfolds not only between ports, but also between production companies and service providers located in or making use of those ports. Furthermore, there is a clearly discernible trend from competition between individual ports to competition between supply chains. Successful ports belong to successful supply chains.

In order to understand present-day port competition, insight is required into the various functions of a port, and the factors that impact on a port's competitiveness. From both a literature review and a series of interviews, it appears that the four most important criteria for port selection are out-of-pocket cost, hinterland connectivity, capacity and reliability. Out-of-pocket cost also turns out to be the key consideration in deciding on hinterland transport modes and hinterland service providers.

Equally, adequate insight is needed into the decision processes of the various port players. It is clear that each port player has an own agenda, including strategic objectives and tools to reach them. Much will depend on the behaviour of the largest and most influential customers of ports, that is, the shipping companies. These players may determine their behaviour individually or within the context of so-called 'strategic alliances'. They may even go so far as to wholly or partially give up their footloose behaviour in favour of a particular port or dedicated terminal. In order to gain a clear understanding of such strategies, a detailed analysis is required at shipping company level.

The speed with which the various market players within the maritime supply chain will take specific initiatives depends on a battery of exogenous and endogenous variables. As is the case with pricing in the maritime sector, and with successfully covering oneself against price fluctuations (compare bunkering) and other risks, timing is what ultimately determines who will emerge as the winner. The extent to which port authorities and/or public authorities will be able to take part in this gain, will be determined by the policies they pursue and the power position they are able to obtain. Attracting and in particular keeping the right players which bring in flows with high value-added will be crucial. To do that, due account will need to be taken of the port's score on the most important port call decision variables.

NOTES

1. A third big evolution might be that among port authorities, there has also been a gradual move towards cooperation. The first initiatives tend to be found mainly in hinterland connections and joint marketing, although there are hardly any significant, concrete examples. Therefore, hardly any scientific literature is available on the industrial–economic and welfare–economic impact of cooperation among ports.
2. An illustration of the dynamics is in the speed with which concentration at the global level increases. In 2008, the top five container handlers possessed 45.6 per cent of world trade, whereas in 2009, that share had gone up to 53.7 per cent (Drewry Shipping Consultants, 2010).
3. A comparable question presents itself in relation to port investments. Port infrastructure and hinterland connections are commonly paid for by the public authorities, but that is not to say that they are necessarily the recipients of the ROI.
4. The output of a port is usually defined in terms of number of passengers or tonnage per unit of time (year/month/day) passing through the port in either direction, that is, 'throughput'.

5. Full lines represent relationships which must always be present, whereas dashed lines refer to optional relationships. Bold lines are linked to the decision field of the sender of the goods, normal lines refer to the decision field of the receiver. This applies under specific types of contract, represented by so-called 'Incoterms'. The border may shift under different contract types.
6. Merchant haulage implies that the shipper or the owner of the goods takes care of hinterland transport, while in carrier haulage this is taken care of by the shipping company.
7. Twenty-seven scientific references, going back to as early as 1985, were selected for in-depth analysis of the criteria which are of importance in port selection. The results of the analysis are summarised in this section.
8. The five ports were chosen such that they are all different in their main characteristics. The aim was to see under what circumstances ports get different valuations of their performance characteristics. The main European container port, Rotterdam, was not included in the analysis, as it was assumed that results should be in line with those of Antwerp, in view of the many common characteristics. For data availability reasons, Antwerp was preferred to Rotterdam as a research subject.
9. The scale used in the Lickert survey is equidistant, for reasons of ease of comparable evaluation of the different criteria.
10. In recent years, most port and higher public authorities have concentrated mainly on the container business. The question arises whether this is or has been a wise strategy. After all, not all cargo can be containerised. Moreover, the added value and profits materialising in, say, project cargo are usually significantly higher than in containerised cargo.
11. Overcapacity is not necessarily assessed negatively by the shipping companies, which tend to assume that the problem of port congestion will absorb some of this excess capacity. This expectation is coupled with longer-haul cargoes, which will alter the tonne/mile ratio. Port congestion mainly shows up now on the hinterland side in Western countries. Congestion therefore reflects in the score that ports get on hinterland connections.
12. One of the most recent examples is the formation of the G6 alliance out of the Grand and the New World Alliances at the end of 2011. Another move is the cooperation agreement between two family-owned shipping companies, MSC and CMA-CGM.

REFERENCES

Aronietis, R., Van de Voorde, E. and Vanelslander, T., 2010. 'Port competitiveness determinants of selected European ports in the containerized cargo market', paper presented at the IAME conference, Lisbon, 7–9 July.

Ben-Akiva, M., Bierlaire, M., Choudbury, C. and Hess, S., 2010. 'Attitudes and value of time heterogeneity', in: Van de Voorde, E. and Vanelslander, T. (eds), *Applied Transport Economics: A Management and Policy Perspective*, Antwerp: De Boeck, pp. 525–48.

Besanko, D., Dranove, D., Shanley, M. and Schaefer, S., 2007. *Economics of Strategy* (4th edn), Hoboken, NJ: John Wiley & Sons.

Blauwens, G., De Baere, P. and Van de Voorde, E., 2010. *Transport economics* (4th edn), Antwerp: De Boeck.

Coppens, F., Lagneaux, F., Meersman, H., Sellekaerts, N., Van de Voorde, E., Van Gastel, G. and Verhetsel, A., 2007. 'Economic impacts of port activity: a disaggregated analysis, the case of Antwerp', Working Paper Series, National Bank of Belgium.

Drewry Shipping Consultants, 2010. *Global Container Terminal Operators 2010*, London.

Dynamar, 2011. *Dynaliners*, May edition.

Ersini, M., Ferrari, C. and Grosso, M., 2011. 'Mediterranean ports: a classification based on container network services', paper presented at the IAME conference, Santiago de Chile, 26–28 October.

Gaur, P., Pundir, S. and Sharma, T., 2001. 'Ports face inadequate capacity, efficiency and competitiveness in a developing country: case of India', *Maritime Policy and Management* **38**, 293–314.

Heaver, T., Meersman, H. and Van de Voorde, E., 2001. 'Co-operation and competition in international container transport: strategies for ports', *Maritime Policy and Management* **28**, 293–305.

Meersman, H., 2009. 'Maritime traffic and the world economy', in: Meersman, H., Van de Voorde, E. and Vanelslander, T. (eds), *Future Challenges for the Port and Shipping Sector*, London: Informa, pp. 89–107.

Meersman, H. and Van de Voorde, E., 2010. 'Port management, operation and competition: a focus on North-Europe', in: Grammenos, C.T. (ed.), *The Handbook of Maritime Economics and Business*, 2nd edn London: Lloyd's List, pp. 891–906.

Meersman, H., Van de Voorde, E. and Vanelslander T., 2010. 'Port competition revisited', *Review of Business and Economics* **55**, 210–32.

Pauwels, T., Meersman, H., Van de Voorde, E. and Vanelslander, T., 2007. 'The relation between port competition and hinterland connections: the case of the Iron Rhine and the Betuweroute', Conference proceedings of the International Forum on Shipping, Ports and Airports (IFSPA), Hong Kong, 10–12 May.

Suykens, F. and Van de Voorde, E., 1998. 'A quarter of a century of port management in Europe: objectives and tools', *Maritime Policy and Management* **25**, 251–61.

Tavasszy, L. and Combes, F., 2010, 'Endogenous value of time in freight transport models', in: Van de Voorde, E. and Vanelslander, T. (eds), *Applied Transport Economics: A Management and Policy Perspective*, Antwerp: De Boeck, pp. 25–40.

Valleri, M. and Van de Voorde, E., 1996. 'Port productivity: what do we know about it?', in: Valleri, M. (ed.), *L'industria portuale: per uno sviluppo sostenibile dei porti*, Bari: Cacucci, pp. 125–41.

Van de Voorde, E. and Vanelslander, T., 2010. 'Demand, costs, markets and policy: the evolution of thought in transport economics', in: Van de Voorde, E. and Vanelslander, T. (eds), *Applied Transport Economics: A Management and Policy Perspective*, Antwerp: De Boeck, pp. 25–40.

Veldman, S., Garcia-Alonso, L. and Vallejo-Pinto, J., 2011. 'Determinants of container port choice in Spain', *Maritime Policy and Management* **38**, 509–22.

Verhoeff, J.M., 1981. 'Zeehavenconcurrentie: overheidsproductie van havendiensten', in: Verhoeff, J.M., (ed.), *Vervoers- en haveneconomie: tussen actie en abstractie*, Leiden: Stenfert Kroese, pp. 181–202.

3. Climate change adaptation and transport: a review

Piet Rietveld*

3.1 INTRODUCTION

Climate change has become a major theme in transportation research and policy. An important starting point was the publication of the Brundtland report (WCED, 1987) on sustainable development. The studies and policies proposed under the heading 'sustainable transport' have been numerous since then. Google gives about 5 million hits for this combination of terms. In the initial phase, the main orientation was on environmental pollution and resource scarcity, in particular the use of fossil fuels. It soon appeared that for some types of pollutants such as NOx it was rather easy to achieve substantial reductions, implying successful cases of decoupling of economic development and pollution. For energy use, the successes were much more modest, the bottom line being that energy use in transport grows more or less at the same rate as transport volumes, whereas in most other sectors improvements in energy efficiency were much easier to achieve (Rothengatter, 2003; EIS, 2010). This means that transport's share in aggregate energy use has been increasing gradually up to some 25 percent.

During the last decade the themes of global warming and climate change have become more prominent (IPCC, 2007; Stern, 2007). To a considerable extent this theme runs parallel to the fossil energy theme, since fossil resources are the main type of energy input. The difference is of course that in the energy theme external effects are less prominent than in the climate change theme. Energy scarcity will be reflected in high energy prices and this will give incentives to increase efficiency in its use, and to speed up the development of renewable resources. In the case of climate change this is different: reducing greenhouse gas emissions in one country will yield benefits at the global level, inducing free-rider tendencies. This explains why it is so difficult to achieve agreement at a global level to reduce greenhouse gas emissions.

Most studies on climate change focus on mitigation with an analysis of how the public and private sectors can reduce greenhouse gas emissions. For example, policy packages consisting of mixtures of technological change, taxes, subsidies, modal shift and spatial policies have been studied in several countries to determine their effectiveness and efficiency in reaching mitigation goals (Banister, 2008). This is a complex area where knowledge from many domains has to be integrated. Important scientific and political debates concern the appropriate policy targets for countries, distributional issues between countries, sector-specific targets, and effectiveness of policy instruments. For example, from an efficiency viewpoint it is not so clear what would be the optimal contribution of the transport sector to the reduction of greenhouse gasses. The fact that its share in the total production of greenhouse gasses is increasing is important to note. But at the same time it remains relevant to compare the social costs of reduction of greenhouse gas emissions in transport with these costs in other sectors such as energy use in manufacturing, or by households for heating and cooling. The level of targets per sector would ideally depend on both the costs of reaching them and the welfare losses related to the decrease in energy use per sector.

The discussion on climate change started with mitigation: policies aimed at reducing greenhouse gas emissions, and thus reducing the speed of climate change. The more recent development is that adaptation to climate change has also become an important policy theme. There are several reasons for this shift. First, it appears difficult to reach agreement on mitigation policies at a world level. So climate change will most probably continue, and it is important for private and public actors to know how to cope with this. Second, even when strict mitigation policies would be implemented, climate change will most probably continue to take place, so it is good to be prepared for proactive policies. Third, an argument that has received little attention thus far: for an appropriate level of mitigation to be chosen, one needs to know how economies will adjust to climate change. For some sectors and in some countries, it might even be that climate change has mainly beneficial consequences or it may be relatively easy or cheap to cope with the consequences of climate change. In such cases, the adaptation theme has low relevance, and this would also apply to mitigation. The reason is that when climate change has little adverse effects there is no need for stringent mitigation policies. Therefore it is important that climate change adaptation is studied at considerable depth for a wide range of sectors and countries in order to find out to what extent there are low-cost adaptation solutions. A World Bank study (2010) has shown that in particular in developing countries the costs of adaptation to climate change can be considerable. Apparently these countries are vulnerable. However, in this study the World Bank focuses on the adaptation costs of *entirely* removing the adverse effects of climate change, which may yield overestimates of the costs of optimal adaptation policies. In the present chapter we shall focus on the adaptation theme. The reason is not that adaptation is necessarily the best way to deal with climate change. The knowledge on the effects of climate change compared with the costs of mitigation and adaptation strategies is not yet sufficient to determine the optimal mix of adaptation and mitigation efforts. The focus on adaptation arises from the fact that this is a rather underdeveloped theme of research.

A feature of adaptation is that it is very local and sector specific. This makes it important to study it in a range of different countries. Coastal flood risk is a major issue in some countries, whereas in other countries drought is the main theme, or the flood theme concerns rivers instead of the sea. A distinguishing difference between mitigation and adaptation is that mitigation benefits materialize at the global level, whereas benefits of adaptation are often local. Protection against coastal flooding in country A will hardly affect the position of country B. Thus, benefits of adaptation policies seldom spill over to other countries, which makes these policies much easier to implement. Depending on the local situation, more complex interactions may occur, however. When countries are small, spillovers may occur. For example, improving robustness of networks in country A may also yield benefits for country B in the case of international linkages. This would be an example of positive spillovers. Negative spillovers of adaptation may also occur: for example, measures in country A to counter the risk of flooding in a river basin may negatively affect flood risks in country B.

Most scientists agree that climate is changing, although large uncertainties exist on how large and fast it will be. A common approach to address the uncertainty is the use of scenarios that indicate a possible range of outcomes. Table 3.1 presents scenarios formulated by KNMI (2007) for the coming 50 years in the Netherlands where the main dimensions of uncertainty relate to the overall temperature increase in the world (1 versus 2°C) and changes in the dominant wind directions (limited versus strong changes). The table shows that there may be a tendency towards drier summers and wetter winters, and this varies considerably between the scenarios.

This chapter reviews the theme of climate change in the transport sector. This is a theme that has received relatively little attention in the literature thus far, and it is no doubt a promising theme of research for the coming years. A review of the literature can be found in Koetse and Rietveld (2009). It is clear that this theme calls for contributions from a range of disciplines including meteorology, hydrology, engineering, economics and other behavioral sciences. After discussing a general framework of climate

Table 3.1   Changes in temperature and precipitation in the Netherlands for 2050 relative to 1990 for four KNMI 2006 climate-change scenarios

Variable	M	M+	W	W+
Summer				
Mean temperature	0.9	1.4	1.7	2.8
Temperature 10% warmest days	1.0	1.8	2.0	3.6
Temperature 10% coldest days	0.9	1.1	1.8	2.2
Mean precipitation (%)	2.8	−9.5	5.5	−19.0
Wet day frequency (%)	−1.6	−9.6	−3.3	−19.3
Mean wet day precipitation (%)	4.6	0.1	9.1	0.3
Median wet day precipitation (%)	−2.5	−6.2	−5.1	−12.4
Winter				
Mean temperature	0.9	1.1	1.8	2.3
Temperature 10% warmest days	0.8	1.0	1.7	1.9
Temperature 10% coldest days	1.0	1.4	2.0	2.8
Mean precipitation (%)	3.6	7.0	7.3	14.2
Wet day frequency (%)	0.1	0.9	0.2	1.9
Mean wet day precipitation (%)	3.6	6.0	7.1	12.1
Median wet day precipitation (%)	3.4	7.3	6.8	14.7

Note: M and W represent a weak and strong change in atmospheric circulation; + indicates a 2°C increase in temperature compared with a reference increase of 1°C.

change impacts on transport in Section 3.2, some impacts of climate conditions on transport networks will be reviewed, in particular delays due to weather related disruptions (Section 3.3). In Section 3.4 the impact of weather on capacity utilization in transport networks will be further examined. The impact of climate-related catastrophes on transport networks will be the subject of Section 3.5. Impacts of weather conditions on travel demand will be surveyed in Section 3.6. Section 3.7 concludes.

3.2   CONCEPTUAL FRAMEWORK

In Figure 3.1 some of the main effects of climate change on transport networks are described. Climate change will impact on transport networks in various ways. For example, high temperatures in summer make asphalt layers more vulnerable, less snow in winter means a reduction of accident risk. Less extreme rainfall implies a reduction in disturbances; more thunderstorms would lead to an increase in the number of disturbances in rail networks. Low water means limited opportunities for inland water

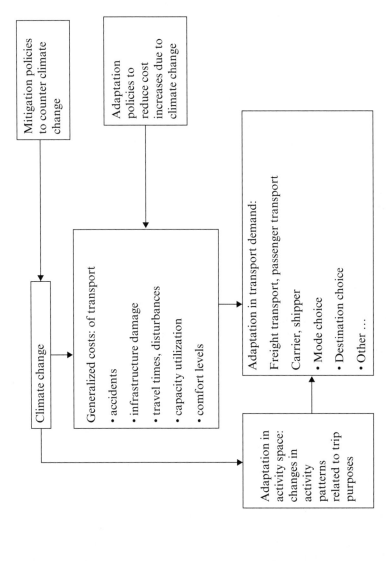

Figure 3.1   Two adaptation routes to climate change in transport systems

transport at full capacity. Weather conditions also affect comfort levels in transport.

Most of the climate-related effects will be small, but occur at high frequency: they lead to limited changes in generalized costs that are felt regularly and by many people, such as the effects of higher frequency of heavy rainfall. The opposite case is that climate conditions have sudden and large impacts such as the collapse of a large bridge, or the breakdown of flood protection in a region, leading to the failure of important parts of transport infrastructure for a longer period. Both will be addressed in this review.

Figure 3.1 distinguishes two types of adaptation strategies in transport with respect to climate change: direct measures to counter the increases in generalized costs of infrastructure construction and use. Examples are snow removal on roads, ice breaking to keep waterways navigable, use of asphalt layers with improved heat resistance, intensified water management to keep waterways navigable when water levels are low, and so on. Many of these measures take place in the infrastructure domain, but also private adaptation may be involved, such as the use of winter tires for cars and the use of aircraft that are less vulnerable to adverse atmospheric conditions. It may be good to reiterate that climate change is not necessarily bad for transport systems: certain elements of generalized costs will decrease. For example, higher temperatures will mean lower frequency of de-icing at airports.

Another type of adaptation is presented in the middle part of Figure 3.1: the changes in generalized costs in transport, being the result of climate change and countervailing actions to changes in its use, will of course lead to responses such as change in travel behavior of individuals, including changes in driving styles under difficult weather conditions, shifts in transport modes in freight transport, and changes in destinations of holidays as a result of weather conditions.

The distinction between both types of adaptation is important for the analysis of welfare effects of climate-change adaptation. The welfare effect of climate change is the cost increase for those actors who will not change their behavior plus the welfare loss of those actors who do change their behavior, computed for example by means of the rule of half. The welfare effect of adaptation measures – given that a climate change will occur – can be computed in a similar way: it equals the reduction of generalized costs of the actors who will not change behavior, plus the welfare gains of those who do change behavior, minus the costs of adaptation.

A final dimension of adaptation to climate change with transport implications is that activity patterns may change. Hence, people may switch from outdoor to indoor activities during adverse weather conditions. This may of course have an impact on travel demand, because it would imply that trip generation would be lower under adverse weather, since at-home activities would become more popular then. A similar reasoning would apply for freight transport: mild winters lead to a reduced demand for fuels so that transport of fuels decreases.

3.3 CLIMATE AND DISRUPTIONS IN TRANSPORT NETWORKS

Transport networks are subject to a large number of disturbances every day, ranging from technical breakdowns in vehicles using the network, collisions, failures in ICT supporting the use of physical networks such as signaling, breakdown of infrastructure components such as switches in rail networks, and so on. Weather conditions play a role in these, but it is not always easy to verify to what extent the disturbances are related to weather conditions. FHWA (2004) indicates that some 15 percent of congestion in road networks can be attributed to adverse weather conditions, although the underpinnings of this figure are not so clear. In the Netherlands some 5 percent of the disturbances in rail networks is usually attributed to weather conditions. This is a modest figure, and it might in reality be somewhat higher (see Xia et al., 2011). Figure 3.2 illustrates that the average number of disturbances on the Netherlands railway network is about 115 per day, but from time to time an extreme number of events are observed, implying a thick tail. Closer examination of this tail reveals that these days tend to be characterized by extreme weather conditions such as a severe storm or snow. This underlines the relevance of weather conditions for large disruptions within transport networks and the need to develop adaptation strategies to cope with these.[1]

Another transport sector that is clearly sensitive to weather variations is aviation. Table 3.2 shows some data on San Francisco International Airport. A study by Eads et al. (2000) demonstrates that poor visibility in the summer months and rain storms in the winter months substantially contribute to delays and cancellations. Compared with good weather, cancellations per day increase by a factor of 2–3 when weather is bad in the morning, and by a factor of 3–4 when weather is bad all day. These results apply in the specific case of San Francisco airport. They cannot be transferred to other airports given the role of specific local climate conditions, the design of an airport and the amount of traffic on it. Nevertheless it gives a clear indication that weather conditions are a potentially important determinant of airport reliability.

Adaptation strategies to cope with the adverse weather conditions on

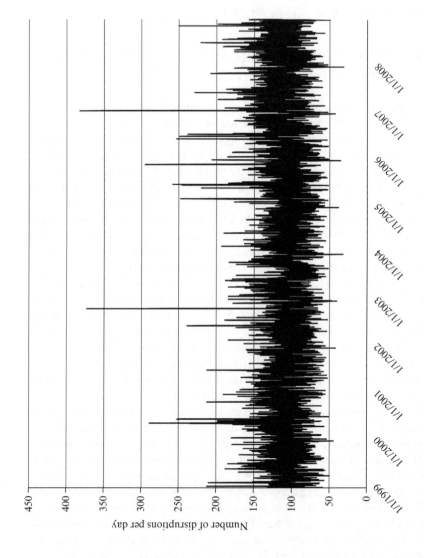

Figure 3.2   Disruptions in railway networks, Netherlands (Prorail)

Table 3.2 Cancellations per day and delay minutes per flight at San Francisco International Airport in various types of weather in 1997, 1998 and 1999

	Year	Good all day	Weather prevailing at airport	
			Bad morning weather	Bad weather all day
Cancellations per	1997	6	10	19
day	1998	8	20	35
	1999	8	18	32
Delay minutes per	1997	20	34	56
flight operated	1998	23	45	89
	1999	20	40	82

Source: Adaptation of Table 4 in Eads et al. (2000).

disturbances go in various directions. At the strategic level it concerns the location choice of transport nodes such as airports, and the orientation of runways (see, for example, CPB, 2002) to reduce sensitivity of airport activity to weather conditions such as fog and wind. For transport infrastructure networks, strategic adaptation may imply the construction of additional links so that network users have route alternatives when a certain link breaks down or becomes strongly unreliable. Other strategic aspects concern the choice for design standards of infrastructures so that they remain robust under adverse conditions. Given the long life of most infrastructures it is important that decisions are made in view of possible climate change. Climate change is uncertain, so this leads to trading-off the additional costs of infrastructure that would function well under more extreme weather conditions, the probability of the occurrence of such conditions, and the additional costs of retrofitting at a later stage. Given the use of discount factors in these cost comparisons of various alternatives, the costs of retrofitting, even when they are substantial would not receive a heavy weight in particular when it would take place decades in the future.

At the operational level, the issue is how to develop optimal strategies to cope with disturbances once they occur. It is clear that the size of welfare loss is strongly dependent on the duration of the disturbance. For example, in road networks the size of the total delays tends to be a quadratic function of the duration of the disturbance (Nam and Mannering, 2000; Koster and Rietveld, 2011). The background is that not only is the average delay proportional to the duration of the disturbance, but also the number of travelers affected. Thus, a quick response is an important element in incident management. In the case of prediction of extremely bad weather, several proactive adaptive responses are possible. One is to reduce access to the network to prevent incidents when extremes are foreseen. Another strategy would be to issue a weather warning with the advice not to make use of the network during a certain timeframe. A less extreme strategy would be to temporarily extend the supply of support services in order to have sufficient capacity for quick responses throughout the network to cope with incidents.

3.4   WEATHER AND CAPACITY UTILIZATION

Weather conditions will have an impact on capacity utilization. For example, speed reduction is a natural response to adverse weather with several transport modes, and this of course will reduce the effective capacity of infrastructure in terms of the flow of vehicles passing per time unit. Note that the speed decrease may be the natural result of an adjustment of the users of a network in view of safety considerations, but it may also be imposed by network managers.

Another mechanism of reduced capacity utilization is that load factors may decrease. This case has been well documented for inland water transport (Jonkeren et al., 2007; Demirel, 2011). The point is that under low water conditions, ships cannot be loaded up to 100 percent. This leads to a shift in the cost curves of ships: the costs per ton transported are inversely related to the load factor. When the load factor decreases to 50 percent, the cost per ton would about double. In the case of the inland water transport market in Western Europe, the supply curve tends to be horizontal, which implies that in the market outcome the price per trip of a barge remains about constant, implying that the price per ton is about proportional to the inverse of the load factor. Only when load factors are lower than some 50 percent, will a tendency of a more than proportional increase in the price per ton be observed (see Table 3.3).

Table 3.3 shows that low water periods may lead to substantial price increases. This induces various adaptation phenomena in the market. First, the price increase leads to a decrease in demand. This decrease is partly in the form of a modal shift away from water transport towards road and rail, although the shift is smaller than one might expect (Jonkeren, 2009). This is because of the lack of capacity on the other infrastructures, and also because the cost advantage of water transport above rail and road is substantial on many important connections. Another response takes place via changes in stocks of bulk products: during low water periods shippers may decide to exhaust their stocks instead of keeping their safety stocks at the standard levels.

Table 3.3   Water levels and load factors on the Rhine (location Kaub)

Waterlevel (cm)	Load factor (%)	Price per ton (euro)
<180	48	13.1
181–190	53	10.1
191–200	58	10.3
201–210	63	9.4
211–220	66	8.8
221–230	71	8.7
231–240	74	8.1
241–250	73	8.2
251–260	79	7.7
>261	84	7.5

Source: Jonkeren (2009).

Water levels fluctuate from week to week, and in some years the share of weeks with serious low water problems is negligible. On the other hand, the year 2003 was a recent year with a very prolonged low water period. During that year the transport-related total welfare loss related to low water were estimated to be about €230 million (ibid.). Figure 3.3 shows the average pattern of water flows which is closely related to water levels on the Rhine at the Lobith location where it enters the Netherlands (dotted line). It appears that on average, autumn is the period with lowest water levels. Climate change uncertainty is incorporated via a series of scenarios for water discharges in 2050. Two of the four scenarios show a considerable decrease of average water discharge during the autumn. This puts the issue of water management on the agenda. The year 2003 with its exceptional long period of low water is close to what is found for the average situation in 2050 described in the W + scenario in Table 3.1. The associated welfare loss would certainly call for an analysis of various adaptation strategies in order to reduce such costs in an efficient manner.

The analysis shows that for inland water transport, annual variations in weather conditions are substantial, which provides a good opportunity to predict the effect of a change in climate. It appears that there is scope for adaptation with all major stakeholders. For example, large clients of inland water transport such as power plants or steel factories may in the long run reconsider the optimality of their location and move towards the sea, implying transport cost savings. These clients may also invest in larger storage facilities and connectivity to other transport modes in order to reduce their dependence on barges for transport. The barge operators may reconsider the present barge types and look for models that are less

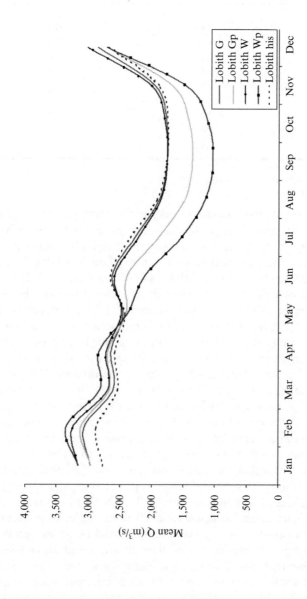

Source: Te Linde (2007).

Figure 3.3 Uncertainty on water discharges in the Rhine, 2050, for four climate change scenarios; Lobith location

sensitive to water-level fluctuations. And finally the public sector may decide to invest in stronger forms of water management, for example by adding locks in order to reduce the effect of low water on capacities. The optimal mixture of efforts is not clear a priori and careful analysis is needed to avoid the situation that governments are under- or overinvesting in the adaptation domain (Demirel, 2011).

3.5 CATASTROPHES AND THEIR IMPACT ON CLIMATE CHANGE

The experience with large catastrophes such as the Hurricane Katrina and the resulting flood shows that risk values are very large, and infrastructures are part of these. Grenzeback and Lukmann (2007) report infrastructure damages of around US$1.1 billion as a consequence of Katrina and this does not cover all infrastructures. Further, there are some studies on the effect of a potential sea-level rise on infrastructure costs. Jacob et al. (2007) indicate that with a 1 meter sea-level rise, the annualized costs of infrastructure damages due to flooding incidents for the Metropolitan East Coast in the US are estimated to rise by a factor of 3. This is substantial, although in absolute terms the effect is still modest.[2]

In addition to the direct costs of flooding that are related to infrastructure damages, indirect costs due to mobility effects may also be substantial. However, there is little empirical evidence on this subject. In a study by AVV (2006) the economic costs associated with changes in traffic and transport due to a single flooding incident in the Netherlands are estimated. The study distinguishes between four transport scenarios, which vary according to the length of the period after the flooding incident and with respect to certain behavioral assumptions and effects. The costs vary from €0.41 billion to € 1.1 billion depending on the scenario (see Table 3.4).

Suarez et al. (2005) also focus on the indirect costs of flooding due to mobility effects. They investigate the impact of climate change on urban transportation in the Boston Metropolitan Area. A transport model is used to study the effects of coastal flooding due to sea-level rise, and of river flooding due to heavy rainfall events, on the performance of the urban transportation system. Effects are expressed in terms of cancellations of trips and in terms of delays due to rerouting and changes in congestion. Assuming a sea-level rise of 0.3 cm per year, and an increase in the magnitude of heavy rainfall events of 0.31 percent per year, the results show an increase in delays and lost trips of around 80 percent in 2100 compared to 2000.

Table 3.4   *Monetary costs of losses in travel time and extra km driven due to a single flooding incident in the Netherlands for four scenarios (2010 €m)*

	Scenario 1	Scenario 2	Scenario 3	Scenario 4
Freight transport	289	163	402	278
Commuting	191	51	318	263
Business trips	415	142	227	170
Other trips	146	58	93	69
Extra kilometers	54	0	74	65
Total	1,095	414	1,114	845

Source: AVV (2006).

Studies of this type demonstrate that climate change impacts do not necessarily make themselves felt at high frequency: they may occur at low frequency, but with a very large impact. Of course, infrastructure is only one of the items next to many other material and non-material costs categories. Studies of the type reviewed here are therefore useful to give a more complete review of the costs of major climate-related events.

3.6   CLIMATE AND TRAVEL DEMAND

As indicated in Section 3.2, adverse weather conditions lead among others to an increase in the average travel time, an increase in the spread of travel times, and to an increased probability of accidents. Hence the generalized costs of transport are affected. Behavioral reactions may occur in various ways such as trip generation, modal choice, and so on.

An important insight is that the relevance of weather conditions for transport not follows only from its impact on generalized costs, but also from its impact on the utility of the activity for which the trip is made. The latter of course will vary according to trip purpose. Participation in activities that have a strong mandatory character such as work and education will not depend that much on weather conditions. The other extreme is outdoor recreation, which will depend strongly on weather conditions.

The most sensitive transport mode appears to be cycling. Richardson (2000) finds that rainfall and both high and low temperatures decrease the number of cycling trips in the metropolitan area of Melbourne, Australia. Goetzke and Rave (2006) and Winters et al. (2007) confirm these findings. However, other transport modes are also affected by weather conditions. Chung et al. (2005) show that the number of car trips made on the Tokyo

Expressway in Japan are lower during rainy days, in particular during weekends. Hofmann and O'Mahony (2005) study urban bus performance on selected routes in Ireland and report that ridership is reduced during rainy days. Bertness (1980) also studied the impact of summer precipitation in the Chicago area. He reported a 3–5 percent reduction in ridership of mass transit systems during rainfall due to a fall in discretionary riders such as shoppers.

Table 3.5, based on Sabir (2011) gives the results of a rather comprehensive study on trip making in the Netherlands where various transport modes and trip purposes are distinguished. The results reported in the table are based on a detailed econometric study of the number of trips per day based on the negative binomial model applied to the results of the Netherlands travel survey between 1995 and 2005. The table gives information on the relative change in the number of trips per person per day under a certain weather condition compared with a reference level for weather, indicated at the bottom of the table. First of all, it is important to note that seasonal dummies have been included and it is found that in spring and autumn considerably more trips are made per person than in summer and winter. For summer the major difference is – not surprisingly – in the decrease of commuting and educational trips related to the holiday period. For winter the largest decrease is due to a smaller number of recreational trips, and visiting friends and relatives. This means that the results reported here for weather circumstances relate to the effects of variations *within* a certain season. The effects of different seasons are not included in the estimates, which means that we provide a lower bound for the estimate of the weather effects on trip making.

When we focus on overall trip making, strong wind (> 6 Bf), high temperature ($> 25°C$) and snow have adverse effects on the number of trips per person per day. The first result indicates that traveling during stormy weather is considered as unattractive, and the same holds true for snow. The result for temperature is not an indication that trip making as such is unattractive with high temperatures, but that the alternative of staying at home, or sitting in the garden is more attractive than doing activities. This can be inferred from the fact that bicycle use increases strongly with high temperatures, apparently making it a very enjoyable travel mode.

Considering the various transport modes, it becomes clear that cycling and walking are to some extent substitutes: for example, low temperatures lead to more walking and less cycling, for high temperatures the opposite is found. A similar result is found for snow. On the other hand, strong wind and precipitation discourage both non-motorized transport modes. A similar result is found for cycling and public transport: cyclists tend to switch to bus/tram/metro when during storms and rain. Temperatures beyond 25°C make

Table 3.5 *Impacts of weather conditions on individuals' daily trips (percentage changes in number of trips)*

	Wind strength	Temperature				Precipitation			Snow	Seasonal		
	Wind > 6 Bft	≤0°C	10–20°C	20–25°C	>25°C	Minutes	Up to 0.1 mm	>0.1 mm	Dummy	Summer	Autumn	Winter
A												
All trips	**-2.04**	-0.20	0.27	-1.17	**-4.87**	**-0.16**	**-0.74**	0.63	**-3.88**	**-3.36**	**6.65**	**-6.84**
B												
Walking	**-3.15**	**12.56**	**-2.60**	**-5.47**	**-9.58**	**-0.25**	-0.65	*-1.61*	1.38	*-1.83*	**-4.10**	-4.10
Bicycle	-1.59	**-7.76**	**9.19**	**18.11**	**21.95**	**-0.73**	**-5.20**	**-7.89**	-4.08	**3.66**	**3.00**	**-14.76**
Car	**-2.07**	-1.40	**-3.90**	**-8.47**	**-14.80**	*0.06*	**0.68**	**2.85**	-2.75	**2.05**	**3.58**	-1.23
Bus/tram/metro	**-21.73**	**16.88**	-3.44	**-12.90**	**-19.62**	**0.26**	**6.19**	4.73	**-14.97**	**-14.39**	2.35	4.52
Train	-2.30	1.21	-2.21	**-7.19**	**-10.45**	-0.05	0.61	2.90	**-10.19**	**-10.65**	**4.41**	-0.79
Other	-1.64	-1.22	**12.32**	**10.97**	**17.53**	**-0.28**	**-4.11**	**-8.30**	**-11.12**	4.02	**-4.04**	**-12.47**
C												
Commuting	-1.07	**-10.94**	0.53	-0.48	-3.86	-0.09	-1.038	*-2.11*	6.77	**-19.42**	**10.13**	**-6.33**
Business	-2.46	**-12.66**	-1.73	-6.88	**-13.69**	-0.06	0.24	0.54	8.34	**-7.37**	1.17	-0.74
Shopping	**-5.50**	**4.64**	-0.05	-1.43	-4.75	-0.19	**1.32**	1.00	**-9.40**	13.71	0.35	-0.74
Recreation	-0.19	**-4.37**	**5.17**	**10.23**	**8.26**	**-0.36**	**-2.64**	*-1.45*	**10.39**	-5.07	**-3.47**	**-10.01**
Educational	-1.65	5.11	**-2.68**	**-5.72**	-7.25	-0.01	**-1.90**	**-3.22**	**-9.16**	**-45.17**	**6.47**	-0.83
Visiting family & friends	**-3.24**	*6.25*	0.80	1.89	**7.97**	**-0.26**	**-3.99**	**-6.05**	-3.19	**4.75**	**-3.59**	**-10.28**

Note: The figures indicate the percentage change in daily number of trips made per person per day. The bold and italic numbers are significant at the 5 and 10% level of statistical significance, respectively. The reference category for wind, temperature, precipitation (mm), snow, visibility and seasonal variables are, respectively, wind strength less than 6 Bft, temperature between 0°C and 10°C, no precipitation, no snow, and Spring.

cycling a substitute for all other modes. This does not mean that exactly the same trip is substituted, of course. It may well be that a long-distance car trip is substituted by a short- to medium-distance bicycle trip.

In terms of trip purposes we find that the mandatory activities such as work and education are indeed rather insensitive to weather conditions. It is interesting that a certain degree of substitution is observed for shopping and recreation: during adverse conditions such as low temperatures and rain, people tend to be more strongly involved in shopping, and less in recreation. The latter must be an indication of changing preferences for indoor versus outdoor activities, not in travel as such.

3.7 CONCLUSIONS

Climate change is generally considered to be a global problem, and it certainly is. An additional dimension is that climate change involves regional and local adaptation challenges. Climate change is strongly linked to a wide range of policy domains such as food security, flood risk, water management, transport system reliability, and land-use planning. Adaptation policies can therefore best be formulated in conjunction with these policy domains. Integration of policy domains such as the joint planning of infrastructure for transport services and infrastructure for flood safety may yield interesting cost savings.[3] In this chapter I have reviewed the theme of climate change in relation to transport planning.

Climate change is slow, and it is uncertain. Furthermore, in most cases there are stronger variations in physical conditions within a certain year, than there are between average scenarios between years. This holds true in particular when climate scenarios are formulated in terms of means. However, when they are formulated in terms of extreme outcomes, stronger variation may occur. The studies reviewed in this chapter give some hints that the climate change theme challenges researchers and policy makers to have a fresh look at quality aspects of transport networks leading to the conclusion that the current level of risk is already so strong that additional measures are needed, even if climate change were not to take place. This suggests a simple bottom line in policies on how to cope with climate change: be proactive by ensuring that even without climate change optimal protection levels have been realized. Given the considerable uncertainty on climate change, it can be understood that governments are reluctant to go beyond what is indicated here. Nevertheless, in some cases governments may be well advised to go further. For example, low-cost measures to make infrastructure more robust may be advisable when the additional costs are low.

Another direction of policy is that the public sector tries to achieve a proper balance of efforts of public versus private actors in the adaptation arena. The private sector may be challenged to contribute according to both dimensions of adaptation in Figure 3.1. First by contributing to reductions in terms of generalized costs of transport, for example by improving the performance of vehicles under bad weather conditions. Second, by adjusting behavior when generalized costs increase.

The theme of weather and climate change is closely related to that of recurrent versus non-recurrent congestion in transport networks. An increase in extreme weather conditions would probably make the non-recurrent part more relevant as a policy theme, in particular also since non-recurrent congestion is more difficult to cope with by transport network users. We also found evidence that adverse weather has strong impacts during the usual peak hours. This indicates that the two congestion concepts are not so easy to distinguish. Providing better insights into the role of weather conditions in both current and non-recurrent congestion is therefore an important theme of research.

NOTES

*   This chapter is partly based on work carried out jointly with Erhan Demirel, Olaf Jonkeren, Mark Koetse, Jos van Ommeren, Muhammad Sabir and Yuanni Xia.
1. Note that most of the examples are taken from the Netherlands, a country with a mild climate. Experiences in other countries with a more extreme climate such as the Nordic countries, or tropical countries may be helpful to study effects of more severe changes in weather conditions and how the public and private sectors are coping with it.
2. Another relevant transport aspect is that transport infrastructure is needed to support evacuation strategies; this dimension is not addressed in this chapter.
3. It is fair to add that policy integration is not always easy, so the cost of policy integration has to be considered here as a countervailing force.

REFERENCES

AVV, 2006. 'Economische Waardering van Mobiliteitseffecten van een Dijkdoorbraak' (Economic Valuation of Mobility Effects of a Flood), AVV, Ministry of Transport, Public Works and Water Management, Rotterdam.

Banister, D., 2008. 'The sustainable mobility paradigm', *Transport Policy* **15**, 73–80.

Bertness, J., 1980. 'Rain-related impacts on selected transportation activities and utility services in the Chicago area', *Journal of Applied Meteorology* **19**, 545–56.

Chung, E., Ohtani, O., Warita, H., Kuwahara, M. and Morita, H., 2005. 'Effects of rain on travel demand and traffic accidents', IEEE Intelligent Transportation Systems Conference Proceedings, Lausanne, Switzerland, 13–15 September.

CPB, 2002. 'Gevolgen van Uitbreiding Schiphol' (Consequences of Extension of Schiphol Airport), CPB, Den Haag.

Demirel, E., 2011. 'Economic models for inland navigation in the context of climate change', PhD dissertation, VU University, Amsterdam.

Eads, G.C., Kiefer, M., Mendiratta, S., McKnight, P., Laing, E. and Kemp, M.A., 2000. 'Reducing Weather-Related Delays and Cancellations at San Francisco International Airport', CRA Report No. D01868-00, prepared for San Francisco International Airport, Charles River Associates, Boston, MA.

EIS, US Energy Information Administration, 2010. 'International Energy Outlook 2010', Washington, DC.

FHWA (Federal Highway Administration), 2004. 'Traffic Congestion and Reliability, Linking Solutions to Problems', Washington, DC.

Goetzke, F. and Rave, T., 2006. 'Bicycle use in Germany: explaining differences between municipalities through network effects', University of West-Virginia, Morgantown, VA.

Grenzeback, L.R. and Lukmann, A.T., 2007. 'Case Study of the Transportation Sector's Response to and Recovery from Hurricanes Katrina and Rita', Cambridge Systematics, Inc., Cambridge, MA.

Hofmann, M. and O'Mahony, M., 2005. 'The Impact of Adverse Weather Conditions on Urban Bus Performance Measures Intelligent Transport System', Proceedings of the 8th International IEEE Conference on Intelligent Transport Systems, Dublin, Ireland, 13–15 September.

IPCC, 2007. *Climate Change 2007: Mitigation of Climate Change*, Contribution of Working Group III to the Fourth Assessment Report of the Intergovernmental Panel on Climate Change, Cambridge and New York: Cambridge University Press.

Jacob, K.H., Gornitz, V. and Rosenzweig, C., 2007. 'Vulnerability of the New York City Metropolitan Area to coastal hazards, including sea-level rise: inferences for urban coastal risk management and adaptation policies', in: McFadden, L., Nicholls, R. and Penning-Rowsell, E. (eds), *Managing Coastal Vulnerability*, Oxford: Elsevier, pp. 139–56.

Jonkeren, O., 2009. 'Adaptation to climate change in inland waterway transport', PhD thesis, VU University, Amsterdam.

Jonkeren, O., Rietveld, P. and van Ommeren, J., 2007. 'Climate change and inland waterway transport: welfare effects of low water levels on the River Rhine', *Journal of Transport Economics and Policy* **41**, 387–412.

KNMI, 2006. 'Climate Change Scenarios 2006 for the Netherlands', WR 2006-01, KNMI, De Bilt, The Netherlands.

Koetse, M.J. and Rietveld, P., 2009. 'The impact of climate change and weather on transport: an overview of empirical findings', *Transportation Research D* **14**, 205–21.

Koster, P. and Rietveld, P., 2011. 'Optimizing incident management on the road', *Journal of Transport Economics and Policy* **45**, 63–81.

Nam, D. and Mannering, F., 2000. 'An exploratory hazard-based analysis of highway incident duration', *Transportation Research A* **34**, 85–102.

Richardson, A.J., 2000. 'Seasonal and Weather Impacts on Urban Cycling Trips', TUTI Report 1-2000, The Urban Transport Institute, Victoria, Australia.

Rothengatter, W., 2003. 'Environmental concepts – physical and economic', in: Hensher, D.A. and Button, K.J. (eds), *Handbook of Transport and the Environment*, Oxford: Elsevier, pp. 9–35.

Sabir, M., 2011. 'Weather and travel behavior', PhD dissertation, VU University, Amsterdam.

Stern, N., 2007. *The Economics of Climate Change: The Stern Review*, Cambridge: Cambridge University Press.

Suarez, P., Anderson, W., Mahal, V. and Lakshmanan, T.R., 2005. 'Impacts of flooding and climate change on urban transportation: a systemwide performance assessment of the Boston Metro Area', *Transportation Research D* **10**, 231–44.

Te Linde, A., 2007. 'The Effects of Climate Change on the Rivers Rhine and Meuse', Delft Hydrolics, Delft.

Winters, M., Friesen, M.C., Koehoorn, M. and Teschke, K., 2007. 'Utilitarian bicycling: a multilevel analysis of climate and personal influences', *American Journal of Preventive Medicine* **32**, 52–8.

World Bank, 2010. *Economics of Adaptation to Climate Change*, Washington, DC: World Bank.

World Commission on Environment and Development (WCED), 1987. *Our Common Future*, Oxford: Oxford University Press.

Xia, Y., van Ommeren, J. and Rietveld, P., 2011. 'Weather conditions and disturbances in railway networks', VU University, Amsterdam.

4. Handling biases in forecasting when making transportation policy

Kenneth Button and Brien Benson*

4.1. INTRODUCTION

To slightly misquote the late American political scientist, Ezra Solomon (1986, p. E1), 'The only function of [traffic] forecasting is to make astrology look respectable'. While Solomon was, of course talking about economics, the sentiment extends to traffic and transportation forecasting in its many guises. Transportation forecasting, as we now understand it, is relatively new, but even an early assessment of traffic forecasting in Britain did not paint a very complementary picture of the engineering-based methods used at the time: 'an assumption of zero change from the base year would not have produced larger forecast errors ... for trips the errors would have been considerably less ... [than those obtained from a transport model]' (Mackinder and Evans, 1981, p. 25). We are simply not very good at it or, in some instances we allow vested interests to manipulate predictions to achieve their own self-serving ends.

The practical challenges of producing good forecasts have perhaps grown over time. Most forms of modern transportation require a substantial amount of expensive, durable, and inflexible infrastructure to be efficient. This infrastructure embraces not only roads, ports, rail lines, and the like that is directly used for movement, but also specialized facilities to build airframes, cars, ships, and railway units. It is also a sector that has traditionally been the subject of significant regulation, generally for economic, military, and political reasons but more recently for environmental protection. In addition, the various transportation networks and their nodes affect the long-term production and locations decisions of those that make use of the different transportation services. To ensure a reasonable degree of efficiency in decision making by both the public and private sectors, it is helpful to have good forecasts of the demands that will be placed on the transportation system, and on its impact on other sectors that society will ultimately have to bear.

Using the term 'bias' as shorthand for a portfolio of issues, if the forecasting bias is exactly, or nearly the same, across modes, space, and time then this may well have little impact on the relative allocation of resources within transport. This type of problem is a second-best, macro one of maldistributing resources between transportation and other possible uses. If, for example forecasts of the public costs of transportation investments and operations are consistently low, but accurate in other sectors of the economy, then transportation will get an unjustified share of taxpayers' money in any form of aggregate cost–benefit analysis. A second-level problem arises when forecast bias is more pronounced for a particular mode that can result in distortions in the resources allocated to various forms of transportation. A final level is when forecast bias in long-term demand can result in an inappropriate capital/operating cost mix for that mode.

Distortions in transportation policy that result from problems in forecasting vary with context, and where the errors or 'interpretations' in forecasting come from a diversity of influences. One of the main problems in separating these out is that it is difficult to know whether poor transportation forecasting is the only, or even the main, problem when conducting activities including investment appraisal or life-cycle costing, in which the elements in the decision-making process, such as the use of cost–benefit analysis, have their own well-known limitations. But, it seems wise as a practical expedient to provide the best and most appropriate forecasts irrespective of other issues (Button, 2010).

The chapter is practical in its orientation, it is concerned almost exclusively with looking at better ways of forecasting; to the extent that this is concerned with modeling philosophy or the institutional structures in which forecasts are developed and used, these are discussed. What the chapter is not is a debate about the nature of planning or of statistical analysis; these are much more fully treated in the works of van Wee, Wachs, Flyvbjerg, and others cited later in the text. It is focused on finding ways of providing better information for decision makers which may involve institutional and intellectual changes, but equally, if this is not possible, second-best, 'dirtier' approaches. Before looking at these 'cures' for the forecasting malaise, or at least some of the possible treatments for the symptom of the disease, we offer a few comments on both the nature of the forecasting biases, and a very brief discussion of what we know about the underlying causes. While attention will be mainly on surface transportation, similar issues emerge regarding forecasting air and maritime modes. The sections provide a foundation for looking at remedial strategies.

4.2 THE SCALE OF THE PROBLEM AND ITS IMPACTS

The poor quality of transportation forecasts has been known for some time. The 1970s saw considerable debate in the UK, for example, over the inaccuracies in the forecasts of car ownership, a major input into traffic modeling, and of the traffic forecasts themselves in the 1980s (UK House of Commons Committee of Public Accounts, 1988). The forecasts for the M25 London orbital road, for instance, were that on 21 of the 26 three-lane sections the traffic flow would be between 50,000 and 79,000 vehicles a day in the 15th year of operation, whereas the flow within a very short time was between 81,400 and 129,000.

In the 1990s, a series of studies in the US, including those by the likes of Kain (1990) and Pickrell (1992) brought into question the forecasts of transit ridership and costs of investments. Pickrell's study of programs funded by the US federal Urban Mass Transportation Administration, for example, found that the 10 projects examined produced major underestimates of costs per passenger (for example, the costs for the Miami heavy rail transit were 872 percent of those forecast, for Detroit's downtown people mover they were 795 percent, and for Buffalo's light rail transit project they were 392 percent); only the Washington heavy rail transit project experienced actual patronage more than half of that forecast. Updating of this work and looking at cost and ridership, forecasts for 47 US transit systems indicates only limited improvements over time (Button et al., 2010); for example, the Los Angeles Orange Line ridership was underestimated by more than 200 percent.

More recently a series of studies by Flyvbjerg and associated co-authors (for example, Flyvbjerg et al., 2005) looking across a range of surface transportation forecasts has shown considerable inaccuracies extending to most Western economies, and provides confirmation of the poor performance of forecasting. There emerges, in particular, a tendency for overprediction of capacity utilization and underprediction of the outcome costs of investments – for example, for 10 rail projects from a variety of countries, the passenger forecasts overestimated traffic by 106 percent, whereas for road projects there is a tendency for the forecasts to be wrong by about 20 percent but with the errors spread equally around the ultimate flows. In terms of costs, an examination of 58 rail projects indicates overruns averaging nearly 45 percent, and for 167 road investments, overruns of 20.4 percent.

It is not just the public sector decision making *per se* that is often based on poor traffic forecasts. A US study by JP Morgan (1997) of 14 private financed and operated toll roads found that only one exceeded the projected return, with four projects overforecasting returns by at least 30 percent. The overall conclusion being, 'reducing the uncertainty associated with these forecasts represent one of the major challenges for transportation agencies, traffic consultants, investment bankers and investors' (p. 12). In a study of over 100 international, privately financed road project appraisals conducted between 2002 and 2005, Bain (2009, p. 48) concludes that, 'in terms of error, the predictive accuracy of traffic models – used for toll road or toll free road forecasts – is poor'. Again there emerges a proclivity to overestimate traffic flows, with the ratio of actual to forecast traffic falling below unity for the majority of studies, although in some cases the predictions underestimated by up to 51 percent. The accuracy of forecasts did not appear to improve over time. If these forecasts were a major factor in both the decisions to make the investments and in their design, then this would imply a serious misuse of resources across modes, and probably between transportation and other activities in the economies concerned. In fact, the problem may well be considerably worse than the quantifications by Pickrell, Flyvbjerg, and others cited earlier, in that there is no way of knowing if forecasts of investments that were rejected were biased and instrumental in the rejections. If so, then resources that would have earned a social return in those projects would have been transferred to some other use where the net benefits are less. We only have data on the investments that actually materialized and on policies that have actually been adopted.

4.3 THE CAUSES OF THE MIS-FORECASTING PROBLEM

There are three broad and entwined reasons why transportation forecasts are generally poor: technical problems, carrying out the forecast, and using the forecast. The importance of each is not constant, and they are often interrelated, but can vary with circumstances over time.

Beginning with more technical matters, the most transparent reason for poor forecast, or at least the one most discussed in academic papers, is that the techniques used are deficient in some way. No one would expect perfection in forecasting, and particularly not over the long lives that most transportation infrastructure will be used, there are too many uncertainties, but one would hope for some improvement in accuracy over time. The abundance of previous forecasts, examined retrospectively using such statistical instruments as meta-analysis, can indicate, by revealing moderator key variables, the common flaws in methodology and application of forecasting procedures (Button et al., 2002).

There seems to be no lack of discussion of methodologies with numerous national and international conferences that are continually being held where, often admittedly exactly the same, experts gather to discuss their work and findings, and there are a plethora of academic journals and monograph series where, again admittedly largely the same people, peer referee and publish their work. Communication on recent findings and best practices, does not, therefore, seem to be lacking, nor do the mathematical skills required to do the technical work seem in short supply. The issue seems more to do with the penetration of this work into practice.

There is a widespread proclivity, however, to look at the technical merits of the models being used, rather than their practical use as forecasting instruments; elegance, sophistication, and the ability to back-cast are often seen as criteria for a good forecasting model, whereas in many cases forecasting exogenous variables is more difficult than predicting traffic flows however well the model fits historical data. The implicit view of Milton Friedman (1953, p. 7) on model performance is often forgotten, 'The ultimate goal of a positive science is the development of a "theory" or "hypothesis" that yields valid and meaningful (i.e., not truistic) predictions about phenomena not yet observed', but is extremely relevant for those who have to produce forecasts in a practical world rather than just a model for academic discussion. To design transportation infrastructure and develop mechanisms for the financing of its construction and maintenance are key public sector responsibilities in most countries, and the private sector has become more involved as various forms of privatization have been introduced. But added to this, the potential users of transportation infrastructure use transportation forecasts to plan location and production decisions, and, in the case of individuals, where to live.

There are, however, clearly challenges in the collection of the data needed to calibrate the parameters of the models required to produce actual forecasts, and in predicting even the short-term future path of many explanatory variables. Most forecasts rely on extrapolations of previous behavior; and thus assume constancy in what influences individuals' decision making. This is difficult to do well, but there are the added complications of trend breaks and of entirely new trends developing. Static economic models, for example, have difficulties not only in incorporating the 'catch-all' variable 'taste' when estimating elasticities but are prone, largely for convenience, to use Cobb–Douglas-based functions that assume the elasticities do not change with variations in other, commonly used independent variables such as income and price. Divergences from historical relationships do occur, and are often reflected in wider institutional changes demonstrating social priorities and attitudes to things such as transportation (Williamson, 2000). The use of such techniques as sensitivity analysis and simulations can provide some insights, but the range of possibilities increases as the length of the forecast period gets longer.

Availability of data is always a problem for forecasters, and, although there have been some positive developments, the problem has become worse in many contexts. There are better survey design techniques and more ways to gather transportation-related data ranging from on-line surveys to the use of global positioning systems for tracking movement. There is also evidence of improvements, although some may disagree, in our ability to produce reasonable medium- and long-term forecasting of such things as income, demographics, and fuel prices that feed into transportation forecasting (D'Agostino et al., 2010). Against this, however, the move towards lighter regulation and privatization of transportation facilities has changed and often reduced the public sources of data, and especially the amount and quality of economic data available to forecasters to carry out their work.

Despite these largely technical and operational challenges, the problems in forecasting accuracy would often seem to lie more in the way forecasting is actually done and the results used. A problem initially highlighted by Kain, and very much in line with the Public Choice School of economic thought (Buchanan and Tullock, 1962), is that forecasts are not politically neutral and many decisions regarding transportation investments and policy are not made in the public interest, but to some degree serve the ends of those who are making or using them. Basically, the forecasting process and output can be captured by those who commission the forecasts and then make use of them. These may be politicians who wish to win re-election and thus positively assess the short-term gains of supporting high-use/low-cost investments provided by some forecasts against other less 'optimistic' projections, or they may be bureaucrats concerned with increasing public sector activities. Under some forms of government, and particularly federal systems, pork-barrel politics can incentivize the use of bias forecasts by local agents to gain central funding; a principal–agent issue. The system is, in strict terms, corrupt and even if forecasters are neutral in their work, this has little influence on the way their output is interpreted and used (van Wee, 2011). Thus to try to close the gap between forecast and actual outcomes is more a matter of institutions than science.

One particular problem is the possibility of game playing, with the authorities consciously keeping cost estimates low at the outset to get a policy accepted, but knowing that subsequent and inevitable modifications will lead to cost escalations. Wachs (1989, 1990), for example, over 20 years ago, gave numerous anecdotal examples in supporting the existence and extent of this situation, whereby, for example, local planners in the US were essentially forced to adjust forecasts so as to gain federal grant aid, or consultants were continually rehired for projects despite a history of biased forecasting. A similar pattern emerges in a study of over 20 US highway agencies by Shane et al. (2009) which finds that a combination of 18 factors contributed to the underestimation of costs, including bias in forecasting assumptions, partly due to simple overconfidence by agencies that they can handle unforeseen problems, local budgetary rules, uncertainty as to what items to include in budget forecasts, and poor forecasting of exogenous factors, such as inflation.

The forecasting problem should not be seen as being unique to the public sector; there are similar institutional issues when considering some forms of private sector forecasts, especially when they involve concessions. The incentive for those tendering for such things as build–operate–transfer projects, according to Bain (2009), is to be optimistic with forecasts so as to win the contract and gain financial support. While the support for this is largely anecdotal in the case of tolled roads, there is more support in the context of airport concessions where *ex post* renegotiations are relatively common when traffic flows fall short of forecasts (Button, 2008).

In assessing ways for improving forecasting accuracy, and making better use of them, some decisions have to be made not just about the forecasting *per se*, but also concerning how technically more accurate forecasts can be incorporated into decision making.

4.4 THE POTENTIAL TREATMENTS

There are a number of possible approaches to handling the poor forecasting that accompanies many transportation appraisals, and resultant poor predictions that are often used to justify suboptimal actions. Some of the options considered are closer to first-best solutions, but most, largely in recognition of institutional realities, are second-best actions that may lead to at least some improvement in forecasts. The options may not be viable or useful in all contexts, but an informal SWOT (strengths, weaknesses, opportunities, threats) style analysis is helpful in isolating which alternatives have merit, and in what situations, as well as offering some insights into the practical problems of adopting them (Hill and Westbrook, 1997). The list of options may not be exhaustive (see Appendix Table 4A.1); the approach is rather one of suggesting that improvement is possible and the types of approach that seem helpful in its attainment. The discussion is also non-technical to avoid the unnecessary obfuscation that itself often surrounds these types of debate, and indeed some of the recent literature on forecasting issues.

4.4.1 Do-nothing

The current situation, if the forecasts form a significant input into the decision process, can clearly lead to a social misallocation of resources. Its strength is one of familiarity; we know what the weaknesses are, although perhaps not the full implications. But weaknesses in themselves do not justify change, after all the costs of developing new methodologies or institutions may outweigh the benefits. In some cases, more accurate forecasts may also not be required even if the existing techniques have shortcomings. For example, the poor performance of national car owner-ships for the UK in the 1970s and 1980s, which comprised an integral part of the traffic forecasting of the time, really had little impact on decision making. Road capacity was clearly inadequate and whether traffic was to grow at 2 percent a year or 4 percent over the next few decades made little difference because of budget constraints. More important was where the demands were likely to be strongest, but even here the trends were manifestly clear, and accurate, detailed projections really would not have helped in prioritization. Another example, crossing the investment-policy boundary is that when road congestion charging was initiated in London in 2003, a round sum of £5 a day was selected as the charge (Leape, 2006). The need for exact demand elasticity was not seen, but the need to imple-ment the charge expeditiously was, and the price on access to London at peak times produced a significant improvement in the city's traffic conditions.

In other cases, traffic forecasts may be of secondary importance because the decision makers place little priority on the pure transporta-tion efficiency of the system. This may in part be a problem of capture, and thus not a desirable situation, but it may also reflect social prefer-ences that elected officials have received votes to attain. There is evidence from studies by Frey (2001) and others regarding general policy making, that wider social objectives may dominate. This, however, is a somewhat weak argument for retaining the status quo if improved forecasts can be attained with little effort; whatever the social objective function, transpor-tation projections are relevant even if only to allow the opportunity costs of options to be transparent.

The potential threat of the do-nothing situation is that it will continue to extend across the whole gamut of transportation projects, even where more-refined and -accurate forecasts are needed for good policy making. The short-term implications may be small, but are likely to be cumulative if forecasting errors are biased in a particular direction. One way of resolv-ing this if current practices are retained is highlighted by Wachs (1990), when he argues for better education concerning the nature of forecasting and the differences between the objective elements and the subjective, which would allow more rational debate.

4.4.2 Improving the Forecast Methodologies

The theoretical methodology of transportation modeling has gradually evolved from the engineering-based four-stage – generation, distribution, mode split, assignment – approach developed in the 1960s (Bates, 2008). It continues to change as a greater appreciation of the importance of human behavior in travel trip-making patterns is recognized and the use of agent-based analysis (Holland and Miller, 1991), behavioral economics (Camerer et al., 2004), activity analysis (McNally and Rindt, 2008) and so on, is adopted. These frameworks, for example, allow for effects of non-linear actions such as hysteresis (Goodwin, 1977), as well as facilitating consideration of more qualitative influences on travel behavior.

But translating transportation models into practical tools for forecasting is not easy, and this may explain why the four-stage process is still widely used. There are challenges in the estimation of parameters, collection of apposite data, prediction of the future paths of independent variables, and so on. The approach of the modelers themselves is not always helpful, and while much attention in the academic literature is paid to how well models explain prior travel patterns, there are few articles that provide actual forecasts that can subsequently be evaluated. Academic tenure and promotion have little to do with the practical needs of the transportation planning community. It is, however, often more difficult to foresee some trend break, or some new influential trend in factors affecting transportation demand, than it is to estimate parameters from historic data that implicitly assume that ongoing trends continue.

But there is another dimension to this: in some cases we do have better techniques but do not use them effectively. Forecasting models have improved over time, but even when better forecasting techniques are demonstrated they are not always adopted. Perhaps the best-known example of this involves the Nobel Prize-winning economist Dan McFadden (2001) who deployed a disaggregate discrete mode split model to examine the construction of the Bay Rapid Transit System (BART) in the San Francisco area. While the conventional aggregate gravity model forecast a 15 percent modal share for BART, McFadden's disaggregate forecast was 6.3 percent and the actuality was 6.2 percent. Despite this, BART has never adopted disaggregate modeling as a policy tool. One can speculate on why this is so: it may be the capture of the system by the vested interests of consultants and others who have developed the four-stage modeling sequence, it may be that decision makers do not seek projections that may contradict their preconceived views, or there may be other reasons.

Simply adopting the state-of-the-art best forecasting techniques would clearly be a way of improving traffic predictions. The weakness is the extent to which this is possible or likely. There is a tendency for many authorities to continue to rely on the traditional four-stage forecasting model that focuses more on engineering flow concepts than on developments and reactions in human behavior. In many cases there are also significant costs involved in changing forecasting models and in collecting the appropriate data, and, thus inertia is a reason for retaining the status quo. The forecasts are also often an integral part of a wider planning and design process embracing interactive suites of programs. The problem is potentially compounded by the capture of much of the system by large consultants interested in selling their four-stage modeling software.

4.4.3   Correction Factors

If the forecasting biases are symmetric and have approximately the same order of magnitude across studies, then it may be possible to apply an adjustment factor to correct the errors: basically if the forecasts always underestimate costs by 20 percent then inflating the forecasts by 20 percent will give better forecasts. This, for example, is essentially what 'reference class forecasting' favored by the American Planning Association involves. The UK Department for Transport (Flyvbjerg with COWI, 2004) has also explored this option along with other departments.

The basic idea is that some sort of benchmark based on previous experiences with similar projects is adopted against which forecasts may be assessed; essentially serious deviations from these benchmarks require specific justification. This form of modified value transfer is relatively easy for policy makers to understand and to implement (Button, 2002). The use of the approach for handling potential cost over-runs has found some favor in a number of UK government departments. It has the strength of being relatively easy to understand and, if used across sectors, can introduce a degree of consistency of approach and in the long term potentially stimulate improved forecasting methodologies.

The major challenge is in defining what the benchmarks should be and drawing the boundaries for when a particular set of forecasts are called in for detailed scrutiny. Essentially, who makes the decisions that the forecasts are overoptimistic and the appropriate correction to apply? There is the additional danger of game playing, with those producing the initial forecasts of, say costs, making even lower forecasts to which the correction factor will apply. There is also the question of how to handle forecasts of essentially novel policies or technologies where benchmarks really do not exist. Overall, there is always the threat that any final decision process to correct is itself captured by those with a strong interest in a particular outcome (Flyvbjerg, 2008).

4.4.4 Bringing More Views into Forecasting

Forecasts are a technical input into decision making; they seldom determine the outcome of a project or policy assessment. They typically inform part of a public consultation process. Engineering demands have often seen single forecasts produced that give limited ideas of the range of uncertainties involved or the potential sources of these problems. Sensitivity analyses are sometimes offered but this relates to risk, where there are pretty well-known error distributions associated with parameters, rather than uncertainty where such distributions are highly opaque. Added to this, the forecasting methodologies are often made almost inaccessible because of their technical nature.

There are two possibilities for greater involvement in thinking about futures: more use of expert opinion and more public participation. In the former context, a number of private transportation entities have embraced the idea of supplementing 'technical' forecasts with adjustments following consultations with experts; Boeing Commercial Airplane started doing this with its traffic forecasts in the 1990s, as did British Airways. These approaches come under the broad umbrella of stated preference methods (Rose and Bleimer, 2008), and often involve the use of Delphi techniques. This may not satisfy the statistical purist, but it does offer the opportunity for introducing insights into possible trend breaks or new trends in traffic patterns.

Regarding the second option, an issue since the advent of standardized appraisal methodologies in the UK, starting with common discount rates across economic sectors in the 1960s, and later with the adoption of standard values across specific transportation projects within the COBA framework (www.cobaquadro.org.uk/downloads), has been for numeric inputs into public investment enquiries to dominate appraisal debates. It is a problem that has not gone unrecognized. Making the forecasting methodologies more transparent and the assumptions made more open to debate has been a longstanding objective. It has the strength of bringing more expertise and views to the decision-making process. The ongoing problem is to make operational something upon which there is considerable agreement: basically to demystify forecasting and open discussion of the possible scenarios to include in the forecasting process.

4.4.5 Engaging the Private Sector More

The analyses of transportation forecasts are, almost by necessity, focused on public sector projections; the forecasts of the private sector are generally not available for retrospective scrutiny. Where it has been possible to compare the forecast performances in the public and private sectors, the evidence is that, for example of 183 transportation projects examined by Flyvbjerg (2007), the private sector forecasts ultimately experienced cost escalations of 34 percent and the public sector 110 percent. More generically, and as an official response to overoptimistic forecasts, the UK Treasury has offered guidance on how public sector agencies can cope with them following the publication of the Mott MacDonald Report (2002).

From an incentive perspective, the difference in the quality of public and private forecasts can be seen in the context of the respective principal–agent situations. Since the spread of stakeholders in the private sector is much less than that in the public sector, where any adverse consequences of inaccurate cost or revenue forecasts fall on all taxpayers, decision makers in the private sector tend to be more conscious of the risks of making mistakes at the project level. The agents are in effect more aware of the interests of their principals in private companies, although admittedly not always entirely responsive. There are fewer ways, for example, for them to disguise a mistake by bundling it with a large number of other projects; and the costs of poor forecasting are borne by a narrower range of stockholders who tend to be more focused. By shifting more investment decisions to the private sector, there is a natural incentive for those involved to be more careful in their forecasting; the incentive for either padding predicted usage or understating costs is diminished when there is close accountability. This shift of responsibility can be done through a variety of mechanisms, including more purely private investments, private sector concessions, or the need for public agencies to seek private sector support for any of their own projects that fail to meet forecast outcomes.

The inherent weakness of this approach is that experience has shown that shifting some types of infrastructure decision making to the private sector is institutionally problematic because of the differences in the mechanisms of financing involved and time horizons taken in decision making (Papajohn et al., 2011). There are also the potentially *ex post* problems in the case of infrastructure, that once built, a private sector provider may exercise monopoly power. But there are ways of dealing with this, including various price-capping regulations and a plethora of options around the build, operate, and transfer framework.

4.4.6 More Flexible Engineering and Financing

Rather than focusing on the improving forecasting accuracy, an alternative is to accept the uncertainties of the future and adjust thinking about investments and policies accordingly. This may be particularly germane regarding large, durable projects that involve sunk costs at a time of concern with global warming effects, and ties in with ideas of robust decision making developed at the Rand Corporation aimed at assisting in decision making under extreme uncertainty (Lempert and Collins, 2007).

The normal discounting procedures used in techniques such as cost–benefit analysis have in the past meant that any errors in long-term projections were weighed lightly in decision making. The increased concern about sustainable development, and in particular the Stern Report's (Stern, 2007) recommendation that very low discount rates should be used in appraisal, means that long-term effects play a more significant role in cost–benefit assessments. Poor forecasts effectively have a larger impact on the welfare calculus. The low discount rate suggested by Stern has not, however, been without its critics (Nordhaus, 2007; Weitzman, 2007).

One method of mitigating the harm that poor long-term demand forecasts could inject into decision making is to build greater flexibility into investments; for example, physically leaving rights of way along roads for possible capacity expansions or the introduction of alternative modes, or financially, leaving the possibility for additional future funding from alternative sources. This is not a new idea and has, for example, been adopted in many recent airport developments (De Neufville, 2008) and is strongly linked with the notion of 'real options' (Amram and Kulatilaka, 1998). It is essentially an engineering design/management approach that allows, for example, for phased construction with the possibility of modifications to meet emerging engineering or financial circumstances as time passes. It has the strength that it can minimize any adverse implications of 'corruption' in the initial forecast, and has the opportunity both to allow for unforeseen events and to adopt new technologies or concepts as they emerge. Against this, there are possible costs of leaving idle capacity as a contingency reserve, or adopting designs that are not in the short term the most productive or cost efficient, and the threat that forecasts required for subsequent decisions regarding modifications will themselves be captured by vested interests.

4.4.7 Improved Incentive Structures

The evidence that many of the problems associated with biased forecasting stem from strategic manipulation of the forecasts suggests that changes in incentives may act to limit the problem. This is the first-best solution in the types of situation on which Kain, Wachs and Flyvbjerg have largely focused. The issue is essentially one of what motivates the mis-use of forecasts. If it is a matter of decision makers simply wanting some association with a piece of transportation hardware (many highways and airports are named after distinguished politicians or bureaucrats), then adapting the US naval approach of never naming a vessel after a living person may suffice. More difficult are cases where the incentive is basically pecuniary or to do with individuals' careers more generally, but there are possibilities. Traditionally in the UK, architects have been responsible for their designs until they die, or the building is demolished. Staying with the UK, contractual agreements for road maintenance have the construction companies having to 'rent' the roads they repair for periods when traffic is disrupted; this reduced the disruption time by about 40 percent as a result of better forecasting of the time required for work.

Changing the incentives for overpredicting use and underpredicting costs, as we have seen, is a particular challenge in systems where budgets are limited and allocated according to techniques based upon cost–benefit analysis–style procedures. The challenge is likely to be greater in federal systems where there are often incentives to escalate the 'doctoring' of cases in the competition for central funds; Wach's examples highlight that problem. At the central level possibly only openness will change practices, although the influence of such bodies as the Government Accountability Office in the US seems rather limited in this context. At the lower levels, the incentives to manipulate forecasts may be reduced by more-rigid criteria in the assessment process, or in some way offer rewards for more-accurate forecasts; details of regime change here depend very much on the exact nature of the existing institutional structure.

4.5   CONCLUSIONS

Producing forecasts is often a hiding for nothing for those responsible, but forecasts are needed for policy formulation, investment decisions and engineering design in transport. Poor forecasting is common and not a new problem. When the US Army Corps of Engineers began the Tennessee–Tombigbee Waterway project in 1975, it forecast construction costs of $323 million and 28 million tons of traffic annually when it opened, and 56 million 20 years later; it cost $2 billion to build, and 20 years later was carrying only 7 million tons of traffic per year. The concern is that there seems to have been little improvement in forecasting accuracy with time.

There appears to be no single, ideal way to improve the accuracy of transportation forecasts, or more importantly the ways in which they are used. For one thing the future is by its nature uncertain, and for another those who make use of forecasts suffer from the inevitable foibles of being human. What may be done is to reduce the errors, make the possibilities of serious mis-forecasts more transparent, and embrace procedures that minimize the implications of 'errors'. There are options for making progress on this issue, some already in train, with a diversity of strengths and weaknesses, but what does not seem to be the case is that any single approach is ideal, especially when account is taken of the way that real-world institutions evolve and function. A portfolio of measures tuned to particular issues and contexts seems a more tractable way forward than attempting to find a single panacea.

NOTE

*   This work forms part of the activities of the Center for Transportation and Economic Development, which is partly funded by the US Department of Transportation. Earlier versions of the chapter or elements of it were given at the Center for Interdepartmental Analysis, University of Bologna; 50th Annual Transportation Research Forum Conference, Fort Worth, 4th CITTA Annual Conference on Planning Research, Porto; and the NECTAR International Conference, Arlington where useful insights were gained. The comments of Martin Wachs on an earlier draft are also greatly appreciated.

REFERENCES

Amram, M. and Kulatilaka, N., 1998. *Real Options: Managing Strategic Investment in an Uncertain World*, Cambridge, MA: Harvard Business School Press.

Bain, R., 2009. 'Error and optimism bias in toll road traffic forecasts', *Transportation* **36**, 469–82.

Bates, J.J., 2008. 'History of demand modeling', in: Hensher, D.A. and Button, K.J. (eds), *Handbook of Transport Modeling* (2nd edn), Amsterdam: Elsevier, pp. 11–33.

Buchanan, J.M. and Tullock, G., 1962. *The Calculus of Consent*, Ann Arbor, MI: University of Michigan Press.

Button, K.J., 2002. 'An evaluation of the potential of meta-analysis and value transfer', in: Florax, R, Nijkamp, P. and Willis, K. (eds), *Comparative Environmental Economic Assessment: Meta-Analysis and Benefit Transfer*, Cheltenham, UK and Northampton, MA, USA: Edward Elgar, pp. 74–89.

Button. K.J., 2008. 'Air transportation infrastructure in developing countries: privatization and deregulation', in: Winston, C. and de Rus, G. (eds), *Aviation Infrastructure Performance: A Study in Comparative Political Economy*, Washington, DC: Brookings Institution, pp. 193–221.

Button, K.J., 2010. 'Does the primary problem of applying cost–benefit analysis to transportation policies lie in the methodology or in the forecasts used?', in: Van de Voorde, E. and Vanelslander, T. (eds), *Papers in Honor of Gust Blauwens*, Antwerp: De Boeck, pp. 477–96.

Button, K.J., Bal, F. and Nijkamp, P., 2002. 'Ceteris paribus, meta-analysis and value transfer', *Socio-economic Planning Sciences* **36**, 127–38.

Button, K.J., Doh, S., Hardy, J., Yuan, M.H. and Zhou, X., 2010. 'The accuracy of transit system ridership forecasts and capital cost estimates', *International Journal of Transport Economics* **37**, 155–68.

Camerer, C.F., Loewenstein, G. and Rabin, M. (eds), 2004. *Advances in Behavioral Economics*, New York: Russell Sage Foundation.

D'Agostino, A., Gambetti, L. and Giannone, D., 2010. 'Macroeconomic forecasting and structural change', Working Paper 1167, European Central Bank, Frankfurt.

De Neufville, R., 2008. 'Low-cost airports for low-cost airlines: flexible design to manage the risks', *Transportation Planning and Technology* **31**, 35–68.

Flyvbjerg, B., 2007. 'Cost overruns and demand shortfalls in urban rail and other infrastructure', Transportation Planning and Technology **30**, 9–30.

Flyvbjerg, B., 2008. 'Curbing optimism bias and strategic misrepresentation in planning: reference class forecasting in practice', *European Planning Studies* **16**, 3–21.

Flyvbjerg, B. with COWI, 2004. 'Procedures for Dealing with Optimism Bias in Transport Planning: Guidance Document', Department for Transport, London.

Flyvbjerg, B., Holm, S. and Buhl, S.L., 2005. 'How (in)accurate are demand forecasts in public works projects? The case of transportation', *Journal of the American Planning Association* **71**, 131–46.

Frey, B., 2001. *Inspiring Economics: Human Motivation in Political Economy*, Cheltenham, UK and Northampton, MA, USA: Edward Elgar.

Friedman, M., 1953. 'The methodology of positive economics', in: Friedman, M. (ed.), *Essays In Positive Economics*, Chicago, IL: University of Chicago Press, pp. 3–43.

Goodwin, P.B., 1977. 'Habit and hysteresis in mode choice', *Urban Studies* **14**, 95–8.

Hill, T. and Westbrook, R., 1997. 'SWOT analysis: it's time for a product recall', *Long Range Planning* **30**, 46–52.

Holland, J.H. and Miller, J.H., 1991. 'Artificial adaptive agents in economic theory', *American Economic Review* **81**, 65–71.

JP Morgan, 1997. 'Examining toll road feasibility studies', *Municipal Finance Journal*, **18**, 1–12.

Kain, J., 1990. 'Deception in Dallas: strategic misrepresentation in rail transit promotion and evaluation', *Journal of the American Planning Association* **56**, 184–96.

Leape, J., 2006. 'The London congestion charge', *Journal of Economic Perspectives* **20**, 157–76.

Lempert, J. and Collins, M.T., 2007. 'Managing the risk of uncertain threshold response: comparison of robust, optimum, and precautionary approaches', *Risk Analysis* **27**, 1009–26.

Mackinder, I. and Evans, S., 1981. 'The Predictive Accuracies of British Transport Studies in Urban Areas', TRRL Report SR 699, Crowthorne.

McFadden, D., 2001. 'Economic choices', *American Economic Review* **91**, 351–78.

McNally, M.G. and Rindt, C.R., 2008. 'The activity-based approach', in: Hensher, D.A. and Button, K.J. (eds), *Handbook of Transport Modeling* (2nd edn), Amsterdam: Elsevier, pp. 55–73.

Mott MacDonald, 2002. 'Review of Large Public Procurement in the UK', Mott MacDonald, Croydon.

Nordhaus, W.D., 2007. 'A review of the "Stern Review on the Economics of Climate Change"', *Journal of Economic Literature* **45**, 686–702.

Papajohn, D., Cui, Q. and Bayraktar, M.E., 2011. 'Public private partnerships in US transportation: a research overview and a path forward', *Journal of Management in Engineering* **27**, 126–35.

Pickrell, D.H., 1992. 'A desire named streetcar: fantasy and fact in rail transit planning', *Journal of the American Planning Association* **58**, 158–76.

Rose, J.M. and Bleimer, M.C.J., 2008. 'Stated preference experimental design strategies', in: Hensher, D.A. and Button, K.J. (eds), *Handbook of Transport Modeling* (2nd edn), Amsterdam: Elsevier, pp. 151–80.

Shane, J.S., Molenaar, K.R., Anderson, S. and Schexnayder, C., 2009. 'Construction project cost escalation factors', *Journal of Management in Engineering* **25**, 221–9.

Solomon, E., 1986. 'Economist: Fed must cut rate again', *Constitution* (Atlanta, GA), July 20.

Stern, N., 2007. *The Economics of Climate Change: The Stern Review*, Cambridge: Cambridge University Press.

UK House of Commons Committee of Public Accounts, 1988. *Road Planning*, London: HMSO.

van Wee, B., 2011. *Transport and Ethics: Ethics and the Evolution of Transport Policies*, Cheltenham, UK and Northampton, MA: Edward Elgar.

Wachs, M., 1989. 'When planners lie with numbers', *Journal of the American Planning Association*, **55**, 476–9.

Wachs, M., 1990. 'Ethics and advocacy in foresting for public policy', *Business and Professional Ethics Journal*, **4**, 141–57.

Weitzman, M.L., 2007. 'A review of the "Stern Review on the Economics of Climate Change"', *Journal of Economic Literature* **45**, 703–24.

Williamson, O.E., 2000. 'The new institutional economics: taking stock, looking ahead', *Journal of Economic Literature*, **38**, 595–613.

APPENDIX

Table 4A.1   Simple SWOT analysis of some alternative ways of handling forecasting uncertainties

	Strengths	Weaknesses	Opportunities	Threats
Do-nothing	Safety of the status quo. Is largely consistent with what is done in other areas of the public sector	Simply leaves the situation as it is	Enhance education of the general public to the objective and subjective nature of forecasts	The system becomes even more captured by vested interests
Improved forecasting methodologies	Inherently good to have better forecasting techniques	The methodologies may not be used. Problems in predicting the future of independent variables. Models are often assessed on historical accuracy and not 'rationality'	May stimulate wider changes in approaches to assessment. May lead to reduced demands on data	New methodologies may be easier to capture because it requires more specialist knowledge. New methodologies may be expensive to deploy
Correction factors	Technically easy to understand. Can consolidate a wealth of prior experiences. Makes the process more mechanical and less political	Deciding on the correction factor. Needs to deal with 'special cases'	Add consistency in approach in forecasting across a variety of public sector activities	Easily becomes fixed in changing conditions. Actors play games by manipulating forecasts to cause adjustments to the correction factor
Adding more views into forecasting	Makes the forecasting process 'less mysterious'	Allows for more qualitative factors to be incorporated in the	Allow more open public discussion about overall decision making	Adds to the complexity of selecting forecast leading to more power to 'experts'

		forecasting. Difficult to decide whose views are useful. Power of numerical over less tangible influences on traffic level		
Engaging the private sector more	Brings in a different perspective. Private sector forecasts generally have a better track record than public sector counterparts	Private sector's methodologies are different from the public sector's. Private sector tends to use forecasting techniques with relatively short time horizons	Develop broader initiatives in public/private cooperation	Can lead to neglect of less commercial effects of transportation investments
More flexible engineering and financing	Easy to understand	Financial costs of having 'stand-by capacity'. Subjectivity in deciding the amount of flexibility to adopt	Allows adoption of broader notions of robust decision making	Leads to missed opportunities by being excessively risk averse
Improved incentive structures	Acts to reduce pressures on forecasters to bias their forecasts	Difficulties in changing ingrained practices. Those it is intended to direct may capture the system	Positive spillover effects elsewhere up and down in the system. May lead to better management of public/private activities	Leads to greater bureaucracy in administering the new incentive systems

5. The functional spaces of major European forwarding ports: study of competition for trade bound to the United States

Mona Kashiha and Jean-Claude Thill

5.1 INTRODUCTION

The escalating liberalization of international trade that occurred during the decades following the Second World War under the impulse of various multilateral agreements and organizations has brought about a fundamental change in the geographical scope of logistics and freight transportation systems. While new trade ties have emerged with East Asia, long-time trading partners such as the United States and European nations have also intensified their trade relationships, to the point that the European Union is the largest trading partner of the United States and this trade represents 4 percent of US gross domestic product (BEA, 2010).

The intensification of long-haul trade routes has reinforced the critical role of seaports, as gateways to economic spaces and as nodes on the global deep-sea liner shipping networks (Goss, 1990; Notteboom and Rodrigue, 2007; Tongzon and Sawant, 2007). A countervailing force has been that shipping lines have now become dominant actors in world trade because they operate at the global scale and often have the option to route their services through one of multiple seaports (Slack, 1993). As Slack puts it, 'no longer can ports expect to attract shipping lines because they are natural gateways to rich hinterlands' (p. 581), and so it is with containerized freight shipping business. Patterns and processes of competition between seaports have changed and can be expected to remain quite dynamic in the face of fast-paced changing business environments (Meersman et al., 2010). The purpose of this chapter is to depict the state of interport competition from a multidimensional perspective. To this end, we adopt the framework of the 'functional economic space' (Gatrell, 1983) whose genesis is to be found in the pioneering work of Perroux on economic spaces and economic relations (1950). In this framework, space is a synthesis of multiple functional linkages (such as trade flows, container shipments and so on) between economic agents, and the structure of this space reveals the forces of economic competition at play between agents. The study of functional spaces of seaports is a critical step towards the depiction of real competitive relationships in deep-sea freight transportation systems, and the identification of challenges that seaports face, as well as their strengths.

There is a sizable body of literature on port competition and the related considerations that influence how seaports are selected for deep-sea shipment of containers. Interview-based research by Slack (1985) and Murphy and Daley (1994) has underscored the preeminence of price and level of service considerations over infrastructure characteristics of ports, while Tongzon and Sawant's (2007) own research points to connectivity, port charges, location, and infrastructure as the most discriminating factors of port choice. A large amount of econometric modeling work has focused on explaining port selection behavior by discrete choice analysis (for example, Nir et al., 2003; Tiwari et al., 2003; Veldman and Buckmann, 2003). Using data on shipments exported from the United States in 1999, Malchow and Kanafani (2001, 2004) identified factors such as inland transportation cost, service frequency, and connectivity as determinants of port choice. Conversely, Tiwari et al. (2003) establish that distance, congestion, and service frequency play a key role in port selection by Chinese shippers. Rather similar conclusions were reached by Blonigen and Wilson (2006) for international trade shipments into US seaports. Meersman et al. (2010) have recently revised the nature and factors of seaport competition. The authors underscore the multifaceted nature of interport competition, and the multiplicity of factors, which tend to dynamically change in response to market structures and world trade conditions.

In this research, we use a large and unique database of containerized door-to-door freight shipments from European countries and bound for the United States to reveal the functional economic space of 22 major European forwarding ports from three different, yet related, perspectives. We look at competition and positioning of these ports with respect to shippers and their geographical location on the European continent. We separately consider their linkages with US ports of entry; finally, we also look at port traffic from the angle of the types of commodity handled. Each analysis produces a functional space of European forwarding ports from one of the three perspectives. All three perspectives are also brought together in a synthetic analysis of interport competition.

Commodity flow databases constitute a rich and multidimensional data source, but this information will not be useful unless some rules and patterns are extracted from data in the form of functional space, for instance. Exploratory spatial data analysis methods play an increasing role in analyzing huge databases. It helps to understand, summarize, and classify the huge unorganized data, and, more importantly, provides new hypotheses about data that can subsequently be applied in spatial modeling. Multivariate statistical methods such as factor analysis, principal component analysis, multidimensional scaling, and self-organizing maps deal with data reduction and have been used effectively to comprehend functional space, either implicitly or explicitly. Berry (1966) applied factor analysis approaches to identify India's salient commodity flow patterns. In this work, R-mode analysis identifies clusters of destination locations with similar profiles of incoming flows, while Q-mode analysis accomplishes the same for origins. Black (1973) proposed dyadic factor analysis to extract fewer factors or components from the various types of commodities entering North America. Yan and Thill (2009) used the data mining technique of self-organizing maps on air travel flows to track change in the US air transportation system. In the present research, we follow an approach that differs from that used in these earlier studies. We are interested in using multidimensional scaling (MDS) to reduce the complexity in Europe-to-US trade data by visualizing hidden patterns in data through proximities in the functional spaces of European forwarding ports. MDS has a long tradition in the fields of geography and spatial sciences (Golledge and Rushton, 1972). One of the earliest geographical applications of MDS is that of Marchand (1973), where the matrix of travel times between Venezuelan cities serves to frame the functional space of Venezuela. Forer (1978) presented another early application of MDS; in this research, intercity travel time data are processed to create two-dimensional airline travel time spaces of New Zealand. More recently, Taylor and Walker (2001) created a service space of world cities that was derived from the service connections between cities across the world.

The rest of this chapter is organized as follows. Section 5.2 introduces the data source of this study and describes the main properties of this dataset. Our methodology is discussed in Section 5.3. Section 5.4 reports on the results of the data analysis, which consists in four functional spaces of European forwarding ports. Conclusions are given in Section 5.5.

5.2   CONTAINERIZED TRADE DATA

5.2.1   Data Source and Data Preparation

Freight shipment flows analyzed in this study consist of a dataset of door-to-door US-bound waterborne containerized export shipments with

European origins. The dataset includes all waterborne containerized US imports during the month of October 2006. The data comprises information submitted through both the US Customs and Border Protection Automated Manifest System (AMS) and manifests submitted at the ports. These original documents were corrected, cross-referenced, and improved by data supplier Port Import Export Reporting Service (PIERS) and distributed to users as the PIERS Trade Intelligence data product (PIERS, 2007). This data source provides appropriate attributes of the shipment of each bill of lading, including shipper company name and address, commodity description and type based on the Harmonized Commodity Description and Coding System (HS), quantity (twenty-foot-equivalent-unit: TEU, value, weight), carrier, forwarding port, pre-carrier location, US port of entry, and US consignee and its address (if the shipment is not in transit to a third country).

Development of machine-learning algorithms and manual methods for verification of data items such as shipment origins (by country and locality), coordinates of shipment origin, and categorization of shipment movement typology, as well as other improvements in support of these processes, was undertaken by the researchers. Data preparation implemented full text search queries and fuzzy matching algorithms to extract and geocode shipper origin localities from shipper company names and addresses. The unique data-cleaning process employed for this dataset included corrections based upon verification of physical origins (production locations) of shipments. Market intelligence was central to this process, as the logistical realities of global commodity chains were connected with production locations for companies with multiple facilities. Production/warehouse facility locations were determined from corporate websites and from evidence within shipment records – such as in the case of a 'precarrier location' data field match with a particular production facility (precarrier location being the point at which a carrier took possession of the cargo, as indicated in the shipment record). Carrier services were also used during this process.

The combination of the implementation of automated machine-learning algorithms and of the market intelligence method enabled us to compile a unique, consistent, and comprehensive database of US-bound containerized door-to-door freight shipments with multiple locational and business attributes, thus allowing for direct study of the hinterland–port–foreland triptych (Robinson, 1970; Charlier, 1992). Records where relevant attributes were suppressed were excluded from the dataset. The October 2006 timeframe is important because it provides a baseline preceding the trade downturn and restructuring associated with the Great Recession of 2008.

Data processing led to the exclusion of 12,169 bill-of-lading records due to suppressed or incomplete information. The resulting usable dataset contains about 107,000 bill-of-lading records, which collectively account for US-bound traffic of 202,837 TEUs. This cross-North-Atlantic trade is estimated to represent about 13.4 percent of US containerized imports (Carluer, 2008) and 21.1 percent of European containerized exports (Amerini, 2010).

5.2.2 Data Description

European waterborne exports to the United States transit through 22 major European forwarding ports, each of which handled at least 500 US-bound TEUs in October 2006. This freight traffic represents 99.0 percent of all TEUs in the dataset. The rest of the analysis in this chapter will be based on this traffic, to the exclusion of the traffic forwarded through the remaining 30 small ports in the European space. Figure 5.1 maps traffic volumes across all 22 major ports, while TEU statistics are listed in Table 5.1. It should be noted that certain European ports may play a significant role in trade with the United States, but as terminal points of a feeder service only and not as forwarding ports. This is why St. Petersburg, Russia, or Constanta, Romania do not appear in this list.

The statistics reported in Table 5.1 identify Bremerhaven/Bremen as the largest forwarding port to the US (20.4 percent of total traffic), followed by Rotterdam (16.4 percent), Antwerp (13.4 percent), La Spezia (8.0 percent), Le Havre (5.4 percent), and Hamburg (5.1 percent). No other port handles more than 5 percent of total European traffic. It should be noted that this ranking is at variance with the 2006 ranking of European ports on the basis of overall container traffic. According to this ranking, Rotterdam is the leader, followed by Hamburg, Antwerp, Bremerhaven/Bremen, Algeciras, Felixstowe, Gioia Tauro, Valencia, Barcelona, and Le Havre, in decreasing order of traffic volume (Amerini, 2010). A very small proportion of the traffic (3.1 percent of TEUs) handled by the above 22 ports is transhipped before reaching the coast of the United States. Particularly, Freeport, Bahamas, is used by Mediterranean Shipping Company as a transhipment hub for Atlantic traffic; Kingston, Caucedo, San Juan, and a few others are used by other operators for the same purpose.

The analysis pertains only to shipments originating in Europe. Several small countries are combined with a larger neighborhood to reduce data sparsity.[1] As a result, a set of 37 'countries' are recognized (Table 5.2).

Shipments represented in the dataset originate from all European countries, as indicated by Figure 5.2. Leading trading countries are Germany (21.6 percent), Italy (18.4 percent), France (9.4 percent), the Netherlands

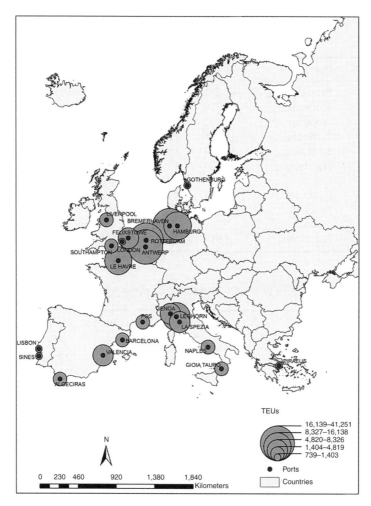

Figure 5.1 US-bound containerized traffic of major European forwarding ports (TEUs)

(8.6 percent), the United Kingdom (8.4 percent), Spain (6.4 percent), and Belgium (4.7 percent). Distributions by shipment value or weight are not markedly different from the distribution based on volume (TEUs). The hinterlands of European forwarding ports studied in this chapter exhibit a clear geographical orientation, in spite of the small size of the European peninsula, and its deep dissection by seas and gulfs. The mapping of port hinterlands by means of desire lines (Appendix 5A) reveals, however, that hinterlands overlap to a significant degree, particularly among ports of

Table 5.1 List of major European ports and their US-bound containerized traffic (TEUs)

Port ID	Port name	TEUs	Port ID	Port name	TEUs
1	Bremerhaven	41,251	12	Liverpool	4,560
2	Rotterdam	33,319	13	Gioia Tauro	4,388
3	Antwerp	27,352	14	Naples	3,682
4	La Spezia	16,138	15	Algeciras	3,464
5	Le Havre	10,914	16	Southampton	3,344
6	Hamburg	10,334	17	Fos	3,201
7	Genoa	8,326	18	Gothenburg	1,403
8	Felixstowe	6,985	19	Lisbon	1,371
9	Leghorn	6,767	20	Piraeus	1,170
10	Valencia	5,739	21	London	1,123
11	Barcelona	4,819	22	Sines	739

Table 5.2 Countries of origin recognized in the analysis

Country code	Country name	Country code	Country name	Country code	Country name
1	Albania	13	Germany	26	Poland
2	Austria	14	Greece	27	Portugal
3	Belarus	15	Hungary	28	Romania
4	Belgium	16	Iceland	29	Russia
5	Bosnia and Herzegovina	17	Ireland	30	Serbia
		18	Italy	31	Slovakia
6	Bulgaria	19	Latvia	32	Slovenia
7	Croatia	20	Lithuania	33	Spain
8	Czech Republic	21	Macedonia	34	Sweden
9	Denmark	22	Malta	35	Switzerland
10	Estonia	23	Moldova	36	Ukraine
11	Finland	24	Netherlands	37	United Kingdom
12	France	25	Norway		

northwestern Europe (in the range from Antwerp to Hamburg), and ports of northern Italy. The ports of Gioia Tauro, Algeciras, and Barcelona are major transhipment centers in the Mediterranean, whose broadly overlapping hinterlands are supported by extensive feeder networks.

US imports of European origin enter the United States through 23 gateways, listed in Table 5.3. Their share of TEU trade is in Figure 5.3. About 70 percent of the traffic is handled by four ports, namely New York/New

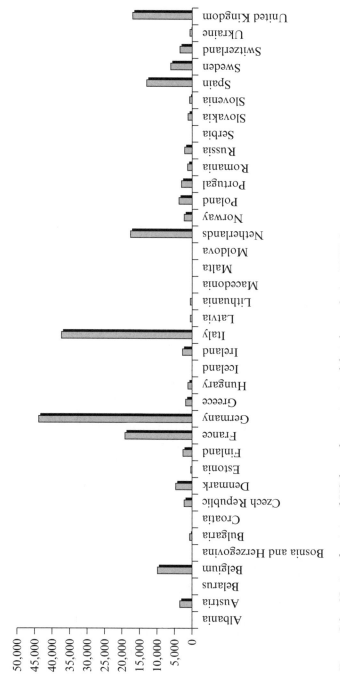

Figure 5.2   National origin of US-bound containerized freight trade (in TEUs)

Table 5.3   US ports of entry recognized in the analysis

Code	US port of entry	Code	US port of entry
1	Baltimore	12	New Westminster, BC
2	Boston	13	New York
3	Charleston	14	Newport News
4	Chester, PA	15	Norfolk
5	Houston	16	Oakland
6	Jacksonville	17	Pt. Everglades
7	Long Beach	18	Richmond, VA
8	Los Angeles	19	San Juan
9	Miami	20	Savannah
10	Mobile	21	Seattle
11	New Orleans	22	Vancouver, BC

Jersey (35.9 percent), Charleston SC (12.3 percent), Houston TX (11.0 percent), and Norfolk VA (10.7 percent). The predominance of ports on the eastern seaboard is a reflection of the Atlantic origin of the trade in question.

For the purpose of analyzing the commodity composition of European freight traffic bound for the United States, we collapsed classes of the Commodity Description and Coding System (USITC, 2007), termed 'HS codes' hereafter, into 17 categories (Table 5.4). Commodity categories comprise groups of similar commodities. As indicated by Figure 5.4, US imports are dominated by Prepared Foods (24.5 percent), Machinery and Mechanical Appliances (11.5 percent), Chemical Products (7.7 percent), Plastics & Rubber (7.4 percent), Articles of Stone, Plaster, Cement, and Asbestos (7.1 percent), and Base Metals and Articles Thereof (7.1 percent).

5.3   METHODOLOGY

MDS is an ordination technique that defines spaces from the matrix of distances between objects while keeping loss of information to a minimum (Cox and Cox, 2001; Kruskal and Wish, 1978). Like other multivariate statistical methods such as principal components analysis, factor analysis, and cluster analysis techniques, MDS deal with data reduction, although it differs from these other methods by taking a dissimilarity matrix as input. The output is a geometric configuration of data points, which represents the hidden structure in the data. Ideally, we would like the configuration to have as few dimensions as possible for the sake of visualization and parsimony.

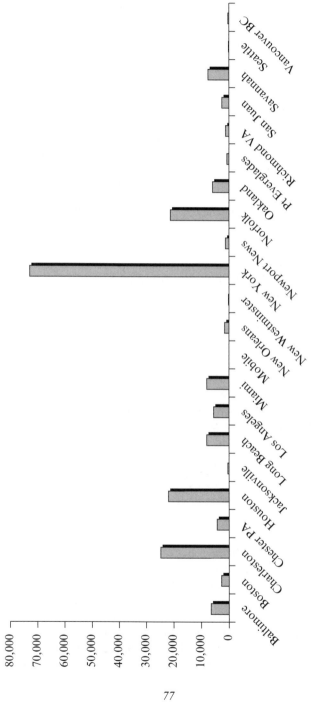

Figure 5.3   TEU share of US ports of entry

Table 5.4   Commodity categories recognized in the analysis

Code	Commodity category	Code	Commodity category
A	Articles of Stone, Plaster, Cement, Asbestos	I	Machinery & Mechanical Appliances
B	Base Metals & Articles Thereof	J	Mineral Products
C	Chemical Products	K	Plastics & Rubber
D	Footwear, Headgear	L	Prepared Foodstuffs
E	General Merchandise	M	Textiles & Textile Articles
F	Handicrafts, Pearls, Semi/ Precious Stones, Metals	N	Transportation Equipment
		O	Vegetables, Animals & their
G	Hides & Skins		Products
H	Instruments – Measuring,	P	Wood & Wood Products
	Musical, Arms & Ammunition	Q	Wood Pulp Products

Let us assume that the proximity or similarity between object i and object j is represented by δ_{ij}. The Euclidean distance between two points, x_i and x_j, that underwent scaling is denoted by d_{ij}. Non-metric MDS, which is applied in this study, does not depend on the numerical metric properties of the dissimilarities and uses only their rank order. The basic concept then takes the form $f(\delta_{ij}) = d_{ij}$, where f can be any transformation function that describes a rising pattern, that is, it preserves the monotonicity constraint. The objective function of MDS minimizes the residuals of the Euclidean distance between scaled points and the monotonic transformation of the corresponding dissimilarities (disparities) $f(\delta_{ij})$. This objective function, also known as the stress, is expressed as:

$$\sqrt{\frac{\sum_i \sum_j [f(\delta_{ij}) - d_{ij}]^2}{scale factor}}$$

Smaller stress values indicate a better fit. A rule of thumb is that a stress value higher than 0.2 indicates poor fit (Kruskal and Wish, 1978).

Computationally, the MDS algorithm involves an iterative analytical fitting process that converges towards a new 'spatial' configuration of the objects that best fits the original one. Mathematically, it is possible to produce MDS solutions of higher dimensions than two or three. Since a four-dimensional space is challenging to visualize in an ordinary sense, it is usually hoped that two- or three-dimensional configurations present good

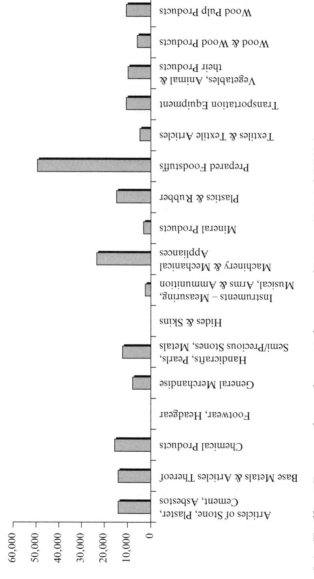

Figure 5.4   Traffic at European forwarding ports by commodity type (in total TEUs)

descriptions of the data. A full description of the computational procedure can be found in Kruskal and Wish.

A good way to see the correspondence between the d_{ij} and the δ_{ij} is by a scatter diagram of distances against dissimilarities, called a Shepard plot. We want small dissimilarities to correspond to small distances, and large dissimilarities to large distances; this means that the points in the scatter diagram should form a rising pattern. The other way to evaluate the quality of results is with the so-called 'stress value'; for any given set of data and for any given configuration, the objective function yields a single number which shows how well (or how poorly) the data fit the configuration.

The research question at the core of this research is manifold. We seek to determine how similarly European ports interact with American ports and how much their interactions relate to the commodity composition of their traffic or the national origin of this traffic on the European continent. These linkages articulate to form a complex structure of factors that shippers consider for port selection in competitive freight networks. We investigate the relative characteristics of European forwarding ports in terms of the composition of their hinterlands, US destination ports and commodity profile to better understand the modalities of interport competition through functional space reconstruction. MDS spaces help us to discover clustering tendencies in flow data associated with forwarding ports and reveal the association between different spaces. They convey the degree of competition in the network of forwarding ports in the context of their export business to the US.

In this research, the MDS algorithm is applied to three distinct matrices capturing the profile of each of the 22 major European forwarding ports (observations or objects), respectively, with respect to US entry ports, national hinterlands, and commodity types handled (variables or attributes). These matrices are populated with TEU counts for the month of October 2006. Similarity between European port objects is calculated by the Euclidean distance between each pair of objects in the associated multidimensional attribute space. Because of the great range disparity of the attributes, it is standard practice to control for the size effect through rescaling. Different rescaling matrix approaches exist, such as an iterative proportional fitting procedure, data normalization, and transformation to proportions. The last approach is applied here. All computations are performed in Matlab 2010a.

In our analyses, stress is usually smaller than 0.2. However, stress value should not be used as the sole indicator of goodness of fit, since it is very much an aspatial measure (Gatrell, 1983). Examining the Shepard plot and also finding meaningful clusters have been our main criteria in selecting appropriate dimensions for mapping European ports.

5.4   MDS RESULTS AND INTERPRETATION

The MDS algorithm is first applied to the dataset of national origination of US-bound container traffic at each of the 22 major European forwarding ports. Figure 5.5 shows the two-dimensional functional space of European ports generated when the measure of port closeness is their similarity in the national composition of hinterlands. The stress function equals 0.18 for this solution; adding one more dimension improves the score to 0.11. To validate whether the three-dimensional solution reflects the existence of additional structures in the data matrix, the three-dimensional results presented in Figure 5.6 can be examined and compared to the configuration in Figure 5.5. The two configurations of ports are rather similar and differ in detail only, which supports the use of a two-dimensional representation for the sake of the ease of interpretation. Shepard plots are presented in Figures 5.7a and 5.7b and demonstrate a good fit. On each plot, disparities $f(\delta_{ij})$ (hollow circles) and distances d_{ij} (dots) are plotted against dissimilarities δ_{ij} for each pair of observations i and j.

   In Figure 5.5, the national composition of each port's hinterland is depicted by a bar chart to facilitate interpretation. The periphery of the MDS map is occupied by several clusters of ports that are geographically close to one another and exhibit significant mutual overlap of their hinterlands, with little or no overlap between clusters. The quartet of British ports – Felixstowe, Liverpool, Southampton, and London – form a cluster in the lower-right portion of the MDS map, with hinterlands focused on the United Kingdom. The Italian quartet of La Spezia, Leghorn, Genoa, and Naples is positioned opposite at the north-central end of the map and their hinterlands are almost exclusively Italian. Iberian ports of Valencia, Sines, and Lisbon to the left, serve Spain and Portugal, while Fos and Le Havre predominantly serve France. Piraeus is the forwarding port of choice of Greek exporters, and a lesser degree for Southeast European countries (especially Romania). Finally, Gothenburg is the primary port of Scandinavia. The very center of the MDS map is occupied by a quartet of ports of Northwestern Europe, Antwerp, Rotterdam, Bremerhaven, and Hamburg, which are also the largest forwarding ports of Europe. All these ports share the characteristic of hinterlands that broadly overlap and span several countries. Two subclusters can be discerned, namely Rotterdam and Antwerp, serving the so-called 'blue Banana', including Belgium, the Netherlands, and other West European countries (France, Switzerland, the United Kingdom, Ireland, western and southwestern Germany[2]), and Hamburg and Bremerhaven, serving Germany as well as East European and Scandinavian countries. From a geographical standpoint, these four ports are generalists that serve businesses from a

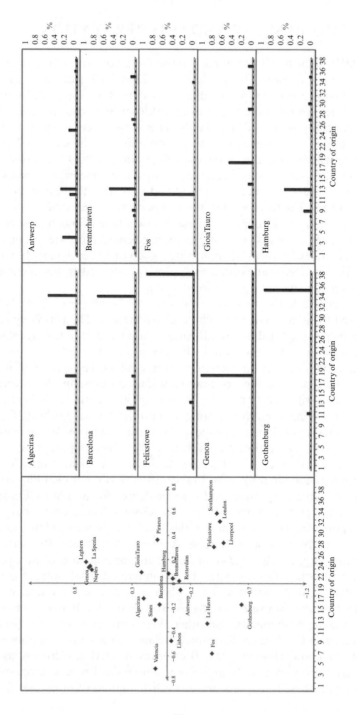

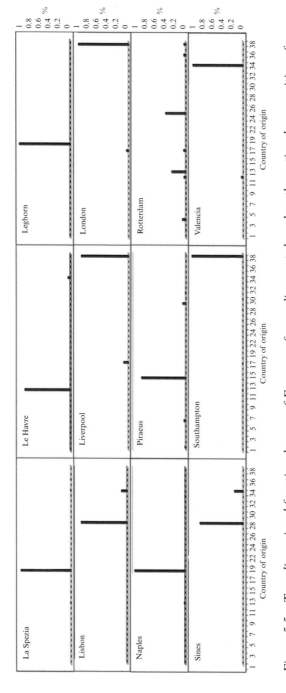

Figure 5.5   Two-dimensional functional space of European forwarding ports based on the national composition of hinterlands (depicted by bar charts)

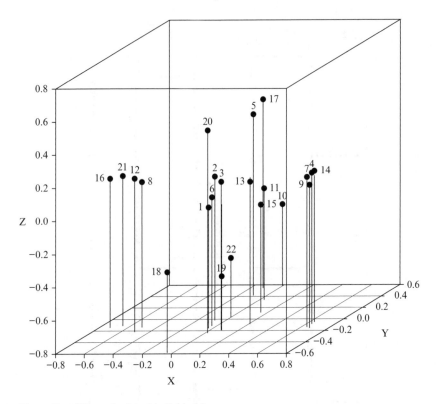

Note: Port IDs can be found in Table 5.1.

Figure 5.6   Three-dimensional functional space of European forwarding ports based on the national composition of hinterlands

large part of Europe, particularly thanks to extensive shortsea and land-based feeder networks. The three Mediterranean ports of Gioia Tauro, Barcelona, and Algeciras, which are positioned just at the periphery of the core group of four ports on the MDS map, strive to play the same role in Southern Europe, although their respective hinterlands are dominated by their national territories.

Overall the hinterland-based functional space of European forwarding ports exhibits clearly defined structures consistent with what is known about the geographical orientation of their hinterlands. While there is little overlap at the periphery, overlap is extreme towards the center. The degree of competition between ports is directly related to the geographical overlap of hinterlands. Finally, one cannot avoid seeing a close isomorphic correspondence between the geographical maps of ports (Figure 5.1) and the hinterland-based functional map depicted in Figure 5.5, where geographically peripheral ports are characterized by more exclusive hinterlands and thus less competition, conversely to core ports that face fierce competition with each other as well as with more peripheral ports.

The functional space of ports created from the perspective of traffic with US ports of entry is shown in Figure 5.8. The stress function equals 0.18 with two dimensions in this case; the Shepard plot is reported in Figure 5.7c. The bar charts depicting US port-of-entry shares reveal a dominant self-sorting of ports on the basis of the share of traffic entering the US through New York/New Jersey (code 13): this share increases gradually from the top to the bottom of the map. As a result, European ports positioned towards the top of the functional space tend to exhibit greater diversification of their interactions with US ports of entry. Southern American ports of Miami (9) and Savannah (20) dominate relatively in the top left corner of this space, while Houston (5) and Charleston (3) are more dominant in the top and right sections of the map. Some self-sorting of ports occurs in relation to their routing to ports of Southern California: Long Beach (7) tends to be more dominant on the left, while Los Angeles (8) tends to dominate on the right. It is clear that this functional space is largely shaped by shipping lines that selectively serve regional ports so as to optimize economies of scale by minimizing berthing times and maximizing foreland coverage.

Figure 5.9 depicts the functional space of European ports where port proximity depicts how similar the commodity type distribution of their traffic is. The commodity categories of Prepared Foodstuffs (L) and Machinery & Mechanical Appliances (I) that dominate US imports from Europe control the configuration of this functional space. Prepared Foodstuffs are seen to be more dominant in the bottom half of the map, while Machinery & Mechanical Appliances are more dominant in the top half. Secondary factors are Base Metals & Articles Thereof (B) (in the top left portion), and Articles of Stone, Plaster, Cement, and Asbestos (A) (in the top right quadrangle), and Instruments (H) in the lower right corner with the port of Sines. What transpires through the self-sorting based on commodity composition of the port traffic shown in Figure 5.9 is the latent regional specialization of industrial production and of export to the United States, with Southern Europe specializing in Prepared Foodstuffs and the rest of Europe showing a stronger orientation towards manufactured goods. As a corollary, the former are more prevalent in traffic handled by ports of Southern Europe than the latter, and vice versa.

The significant differences observed between the three separate mappings of Figures 5.5, 5.8, and 5.9 open the question of the relative

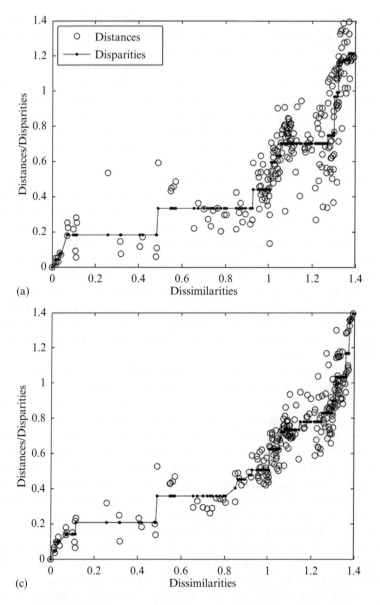

Figure 5.7　Shepard plots: (a) two-dimensional solution for national
composition of hinterlands; (b) three-dimensional solution
for national composition of hinterlands; (c) two-dimensional
solution for American ports of entry; (d) two-dimensional
solution for commodity composition

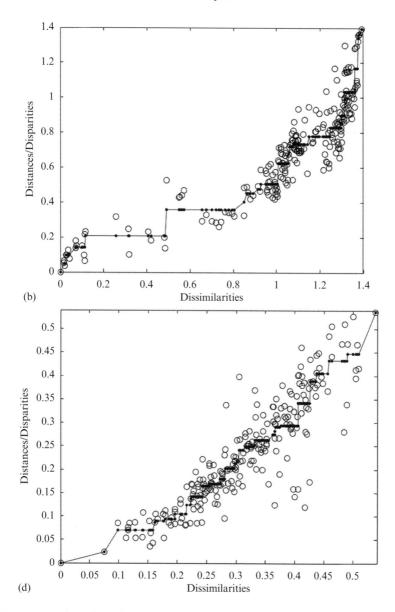

(b)

(d)

Figure 5.7 (continued)

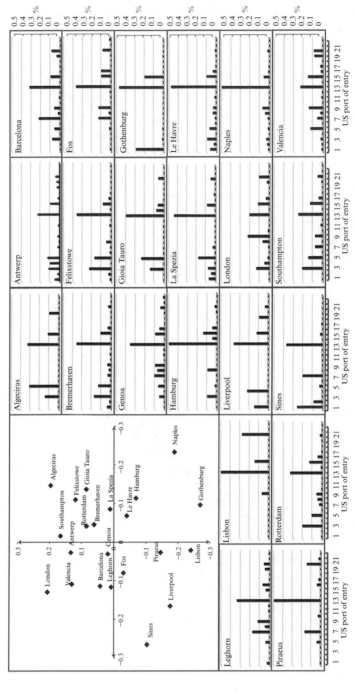

Figure 5.8   Two-dimensional functional space of European forwarding ports based on their interaction with American ports on entry (shares depicted by bar charts)

88

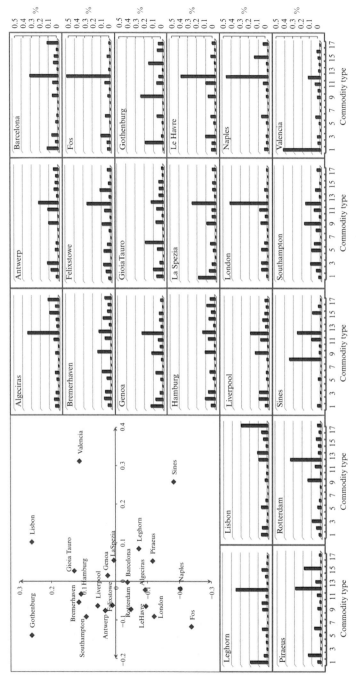

Figure 5.9 Two-dimensional functional space of European forwarding ports based on commodity composition (bar charts represent commodity shares)

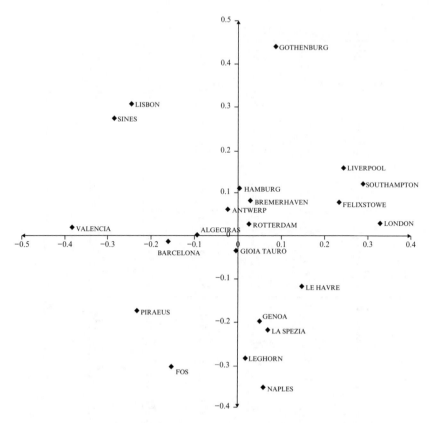

Figure 5.10   Composite functional space

importance of commodity type, origin and destination of shipments in the selection of forwarding ports by shippers and in shaping the competitive environment that European ports face when forwarding European products to the United States. The partial views captured by Figures 5.5, 5.8, and 5.9 can now be brought together in a synthetic mapping of the functional space of European forwarding ports. This is accomplished here by simple addition of the three partial mappings. The result is given in Figure 5.10.

The composite functional space exhibits keen similarities with the space defined by the national orientation of hinterlands (Figures 5.5 and 5.6). The key features of this space are as follows. The four ports of the northwestern range (Antwerp, Rotterdam, Hamburg, and Bremerhaven) form the focal point of the entire system. This core group is surrounded by ports that are more niche players, serving select routes, with greater product specialization, and deeper reliance on regional hinterlands. Different groupings can be identified here, namely taken clockwise, the Swedish, the British, the Italian, and finally the Greek and Iberian. France stands out as the exception, with Le Havre and Fos being separated. The explanation here is to be found in the geography of France, with both Atlantic and Mediterranean orientations. Le Havre shares some commonalities with ports of the northwestern range (less Prepared Foodstuffs traffic, business from the Low Countries, and also from Portugal and Eastern Europe thanks to feeder services), while Fos has some business with Spanish exporters. Each of the regional clusters identified is itself organized internally: from the more diverse and more competitive on the side oriented towards the center of the functional space to the less diverse and affected by competition on the opposite side of the cluster. Hence, the contrast between Felixstowe and London in the United Kingdom, Gioia Tauro and Naples in Italy, Algeciras and Sines or Valencia on the Iberian Peninsula. Finally, given their position at the very center of the composite functional space, Rotterdam, Antwerp, Bremerhaven, and Hamburg emerge as the European ports exposed to the most intense competitive forces. A surprise here may be that Rotterdam does not stand out more in comparison to its Belgian and German rivals. The positioning of Algeciras and Gioia Tauro in close proximity to the four ports of the northwestern range is revealing of the effective strategy followed by these two Spanish and Italian ports to serve as major gateways to transatlantic trade (and not only Mediterranean) and in fact global trade.

5.5 CONCLUSIONS

The purpose of this chapter was to study the structure of the system of deep-sea forwarding ports in Europe from a multidimensional perspective, and particularly the competitive relationships that prevail among them in their trade with the United States. The construct of 'functional economic space' was adopted as a framework to anchor the study in the complex patterns of freight shipping flows that transit through major European ports. The technique of multidimensional scaling was used to reveal the geometry of functional spaces of major European forwarding ports out of detailed commodity flow data compiled from the PIERS Trade Intelligence database. Functional spaces were created that captured the national composition of port hinterlands, the commodity profile of port traffic, the US port of entry profile, and finally the combination of these three dimensions.

Non-metric MDS was successful at creating meaningful functional spaces of forwarding ports. The configurations of functional spaces revealed the degree of competition facing ports from each perspective, and more fundamentally the complex structure of freight forwarding from Europe to the United States. The composite functional space was found to exhibit close topological similarities with the geographical space. It also identified the quartet of Rotterdam, Antwerp, Hamburg, and Bremerhaven, as the most competitive ports in Europe. Other ports form clusters configured around this core quartet and can be seen more as niche players, serving select routes, with greater product specialization, and deeper reliance of regional hinterlands. It is clear that the hybrid approach based on the data reduction algorithm of MDS and geovisualization is highly effective in extracting clustering tendencies in flow data and in establishing the fundamental properties of the European system of deep-sea forwarding ports.

The analytical approach presented in this chapter will be of use to researchers interested in studying the spatial–temporal organization of the ports systems at the regional or hemispheric scale, and the structure of logistics systems. Ports, carriers, shippers, and regional policy stakeholders can learn emerging trends in the fast-changing world of international trade and logistics by letting the data speak for themselves, so as to take advantage of new business opportunities or reposition themselves *vis-à-vis* competitors.

The work reported in this chapter can be further enhanced to deepen the understanding of the European system of deep-sea forwarding ports. First, the dataset should be extended to multiple months to remove possible seasonality. Also, a longitudinal study including trade flow data for multiple years may reveal interesting shifts in world trade relationships in response to continental or global and mid- to long-term economic conditions. Second, the spatial definition of port hinterlands can be apprehended at a subnational geographical resolution to better capture the role of short-sea and land-based feeder services. Furthermore, MDS and geovisualization can be combined with a multivariate model of port choice to integrate a broader range of factors at once and more precisely characterize the nature and scope of competitive behaviors between ports and between agents using port infrastructures, such as shipping lines and shippers. Preliminary results with decision trees of port selection point to the greater depth of analysis afforded by this approach. Finally, the MDS-based approach of analysis is conducive to studying the temporal evolution of competitive structures exhibited by international logistics and freight transportation systems.

NOTES

1. Andorra and Monaco are collapsed with France; Lichtenstein with Switzerland; Luxembourg with Belgium; San Marino with Italy; the Faroe Islands with Denmark; and the Isle of Man and the Channel Islands with the United Kingdom.
2. The fact that western and southwestern Germany are core regions of the hinterlands of Antwerp and Rotterdam is not revealed by MDS analysis because this analysis is conducted at the national scale. See the maps of port hinterlands in Appendix 5A for further evidence.

REFERENCES

Amerini, G., 2010. 'European port activity in 2009 hit by the general economic crisis', Eurostat, European Union, Luxembourg, available at: http://epp.eurostat. ec.europa.eu/cache/ITY_OFFPUB/KS-SF-10-065/EN/KS-SF-10-065-EN.PDF (accessed September 12, 2011).

BEA, 2010. 'Current-dollar and "real" GDP', Bureau of Economic Analysis, Washington, DC, available at: www.bea.gov/national/xls/gdplev.xls (accessed August 2, 2011).

Berry, B.J.L., 1966. 'Essays on commodity flows and the spatial structure of the Indian economy', RP III, Department of Geography, University of Chicago, Chicago, IL.

Black, W.R., 1973. 'Toward a factorial ecology of flows', *Economic Geography* **49**, 59–67.

Blonigen, B.A. and Wilson, W.W., 2006. 'International trade, transportation networks and port choice', American Economic Association Annual Meetings, available at: http://www.aeaweb.org/annual_mtg_papers/2007/0105_1430_2103. pdf. (accessed October 10, 2011).

Carluer, F., 2008. *Global Logistic Chain Security: Economic Impacts of the US 100 % Container Scanning Law*, Brussels: World Customs Organization.

Charlier, J., 1992. 'Ports and hinterland connections', in: Dolman, A.J. and Van Ettinger, J. (eds), *Ports as Nodal Points in a Global Transport System*, Oxford: Pergamon, pp. 105–21.

Cox, T.F. and Cox, M.A.A., 2001. *Multidimensional Scaling*, London: Chapman & Hall.

Forer, P.C., 1978. 'A place for plastic space', *Progress in Human Geography* **2**, 230–67.

Gatrell, A., 1983. *Distance and Space: A Geographical Perspective*, Oxford: Clarendon.

Golledge, R. and Rushton, G., 1972. *Multidimensional Scaling: Review and Geographical Applications*, Washington, DC: Association of American Geographers.

Goss, R.A., 1990. 'Economic policies and seaports: 1. The economic functions of seaports', *Maritime Policy & Management* **17**, 207–19.

Kruskal, J.B. and Wish, M., 1978. *Multidimensional Scaling*, Beverly Hills, CA: Sage.

Malchow, M.B. and Kanafani, A., 2001. 'A disaggregate analysis of factors influencing a port's attractiveness', *Maritime Policy & Management* **28**, 361–73.

Malchow, M.B. and Kanafani, A., 2004. 'A disaggregate analysis of port selection', *Transportation Research E* **40**, 317–37.

Marchand, B., 1973. 'Deformation of a transportation surface', *Annals of the Association of American Geographers* **63**, 507–21.

Meersman, H., van de Voorde, E. and Vanelslander, T., 2010. 'Ports competition revisited', *Review of Business and Economics* **55**, 210–32.

Murphy, P.R. and Daley, J.M., 1994. 'A comparative analysis of port selection factors', *Transportation Journal* **34**, 15–21.

Nir, A., Lin, K. and Liang, G., 2003. 'Port choice behavior: from the perspective of the shipper', *Maritime Policy & Management* **30**, 165–73.

Notteboom, T. and Rodrigue, J.-P., 2007. 'Re-assessing port hinterland relationships in the context of global supply chains', in: Wang, J., Olivier, D., Notteboom, T. and Slack, B. (eds), *Ports, Cities, and Global Supply Chains*, London: Ashgate, pp. 51–68.

Perroux, F., 1950. 'Economic space: theory and applications', *Quarterly Journal of Economics* **64**, 21–36.

PIERS, 2007. 'July 1, 2006–June 30, 2007 – PIERS TI U.S. Waterborne Imports Dataset' (Data file), UBM Global Trade, Newark, NJ.

Robinson, R., 1970. 'The hinterland–foreland continuum: concept and methodology', *Professional Geographer* **22**, 307–10.

Slack, B., 1985. 'Containerization, inter-port competition and port selection', *Maritime Policy & Management* **12**, 293–303.

Slack, B., 1993. 'Pawns in the game: ports in a global transportation system', *Growth and Change* **24**, 579–88.

Taylor, P.J. and Walker, D., 2001. 'World cities: a first multivariate analysis of their service complexes', *Urban Studies* **38**, 23–47.

Tiwari, P., Itoh, H. and Doi, M., 2003. 'Shippers' port and carrier selection criteria in China: a discrete choice analysis', *Maritime Economics & Logistics* **5**, 23–39.

Tongzon, J.L. and Sawant, L., 2007. 'Port choice in a competitive environment from the shipping lines' perspective', *Applied Economics* **39**, 447–92.

United States International Trade Commission (USITC), 2007. 'HTS: 2007-07-02 – Revision 2, Official Harmonized Tariff Schedule of the United States Annotated', available at: http://www.usitc.gov/tata/hts/bychapter/_0702.htm (accessed September 15, 2011).

Veldman, S.J. and Buckmann, E.H., 2003. 'A model on container port competition: an application for the West European container hub ports', *Maritime Economics & Logistics* **5**, 3–22.

Yan, J. and Thill, J.-C., 2009. 'Visual data mining in spatial interaction analysis with self-organizing maps', *Environment and Planning* **B 36**, 466–86.

APPENDIX 5A HINTERLANDS OF MAJOR FORWARDING EUROPEAN PORTS

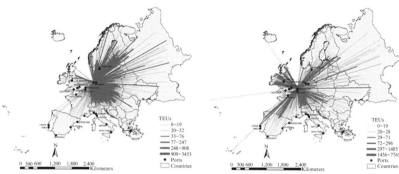

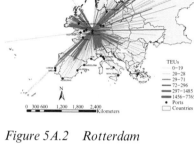

Figure 5A.1   Bremerhaven

Figure 5A.2   Rotterdam

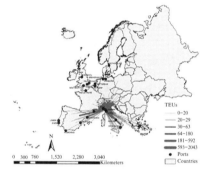

Figure 5A.3   Antwerp

Figure 5A.4   La Spezia

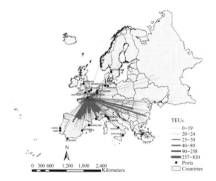

Figure 5A.5   Le Havre

Figure 5A.6   Hamburg

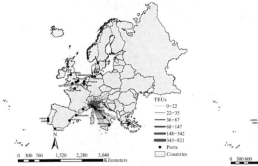

Figure 5A.7   Genoa

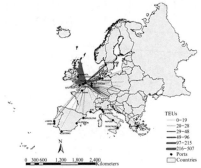

Figure 5A.8   Felixstowe

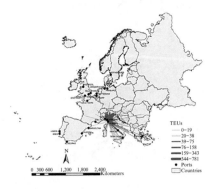

Figure 5A.9   Leghorn

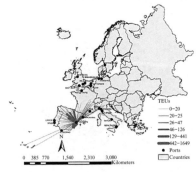

Figure 5A.10   Valencia

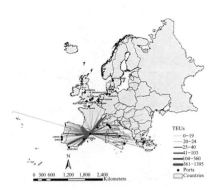

Figure 5A.11   Barcelona

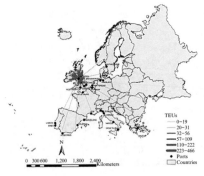

Figure 5A.12   Liverpool

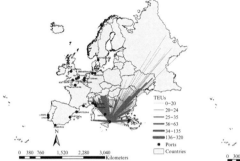

Figure 5A.13   Gioia Tauro

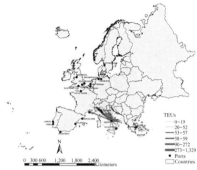

Figure 5A.14   Naples

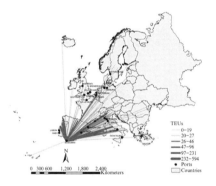

Figure 5A.15   Algeciras

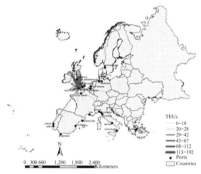

Figure 5A.16   Southampton

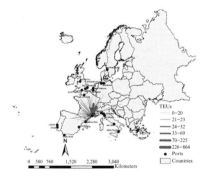

Figure 5A.17   Fos

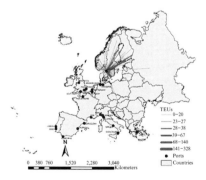

Figure 5A.18   Gothenburg

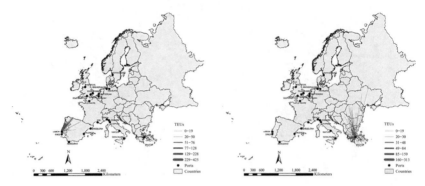

Figure 5A.19   Lisbon   *Figure 5A.20   Piraeus*

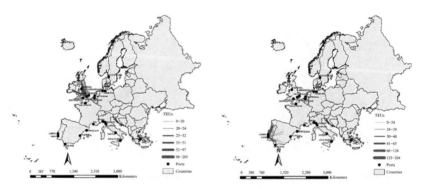

Figure 5A.21   London   *Figure 5A.22   Sines*

6. Persistence of profits in the container liner shipping industry

Christa Sys*

6.1 INTRODUCTION

Since the seminal work of Bain (*Barriers to New Competition*: 1956) and Baumol et al. (*Contestable Markets*: 1982), a vast amount of literature has studied the entry/exit conditions for various industries to determine the extent to which established firms or incumbents need to fear competition from outside the market. While the role of entry and exit has been dealt with in shipping literature in general (for example, Brooks, 2000; Cullinane and Khanna, 2000) and with regard to liner conferences (for example, Heaver, 1973; Davies, 1983 and 1986), the study of entry and exit conditions has been ignored for the containerised liner shipping industry.

Entry conditions should determine the extent to which established liner operators need to fear competition from potential entrants. The threat of entry cannot be neglected.[1] Geroski and Jacquemin (1988, p. 375) stated that 'entry does not need to occur in order to have effect on the behaviour of firms in markets, the mere threat of large scale imitation may lead incumbent firms to take pre-emptive actions which both lower their current period profit and discourage potential entrants from actually entering'. Observing patterns in time-series variation of firm-level profit rate data allows us to draw inferences about the actual and potential entry/exit.

The market structure of the container liner shipping industry (CLSI) could be described as a monopolistic competition for the 1999–2008 period; meaning welfare losses (Sys et al., 2011). According to economic theory, firms under monopolistic competition and oligopoly earn supernormal profit in the short run. In practice, there are no indications of earning such large profits in this sector. Can an explanation be found in the threat of entry?

This chapter addresses the following research question: are the competitive forces in the containerised liner shipping industry sufficiently powerful to bring any abnormal profits (positive or negative) into line with the competitive rate of return?

In studying the dynamics of entry/exit conditions for the CLSI,[2] the relevant market is the first element to be considered. Although the importance of non-vessel operating common carriers (NVOCCs) and global forwarders is growing, here, the relevant market consists of all vessel operating common carriers (for example, Maersk Line, MSC and CMA CGM) offering container liner shipping services, including actual or potential competitors. The transportation of a box is the product dimension. The relevant geographical dimension of the market is defined globally and at trade level, respectively.

The remainder of this chapter is structured as follows: Section 6.2 analyses the profitability of the CLSI. To answer the research question, Section 6.3 first outlines the persistence of profit approach. The model is explained in Subsection 6.3.1. Subsection 6.3.2 presents the sample and data. Section 6.4 reports and discusses the econometric results. Finally, Section 6.5 gives concluding remarks.

6.2   PROFITABILITY OF THE CONTAINER LINER SHIPPING INDUSTRY

As background for the empirical part of this chapter, this section provides an overview of the profitability of the CLSI from 2000 to mid-2010.

To study the profitability of the CLSI, the evolution of three profitability measures will be examined.[3] First, Table 6A.1 in the appendix gives an overview of the evolution of the operating profit or earnings before interest, tax, depreciation and amortisation (EBITDA)[4] in absolute values (upper panel) and year-on-year percentage change (lower panel). Second, a barometer of long-term industry profitability, namely the evolution of return on sales (ROS)[5] is shown in Table 6A.2. Third, Table 6A.3 lists both in absolute values and year-on-year per cent change the evolution of the bottom-line performance or net profit for the selected firms engaged in the CLSI.

The sample selection process is driven by those liner operators that publish accounts at the level of the container shipping division and resulted in a sample of 20 liner operators covering the 2000–08 period.[6] Table 6.1 provides a short description of the selected carriers.

As shown in Tables 6A.1–3, the financial results for the year 2000 were generally good. Focusing on the operating results of the liner operators, the year 2003 was a much better year than either 2001 (that is, influence of currency exchange factors on liner operators' bottom-line performance) and 2002 (that is, weaker results posted in 2001 continued in 2002). The most impressive improvements were witnessed by Asian-based carriers

Table 6.1 Sample of liner operators

Rank	Liner operator	TEU	Ships	Number of services	Market share %	Alliances	Webpage
4	APL/NOL	549,508	139	70	4.41	X	www.nol.com.sg
29	CCNI	36,712	16	10	0.30	–	www.ccni.cl
8	China Shg C.L. (CSCL)	453,009	125	46	3.64	–	www.cscl.com.cn
3	CMA CGM	1,031,327	353	91	8.29	–	www.cma-cgm.com
7	COSCO Container L.	453,204	134	88	3.64	X	www.coscon.com
13	CSAV	328,721	96	22	2.64	–	www.csav.com
9	Hanjin Shipping	440,299	99	52	3.54	X	www.hanjin.com
6	Hapag Lloyd	462,288	113	68	3.72	X	ww.hapag-lloyd.com
11	K-Line	342,043	90	66	2.75	X	www.kline.com
1	Maersk Line	2,044,981	538	104	16.44	–	www.maerskline.com
36	Matson	29,074	15	5	0.23	–	www.matson.com
21	MISC Berhad	125,101	39	22	1.01	–	www.misc.com.my
12	Mitsui-OSK L. (MOL)	341,820	91	85	2.75	X	www.mol.co.jp
10	NYK	407,300	106	41	3.27	X	www.nykline.com
14	OOCL	324,209	71	69	2.61	X	www.oocl.com
25	RCL	53,435	39	36	0.43	–	www.rclgroup.com
19	UASC	196,237	49	15	1.58	–	www.uasc.net
22	Wan Hai Lines	125,060	66	34	1.01	–	www.wanhai.com
15	Yang Ming Line	312,962	77	51	2.52%	X	www.yml.com.tw
17	ZIM	305,523	94	47	2.46%	–	www.zim.co.il

(for example, CSCL, COSCO Container line). The improved financial performance posted by liner operators in 2003 continued into the year 2004. By comparison, the number of liner operators realising a ROS above 10 per cent, doubled (see Table 6A.2). During the last two years, the container market improved due to a combination of factors (for example, general freight rate recovery programmes, network optimisation, (tight) cost control, better performance and a strong demand on all main trade routes even faster than the increase in available vessel capacity). However, the improvement in the container market was tempered by the adverse impact of continuous increases in rates for chartered tonnage, high fuel prices, high land operation costs and increased costs relating to the repositioning of empty containers.

The year 2005 was the last year of strong profitability. Increased costs, especially those relating to bunkering and chartered tonnage yet again neutralised the freight rates which were on average above the level of 2004. Higher bunker recoveries were introduced. The optimistic expectations for continued economic growth led to extra contracts for new and larger container vessel tonnage. One year later, looking at the percentage change (lower panel of Tables 6A.1 and 6A.3), a reduction in profit levels is clearly observable. Operating profits plummeted by an average of 30 per cent (see sample average, Table 6A.1) and some liner operators even slipped into the red at net level (see Table 6A.3). Excepting some liner operators, Beddow and Ajala (2007) note that diversified groups better maintain their profit than pure container liner operators. Following the dramatic decrease seen in 2006, liner operators' profits increased again in 2007. The recovery experienced in 2007 was only temporary since the container vessel capacity increased more than the volumes transported, causing freight rates to develop negatively.

A reversing trend is noticeable starting in the last quarter of 2008 as global demand slows drastically following the global financial and economic crisis. The period from the end of 2008 to the beginning of 2009 is characterised by a downswing in demand and freight rates across all trade lanes caused by the global downturn, higher operating costs caused by escalating bunker fuel prices and costs associated with the restructuring process. Some financially challenged liner operators stopped reporting net profit at container division.

By the end of 2009, most liner operators' financial results have reached negative results. Focusing on the container division results, some examples illustrate the impact of the new market downturn on liner carriers' ongoing profitability. First, AP Møller-Maersk posted a post-tax loss of US$373 million, dragged down by the segment result after tax for Maersk Line of US$–555 million. Next, Hapag-Lloyd posted a US$300 million operating loss for the first quarter of 2009. Hapag-Lloyd as well as other carriers (for example, CMA CGM) applied for state aid. Furthermore, Taiwan's duo of ocean carriers – Yang Ming and Wan Hai Line – as well as the Japanese ocean carriers NYK Line, MOL and K-Line have all seen their 2009 financial results falling. Their net profit sank into the red compared to previous years' profit. The list of carriers posting substantially lower financial results in 2009 grew, such as Hanjin Shipping's container division, China Cosco Holdings' container shipping arm COSCON and fellow Chinese ocean carrier China Shipping Container Lines (CSCL) as well as the Malaysian transport group, MISC Berhad. Furthermore, the Chilean shipping line, CSAV and the Intra-Asia feeder and domestic carrier, Regional Container Lines (RCL) also reported considerable losses in 2009. In fighting to keep their cost base in check, both carriers trimmed operating costs (that is, a lower fuel bill and renegotiated charter rates).

For the first quarter of 2010, Maersk Line, CMA CGM, Hapag-Lloyd and China Cosco Holdings turned back into operating profits. Even with a significant improvement in carryings and turnover, Singapore's leading liner shipping and logistics group, APL, still reported heavy losses. An explanation might be found in its much smaller share of the Asia–Europe trade and its heavier reliance on the transpacific than other Top 10 liner operators. Other carriers forecast a return to profit.

Mid-2010, most liner operators expected to make a much bigger profit in 2010 than previously forecast, assuming that freight rates, oil prices and exchange rates remained stable over the remainder of the year (Beddow and Ajala, 2006, 2007, 2008; Beddow, 2009, 2010; Drewry, 2000–09).

Summing up, the CLSI suffers from the current economic downturn like most other industries. Knowing that the liner operators have taken action to cut costs (for example, reduced number of sailings, introducing bigger cost-effective tonnage, slow-steaming to save fuel, sailing via the Cape of Good Hope to save on Suez canal transit fees, off-hiring vessels, scrapping vessels, cutting overheads, selling some of their profitable terminal operations (for example, Hanjin, Hapag-Lloyd Maersk Line, OOCL), one might conclude that there is no indication of earning supernormal profits at current profitability levels. Moreover, financially it was a grim five-year period for liner operators.

As stated above, the aim of this chapter is to seek an explanation in the threat of entry. The persistence of profit methodology makes it possible to capture the threat of entry.

6.3   PERSISTENCE OF PROFIT APPROACH

The threat of entry determines the market performance in a fundamental way. From an econometric view, assessing the likelihood of potential entry is a problem since the threat of entry is an unobservable variable. In addition, Martin (2002) states that even actual entry of the kind that affects the performance of established firms is an unobservable variable. To deal with this issue, a body of literature, known as the Persistence of Profit (PoP) approach, observes profit outcomes over time to make inferences about the nature of competition.

The literature distinguishes two representations of the competitive processes, namely, the static and dynamic views. The static view is based on the Structure–Conduct–Performance (SCP) model. According to SCP, the structure of the market (reflected in characteristics, such as the number and size distribution of firms, the extent of product differentiation and the strength of entry and exit barriers) affects the conduct of the firms operating in that market which in turn influences their performances. Competition among an existing set of firms suffices to produce zero profits at each point in time. This static view does little to explain the dynamics of competition. The dynamic view owes its origin to Joseph Schumpeter. Under the dynamic view, the entry and exit of firms drives profits to zero in the long run, and is thus consistent with there being non-zero economic profits at different points in time. This Schumpeterian perspective on the competitive process is adopted in PoP studies[7] (Mueller, 1977, 1986; Geroski, 1990; Lipczynski et al., 2009).

In this chapter, the persistence of profits will be studied for the CLSI. To this end, Mueller's (1977, 1986) PoP hypothesis will be tested for a sample of container liner operators between 2000 and 2008. A time-series analysis on firm-level profits is used to estimate the short- and long-run persistence. Persistence should be interpreted as the percentage of a firm's rent in any period before period t that systematically remains in period t (Waring, 1996). The hypothesis states that (potential and actual) entry/exit conditions are sufficiently powerful to ensure that no firm persistently earns profits above or below the norm (Lipczynski et al., 2009).

6.3.1   Model

This chapter applies the well-established profit persistence methodology pioneered by Mueller (1977, 1986) and extended in contributions by Geroski and Jacquemin (1988) and Geroski (1990) in modelling variations in company profitability over time.

First, Mueller (1986) shows that persistence of profits can be estimated using a first-order autoregressive (AR(1)) equation for each firm's stand-ardised profit rate as follows:

$$\pi_{i,t}^s = (1 - \lambda_i)\pi_{i,p} + \lambda_i \pi_{i,t-1}^s + \mu_{i,t}, \tag{6.1}$$

where λ_i and $\pi_{i,p}$ are the key parameters. These parameters of interest describe the impact of the previous year's firm-specific profits to the current year's profit rates by regressing $\pi_{i,t-1}^s$ on $\pi_{i,t}^s$ and reflecting the strength of persistence of profit in both the short and the long runs (Lipczynski et al., 2009). The measure of persistence is the slope coefficient, λ_i. The value of λ_i predicts the intensity of competition or the speed with which profits converge on $\pi_{i,p}$. For convergence, λ_i must lie between zero and one (Cable and Mueller, 2008). $\pi_{i,p}$ represents the permanent profitability level of firm i. The permanent component $\pi_{i,p}$ can itself be partitioned into two terms as $\pi_{i,p} = c + r_i$ where c is the competitive rate of return common to all firms and r_i equals a permanent rent specific to firm i. The cost of entry/exit into/from the industry is assumed to be reflected by the latter term. The error term, $\mu_{i,t}$ captures the effect of random shocks to these profits which is assumed to satisfy the usual conditions for OLS.

Letting $\hat{\alpha}_i$ and $\hat{\lambda}_i$ be the estimates of the autoregressive equation, this reduces equation (6.1) to the following testable empirical model:

$$\pi_{i,t}^s = \hat{\alpha}_i + \hat{\lambda}_i \pi_{i,t-1}^s + \mu_{i,t}, \tag{6.2}$$

where $\hat{\alpha}_i = (1 - \hat{\lambda}_i)\pi_{i,p}$. If $\hat{\alpha}_i$ and $\hat{\lambda}_i$ are the generalised least squares esti-mators of α_i and λ_i, then the permanent profitability level of firm i, $\pi_{i,p}$ can be derived and estimated as:

$$\pi_{i,p} = \frac{\hat{\alpha}_i}{1 - \hat{\lambda}_i}. \tag{6.3}$$

An overview of the interpretation of short- and long-run persistence and with it the link to barriers to entry is given in Table 6.2.

Second, Geroski and Jacquemin (1988) and Geroski (1990) have shown that equation (6.1) is a reduced form of a more elaborate two-equation structural model which makes explicit the role of actual and potential entry (and exit) in the model, but which does not affect the specification of the reduced form. The central idea is that profits can be expected to attract entry, and entry drives down profits.

Table 6.2   Interpretation of persistence

		Barriers to entry
Short-run persistence: λ_i		
$\lambda_i = 0$	Year-on-year variation in $\pi_{i,t}^s$ is random	No
	No association between $\pi_{i,t-1}^s$ and $\pi_{i,t}^s$	
$0 < \lambda_i < 1$	If $\pi_{i,t-1}^s$ is above (below) zero, it is likely that $\pi_{i,t}^s$ will also be above (below)	Yes
	Positive association between $\pi_{i,t-1}^s$ and $\pi_{i,t}^s$	
Long-run persistence: α_i		
Positive	Firm i's actual long-run average profit rate is above average for all firms	
Negative	Firm i's actual long-run average profit rate is below average for all firms	
Permanent component: $\pi_{i,p}$		
$\pi_{i,p} = 0$	Standardised profit rates of all firms tend to fluctuate around the same long-run convergence	No or surmountable
$\pi_{i,p} \neq 0$	Standardised profit rates of all firms tend to fluctuate around different long-run average values	Yes
	No convergence	

In the first structural equation, profits are assumed to depend on the threat of entry in the market, $E_{i,t}$:

$$\pi_{i,t}^s = \gamma_{i0} + \gamma_{i1} E_{i,t} + \gamma_{i2} \pi_{i,t-1}^s + \mu_{i,t}, \tag{6.4}$$

where $\gamma_{i1} < 0$, $0 < \gamma_{i2} < 1$ and γ_{i0} may take any value. The parameter γ_{i1} measures the direct impact through actual entry or indirectly by forcing established firms to undertake pre-emptive actions, and varies inversely with the level of entry barriers protecting firm i, while γ_{i2} describes the effect of entry on $\pi_{i,t}^s$. The error term, $\mu_{i,t}$ is characterised as a normally distributed iid (independently and identically distributed) stochastic process with mean, $E(\mu_{i,t}) = 0$ and variance, $E(\mu_{i,t}^s) = $ constant (Geroski, 1990).

Next, the threat of (actual and potential) entry and exit is assumed to depend on the standardised profits observed in the last period. The second structural equation can be written as follows:

$$E_{i,t} = \gamma_{i3}(\pi_{i,t-1}^s - \gamma_{i4}) + \varepsilon_{i,t} \tag{6.5}$$

where $\gamma_{i3}, \gamma_{i4} > 0$. The amount of entry attracted by a unit increase in excess profit (that is, those profits that can be bid away) is measured by the parameter, γ_{i3}. According to Geroski, this parameter reflects the number of potential entrants. The exogenous flow of entry or exit is captured in the white noise error term, $\varepsilon_{i,t}$ which is assumed to be independent of $\mu_{i,t}$.

Equations (6.4) and (6.5) cannot be estimated directly since the variable $E_{i,t}$ cannot be quantified. This unobservable variable can be eliminated by solving for the reduced form. Substituting (6.5) into (6.4), and rearranging again yields equation (6.2) where:

$$\hat{\alpha}_i = (\gamma_{i0} - \gamma_{i1}\gamma_{i3}\gamma_{i4}),$$

$$\hat{\lambda}_i = (\gamma_{i2} + \gamma_{i1}\gamma_{i3}),$$

$$\mu_{i,t} = (\mu_{i,t} + \gamma_{i1}\varepsilon_{i,t})$$

Despite the fact that the model is built around an unobservable variable called 'threat of entry', (6.2) can be estimated with observable data, namely, firm-level profit rates.

6.3.2 Sample, Variable and Data

The PoP approach analyses time-series data on firm-level profit rates. A time-series study requires time series as long as possible. In contrast to other industries, the CLSI suffers from a lack of long time-series data. Consequently, it puts a restriction on the number of liner operators that may be included in the sample.[8] For this purpose, and in function of data availability, the empirical specifications at container division level are based on an unbalanced panel dataset for a sample of 21 major liner operators covering the period from 2000 to 2008 inclusive.

To control for business cycles and to remove the effects of any macroeconomic fluctuations, the PoP literature concentrates on the persistence of a firm's standardised profit rate denoted $\pi_{i,t}^s$. The persistence of a liner operator's standardised profit rate is defined as $\pi_{i,t}^s = \pi_{i,t} - \bar{\pi}_t$, where $\pi_{i,t}$ is firm i's actual profit rate at time t and $\bar{\pi}_t = \sum_{i=1}^{n} \frac{\pi_{i,t}}{n}$ the average profitability of the industry profit rate in year t. In other words, $\pi_{i,t}^s$ represents the deviation of the profitability of liner operator i at time t from the average profitability of all liner operators in the sample at a given time.

Most PoP studies measure profit as the firm's return on assets (ROA). The interpretation of this main variable varies, however. First, some studies define the profit rate as the ratio of *before* taxes to total assets (for example, Mueller, 1977, 1990a; Geroski and Jacquemin, 1988; Glen et al., 2001; Yurtoglu, 2004; Eklund and Wiberg, 2007). Mueller (1977) argues that before-tax profits were used to avoid noise as a result of differences in tax treatment. In the same study, Mueller tested all of the models using an after-tax definition of profits. He obtained the same qualitative results. Second, other studies used net profit *after* tax plus interest payments (for example, Goddard and Wilson, 1996, 1999; Waring, 1996; Maruyama and Odagiri, 2002; Bektas, 2007; Gschwandtner, 2009). On the topic of 'after tax', Maruyama and Odagiri (2002) reason that entrants should make their entry decisions based on after-tax profits if effective tax rates differ across industries. In addition, they argue that interest should be included because total assets in the denominator include those financed by debt and, so, the numerator should also take account of the returns to debt. Another viewpoint is offered by Mueller (1990a), who defined a company's return on capital as its profits net of taxes and *gross* of interest divided by total assets. This line of reasoning is based on the assumption that the convergence of profits to the competitive return is driven by exit and entry of other firms and that this entry and exit respond to after-tax profit levels. Finally, Stephan and Tsapin (2008) used two measures of profit rate: price–cost margin (or revenue minus costs relative to revenue) and ROA, which is defined as operating profits divided by the assets of the firm.

A study of the persistence of profit for the CLSI differs from other PoP studies where the persistence of profit is investigated across industries or across firms located in a specific country (for example, *Japan*: Maruyama and Odagiri, 2002; *Spain*: Bou and Santorra, 2007; *Turkey*: Bektas, 2007, Yurtoglu, 2004; *United Kingdom*: Goddard and Wilson, 1996, Cubbin and Geroski, 1990; *United States*: Mueller, 1990b). The CLSI is a global industry with liner operators having their headquarters all over the world. Different accounting methods are used. Leasing and/or chartering of ships is common practice, certainly of carriers-to-be. In addition, this study focuses on the business segment of container liner shipping. Therefore, assuming that entry into and exit from the CLSI is driven by operational profit, this PoP study measures profit as the return on sales (ROS or EBITDA[9] to turnover, where the denominator equals a proxy for total assets). EBITDA is a useful parameter for an entrant in evaluating the operating performance as it removes depreciation and amortisation which can vary depending upon accounting methods as well as interest and taxes.

To test/confirm the validity of this assumption, regressions were run using ROA (or net income to total assets at container-level division) and return on capital employed (ROCE or EBITDA to total assets). In the case of 100 per cent liner operators, the results of these three profitability measures do not differ significantly. In the case of liner operators with diversified operations portfolio, the results of ROA differ from the other results. This difference can largely be attributed to the fact that not all liner operators report net income at container division level (for example, Evergreen, Hamburg Süd, Hyundai Merchant Marine) or stopped reporting it (for example, Hapag-Lloyd). The above arguments argue in favour of the profitability measure, ROS.[10]

The data for the empirical investigation were collected from Liner Intelligence financial analysis (www.ci-online.co.uk) and from investor/ annual reports published on the publicly available internet websites of the selected liner operators.

6.4 EMPIRICAL RESULTS AND DISCUSSION

This section will first test the admissibility of the data. Second, the empirical results are reported and discussed.

6.4.1 Admissibility of Dataset

This study works with a relatively short time dimension of the data (see also Glen et al., 2001). This is a disadvantage of time series with a short time dimension. Conversely, an advantage of a short time series is that the time series is less likely to be subject to the kinds of shocks that would change the profits dynamics of a firm (Cable and Mueller, 2008).

However, since some econometric issues can arise, it is necessary to test the admissibility of the data. The analysis starts with the test whether the time series are stationary or not, then the lag structure of the equation is investigated and finally, the serial correlation of the disturbances in equation (6.2) are checked.

A first econometric issue in estimating equation (6.2) is stationarity. Empirical work based on times-series data as in the analysis of the speed of adjustment of profitability assumes that the underlying time series is stationary. The existence of non-stationarity (or unit root) in the firm-level profitability series would indicate that shocks to profitability persist indefinitely and that competitive pressures never erode differences in profitability (Yurtoglu, 2004).

Studies testing for unit root mostly used the augmented Dickey–Fuller (ADF) test and the Phillips–Perron test (for example, Glen et al., 2001; Yurtoglu, 2004; Bektas, 2007). Both tests have a null hypothesis of a unit root process. Cable and Mueller (2008) concluded that the right null hypothesis for times-series profits should be one of stationarity. Following these authors, here, stationarity is tested by using the Kwiatkowski–Phillips–Schmidt–Shin (KPSS) procedure. The KPSS test is an inverse of the Phillips–Peron test, so it reverses the null (stationary) and alternative (non-stationary) hypothesis. An extra advantage of this procedure is its robustness in small samples. The results of the KPSS test show that the times series were stationary.[11]

The second econometric issue concerns the introduction of more lagged dependent variables to the right-hand side of equation (6.2). To decide on the appropriate lag structure, the Akaike Information Criterion (AIC) and the Schwarz Bayesian Criterion (SBC) were computed. Both criteria favoured equation (6.2) above alternative higher-order autoregressive models.

Testing for the presence of serial correlation is a third econometric issue. Before using an estimated equation for statistical inference (for example, hypothesis tests), it is essential to examine the residuals for evidence of serial correlation. The Breusch–Godfrey LM test and the Ljung–Box Q-statistic were performed.[12] Both tests for serial correlation indicate that the residuals are not serially correlated and equation (6.2) should not be re-specified before using it for hypothesis tests.

6.4.2   Empirical Results

A point of interest arising from the empirical results is the different behaviour of independent carriers and liner operators involved in an alliance. Mediterranean Shipping Company (MSC – ranked 2nd), Hyundai Merchant Marine (HMM, member of The New World Alliance) and Evergreen[13] are not integrated in the sample. MSC does not report its financial results and HMM and Evergreen publish no disaggregated data (that is, for their business segment 'container'). In addition, in the annual report 2008 the TUI group, former parent of Hapag-Lloyd (which participates in the Grand Alliance) stopped reporting disaggregated data. Therefore, the present study compares the empirical results of two independent Top 3 liner operators (that is, CMA CGM and Maersk Line) with the CHKY alliance formed by COSCO, K-Line, Hanjin and Yang Ming Line.

A visual plot of data is usually the first step in the analysis of any time series. Figure 6.1 sets out plots of the excess profit, $\pi_{i,t}^s$ for Maersk Line (ranked 1st) and CMA CGM (ranked 3rd) against time (left-hand panel). The right-hand panel of Figure 6.1 plots their associated phase diagrams with $\pi_{i,t-1}^s$ on the horizontal axis and $\pi_{i,t}^s$ on the vertical axis.

Both carriers are European-based and family-owned companies. Their growth is driven partly by mergers and acquisitions and partly by organic growth (Sys, 2009). Maersk Line is part of the A.P. Møller-Maersk group which is engaged in a multitude of activities (for example, liner shipping; tanker, offshore and other shipping operations; oil and gas activities; APM terminals). CMA CGM dates from the merger of CMA and CGM, which were two separate entities in 1999. Maersk Line accounts for 52 per

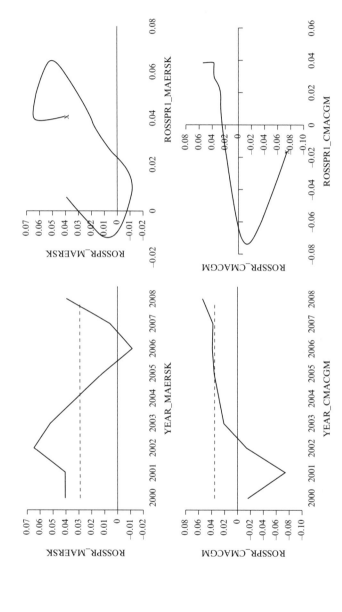

Note: The marker option x corresponds with the first observation.

Figure 6.1   Profit time series

111

cent of group turnover whereas the container liner shipping division of CMA CGM accounts for +90 per cent.

The phase diagrams give a visual impression of the persistence category (Cable and Mueller, 2008). With two exceptions, Maersk's data points are situated in the first quadrant. The first quadrant corresponds with the scenario 'profits are consistently above the norm'. The discomfort from PONL integration (2005) is observable in both graphs. Since, Maersk Line no longer has to absorb extra costs associated with the integration of P&O Nedlloyd, they turned back in the first quadrant. In the case of CMA CMG, the phase diagram indicates an evolution from below the norm (third quadrant) to above the norm. This might suggest that the acquisitions of CMA CGM were more successful. In order to preserve space, the graphs of the members of the CHKY alliance are not reported. Except for Hanjin which strays occasionally into the other quadrants, the observations of the other members are located in the third quadrant, that is, profits below the norm.[14]

Turning to the formal analysis, separate regressions for each liner operator were estimated following equation (6.2). Estimation is carried out with the aid of E-views. The OLS estimates of (6.2) for CMA CGM, Maersk Line and the CHKY alliance are reported in Table 6.3 (*t*-statistics in parentheses). The table is arranged in descending order of estimated $\hat{\lambda}_i$.

Table 6.3 Empirical results

Rank	Liner operator	α_i	λ_i	$1-\lambda_i$	$\pi_{i,p}$
Top 3 liner operators					
3	CMA CGM	0.011	0.682	0.318	0.035
		(0.813)	(2.258)	(1.051)	(1.496)
1	Maersk	0.011	0.612	0.388	0.029
		(0.950)	(2.715)	(1.721)	(1.453)
CHKY alliance					
11	Kline	−0.018	0.080	0.920	−0.019
		(−1.043)	(0.255)		
7	COSCO	−0.020	0.071	0.929	−0.022
		(−0.472)	(0.055)		
15	YML	−0.068	0.062	0.938	−0.073
		(−2.633)	(0.245)		
9	Hanjin	−0.025	−0.096	1.096	−0.023
		(−3.116)	(−0.465)		
	Average	0.029			
Sample strength of persistence		0.198			

Firm-level PoP literature examines two forms of persistence, namely, short- and long-run persistence (see Table 6.2).

First, short-run persistence refers to the percentage of a firm's standardised profit rate in any period before period t that remains in period t. The first-order autocorrelation coefficient $\hat{\lambda}_i$ can be interpreted as a measure of short-run persistence of profit.[15] As reflected in Table 6.2, the estimated $\hat{\lambda}_i$'s are positive and significant for CMA CGM and Maersk Line. The closer $\hat{\lambda}_i$ is to one, the more rapidly liner operators' profits converge to their long-run level. In the case of CHKY, $\hat{\lambda}_i$ is close to zero, and there is low persistence of profits. In other words, profits in year t do not depend largely on profits in year $t - 1$. Regarding the low average value (that is, 0.02941), no generalisation for all alliances can be formulated since there are no data for HMM. Furthermore, the ranking of the liner operators (see column 2) differs from the ranking based on market share (see column 1). Sorting for long-run persistence leads to another hierarchisation, namely, MISC, RCL, OOCL, CMA CGM and Maersk Line. This might be an indication that large operators give up profit to preserve their market share. Next, the $\hat{\lambda}_i$'s of the independent carriers are significantly larger than those of the members of the CHKY alliance. This leads us to the values of the speed of profit adjustment parameter, $(1 - \hat{\lambda}_i)$ (see column 5). The expression $(1 - \hat{\lambda}_i)$ is an estimate of the speed of erosion of short-run rents and indicates how quickly the profit rate $\pi_{i,t}^s$ approaches its long-run equilibrium level $\pi_{i,p}$. On a longer time series, the lower value of $(1 - \hat{\lambda}_{i,t})$ for CMA CGM and Maersk Line would be interpreted as if it is more than likely that both carriers will reap an abnormal profit the following year (Lipczynski et al., 2009). Currently it is difficult to formulate such a statement, but the financial and economic downturn might be indicated in future research as a structural break since some liner operators wrestle with cash flow problems and heavy expansion-induced debt burdens and have announced substantially poorer financial results for 2009. Certainly and not surprisingly, the short-run rents of CMA CGM and Maersk Line erode more slowly. Conversely, if $(1 - \hat{\lambda}_i)$ is high, then the degree of persistence of past profits is also small and consequently short-run rents are quickly eroded. Quick erosion is a sign of increased competition (Gschwandter, 2009). Another indication of quick erosion can be found, in common with previous studies, in the explanatory power of the regressions for $\hat{\lambda}_i$ which is quite low with a mean R^2 value of 0.15. Thus the transitory component of a firm's profit rate would seem to require no more than a year for it to be eliminated (Mueller, 1986).

Second, the degree of variation in the long-run average standardised profit rates between liner operators is known as long-run persistence. $\pi_{i,p}$ is a measure of permanent rents which are not eroded by competitive forces. The long-run $\pi_{i,p}$ is calculated as $\hat{\alpha}_i/1 - \hat{\lambda}_i$ (see equation (6.3)). In the case of CMA CGM, a $\pi_{i,p}$ of 0.03536 implies that CMA CMG's profit to assets/sales ratio (at container division level) is on average permanently 3.5 per cent above the sample mean. In the left-hand panel of Figure 6.1, the dashed horizontal line corresponds with the average of equilibrium value of $\pi_{i,p}$.

The sign of the parameter $\hat{\alpha}_i$ determines whether firm i's long-run averaged standardised profit is positive or negative. In Figure 6.1, the positive value of $\hat{\alpha}_i$ for CMA CGM and Maersk Line indicates that those liner operators earn returns above the competitive norm.[16] In the case of the CHKY alliance, there is an indication that members' returns are below the competitive norm. This corresponds with the observations of the informal method. Except for APL and OOCL, a look at the sample shows us that the returns for all liner operators participating in an alliance are below the competitive norm. This would be an interesting topic for future research.

To formally test the hypothesis that (potential and actual) entry into and exit from any market are sufficiently free to bring abnormal profits quickly into line with the competitive rate of return, would be to assess whether $\pi_{i,p}$ differs significantly across firms. If $\pi_{i,p}$ equals zero for all i, one would accept the hypothesis that all long-run rents are zero (Mueller, 1990a/b; Lipczynski et al., 2009). If $\pi_{i,p} \neq 0$ for some liner operators, there is long-run persistence, in the sense that these liner operators earn profits which tend to differ permanently from the average profitability of liner operators in general (see Figure 6.1). The Wald test is applied to test the significance of estimated 'permanent' profits or 'long-run projected profits', $\pi_{i,p}$. As reflected in Table 6.2, $\pi_{i,p}$ is > 0 for CMA CGM and Maersk Line; [17] and $\pi_{i,p} < 0$ for the CHKY alliance. In the containerised liner shipping case, the empirical results suggest that the hypothesis can be rejected.

The aim of observing patterns in the time-series variation of firm-level profit rate data was to draw inferences about entry and exit as well as whether barriers to entry exits. Goddard and Wilson (1996, p.109) state:

'$\hat{\lambda}_i$ summarises information on the extent to which high profits in the previous time period induces entry in the current period, the extent to which such entry affects profit in the current period and the extent to which such the firm would have be able to maintain its advantages in absence of entry'.

The quick erosion of the short-run persistence indicates the existence of entry. The fact that some liner operators do earn long-run rents implies that barriers to entry and exit do exist (see Table 6.3).

Finally, for the sample, the estimated $\hat{\lambda}_i$'s range from 0.68 to $- 0.39$

around a mean of 0.19775 (see bottom line of Table 6.3). The values of $\hat{\lambda}_i$ are negative in five cases but of these none is statistically significant at the 5 per cent level. The average estimated value 0.19775 for $\hat{\lambda}_i$ suggests relatively low persistence of profit. This result is significantly lower than those obtained in other industries (see Gschwandtner, 2009; Lipczynski et al., 2009).

6.5 CONCLUDING REMARKS

Barriers to entry constitute a major structural attribute of industry sectors. Liner operators should know the entry and exit conditions of their industry, since both are powerful forces because they strongly influence behaviour. To this end, this chapter studied both the (actual and potential) entry and exit.

The study addressed the research question whether the competitive forces in the CLSI are sufficiently powerful to bring any abnormal profits (positive or negative) into line with the competitive rate of return.

To model both actual and potential entry, the study adopted the growing persistence of profits literature. This dynamic methodology observes firm-level profit outcomes over time to draw inferences about the nature of competition as both actual and potential entry are unobservable variables. The central idea is that profits should persist if there are impediments to the competitive dynamic (for example, entry barriers). This PoP study measures profit as the return on sales, and the methodology is applied to a panel of 21 liner operators observed over the 2000–08 period.

Five major conclusions follow from the time-series analysis on firm-level profits. First, short-run persistence refers to the percentage of a firm's standardised profit rate in any period before period t that remains in period t. The econometric results reveal a significant positive impact on profit persistence for independent carriers (for example, CMA CGM, Maersk Line). Such a result indicates that those liner operators earn returns above the competitive norm. Conversely, in the case of the CHKY alliance, the results show a low persistence of profits. In other words, the profits in year t of liner carriers involved in the CHKY alliance do not largely depend on profits in year $t - 1$. No generalisation for all alliances can be formulated as there are no data for Hapag-Lloyd and HMM.

Second, the values of the speed of profit adjustment parameter indicate how quickly the profit rate approaches its long-run equilibrium level. The short-run rents of CMA CGM and Maersk Line erode more slowly than those of liner operators involved in the CHKY alliance. This can be taken as an indication of the existence of entry barriers.

Third, turning to long-run persistence, the hypothesis was tested that (actual and potential) entry into and exit from any market is sufficiently free to bring any abnormal profits quickly into line with the competitive rate of return. If the permanent profitability equals zero for all liner operators, this would support the hypothesis that all long-run rents are zero. Otherwise, there is long-run persistence in the sense that these liner operators earn profits which tend to differ permanently from the average profitability of liner operators in general. In the case of CMA CGM, a permanent level of profitability of 0.03536 implies that their profit to assets/sales ratio (at container division level) is on average permanently 3.5 per cent above the sample mean. Since the permanent level of profitability does not equal zero for all liner operators, the results imply that there is long-run persistence. Therefore, in the containerised liner shipping case, the empirical results suggest that the hypothesis can be rejected. The 'persistence of profit' approach demonstrates that independent carriers are able to preserve their profits over time. However, abnormal profit erodes at a faster pace than in other industries.

The results further suggest that the abnormal profit (if any) of shipping companies involved in strategic alliances erodes more quickly by forces of competition than those of independent carriers. Another observation is that the ranking of the liner operators differs from a ranking based on market share.

Fifth, the excess returns erode at a faster pace than in other industries. This might be an indication that large operators sacrifice profit to preserve their market share.

These conclusions are highly relevant for the liner operators, in understanding the effects of (actual and potential) entry and exit on the operators' behaviour. From a policy viewpoint, the findings of this study have a high economic relevance, since stability in the market is most important. A critical reflection might concern the short time horizon of the research. In general, the CLSI suffers from a lack of long time-series data. An interesting suggestion for future research might be to examine whether liner operators that persistently reap profits above the norm today should continue to do so in subsequent periods.

NOTES

*   The author is grateful to Prof. dr. H. Meersman and Prof. dr. E. Van de Voorde for their valuable comments and suggestions which contributed to the writing of this chapter. The author remains solely responsible for the chapter's content.
1.   Davies (1983 and 1986) has studied the entry and exit of liner operators into/from liner conferences serving Canada covering the 1975–82 period as well as the actual entries

and exits of ships into/from Canadian liner trades between 1977 and 1979 to validate the contestability theory. On the basis of this empirical analysis, the conclusions were that entry and exit occur often and that liner shipping markets can accurately be described as being contestable. In their critique on contestability, both Pearson (1987) and Jankowski (1989) argued that the focus was solely on actual entry and neglected the threat of entry.

2. The Container shipping industry, a major segment of the liner shipping industry, is a maritime industry, international if not global in scope. This industry operates vessels transporting containers with various but standardised dimensions/sizes, regardless of the content. Whether filled or not, these (container) vessels are put into service on a regular basis and often according to a fixed sailing schedule, loading and discharging at specified ports (Sys, 2009).

3. Data were collected from Liner Intelligence financial analysis (www.ci-online.co.uk), annual reports, the notes to financial statements as well as fact books and Powerpoint presentations. Data in currencies other than US dollars were converted into US dollars using the currency convertor www.oanda.com/currency/convertor at the currency exchange rate prevailing when the balance sheet data were compiled (end of March or December). All figures in Tables 6A.1–3 are in US$ millions except % changes.

4. Not all liner operators have the same accounting rules on vessel depreciation. Therefore, EBITDA is preferred to EBIT.

5. Return on sales is defined as EBITA divided by sales revenue, and measures the ability to extract operating profit out of every dollar earned before financial interest and tax.

6. Note: some Top 20 liner operators are not included in the sample. Due to missing data for operating income and net profit, for instance, Hamburg Süd and Pacific International Line are not included in the sample. Furthermore, some liner operators are excluded as segmented figures for container division were not available (for example, Evergreen, Hyundai Merchant Marine).

7. For an overview of firm-level PoP studies, see Gschwandter (2009); Lipczynski et al. (2009).

8. The dataset comprises the following 21 liner operators in alphabetical order: APL (5), CCNI (29), CMA CGM (3), COSCO (7), CSAV (13), CSCL (8), Hapag-Lloyd (6), Horizon Line (30), Hanjin (9), K-Line (11), Maersk Line (1), Matson (36), MISC (21), MOL (12), NYK (10), OOCL (14), RCL (25), UASC (19), Wan Hai Line (22), Yang Ming Line (15) and ZIM (17). The number in parentheses denotes their ranking at 1 January 2010.

9. Reconciliation from EBITDA to net income: subtract non-cash charges (that is, depreciation and amortisation expenses), non-operating expenses (such as interest and 'other' non-core expenses) as well as income tax from EBITDA.

10. Neglecting the owned versus chartered ships ratio might obtain biased results.

11. This study also applied a unit root test provided by Im et al. (2003) to the panel data which has time and cross-section dimensions. The test is based on the average value of the ADF statistics obtained for each of the individual firms' data. The result is equal to –2.7084 for the sample of 21 liner operators observed over the 2000–08 period. Since the calculated t-statistic is lower than the critical value of the standardised t-bar test at the 5% level, the null hypothesis of non-stationarity is rejected.

12. If there are lagged dependent variables on the right-hand side of the regression, the DW test is no longer valid.

13. Studying the behaviour of Evergreen would have been interesting as this liner operator decided not to follow the trend of buying/chartering ultra-large container ships. Evergreen is now the only large operator with an empty order book. Will the present economic slowdown and the difficult situation of the liner business contribute to Evergreen's corporate strategy?

14. The observations of CCNI, COSCO, CSAV, NYK, Wan Hai Line and ZIM are located in the third quadrant. In contrast, the observations of MISC, RCL, OOCL (with one exception) and Matson (with two exceptions) are situated in the first quadrant. The other liner operators stray occasionally into the other quadrants.

15.   One side note urges: since the sample size is small, some caution is required for interpreting the estimated $\hat{\lambda}_i$ and accordingly, the estimated long-run profit rate. From theory, the least-squares estimate of an autoregressive model is known to be biased downward, when the sample size is small (Patterson, 2000). Adjusting for this bias, the mean of $\hat{\lambda}_i$ equals 0.2636. The adjusted $\hat{\lambda}_i$ still corresponds with low persistence.
16.   The estimated value of $\hat{\alpha}_i$ is also positive for APL, CSCL, Horizon Line, Matson, MISC, OOCL and RCL.
17.   This outcome also applies for APL, CSCL, Horizon Line, Matson and UASC. The remaining carriers show a $\pi_{i,p} < 0$.

REFERENCES

Bain, J., 1956. *Barriers to New Competition*, Cambridge, MA: Harvard University Press.

Baumol, W.J., Panzar, J. C. and Willing, R. 1982. *Contestable Markets and the Theory of Industry Structure*, New York: Harcourt Brace Jovanovich.

Beddow, M., 2009. 'Battered & bruised', *Containerisation International*, October, 28–33.

Beddow, M., 2010. 'A dash for cash', *Containerisation International*, January, 36–7.

Beddow, M. and Ajala, L., 2006. 'Bleeding bucks', *Containerisation International*, October, 34–9.

Beddow, M. and Ajala, L., 2007. 'Container carriers take a cold bath', *Containerisation International*, October, 42–5.

Beddow, M. and Ajala, L., 2008. 'A gloomy outlook', *Containerisation International*, October, 42–6.

Bektas, E., 2007. 'The persistence of profits in the Turkish banking system', *Applied Economics Letters* **14**, 187–90.

Bou, J.C. and Satorra, A., 2007. 'The persistence of abnormal returns at industry and firm levels: evidence from Spain', *Strategic Management Journal* **28**, 707–22.

Brooks, M.R., 2000. *Sea Change in Liner Shipping: Regulation and Managerial Decision-Making in a Global Industry*, Oxford: Pergamon.

Cable, J.R. and Mueller, D.C., 2008. 'Testing for persistence of profits' differences across firms', *International Journal of the Economics of Business* **152**, 201–28.

Cubbin, J.S. and Geroski, P.A. 1990. 'The persistence of profits in the United Kingdom', in: Mueller (ed.), (1990a), pp. 147–67.

Cullinane, K. and Khanna, M., 2000. 'Economies of scale in large containerships: optimal size and geographical implications', *Journal of Transport Geography* **83**, 181–95.

Davies, J.E., 1983. 'Pricing in the Liner Shipping Industry: A Survey of Conceptual Models', Transport Research Analysis Report no. 1983/04E, Canadian Transport Commission Research Branch.

Davies, J.E., 1986. 'Competition, contestability and the liner shipping industry', *Journal of Transport Economics and Policy* **203**, 299–312.

Drewry, 2000–09. *Container Market Annual Review and Forecast*, London: Drewry Shipping Consultants Limited.

Eklund, J.E. and, Wiberg, D., 2007. 'Persistence of profits and the systematic search for knowledge – R&D links to firms above-norm profits', CESIS Electronic Working Paper Series, No. 85.

Geroski, P.A., 1990. 'Modelling persistent profitability', in: Mueller (ed.) (1990a), pp. 15–34.

Geroski, P.A. and Jacquemin, A., 1988. 'The persistence of profits: a European comparison', *Economic Journal* **98**, 375–89.

Glen, J., Lee, K. and Singh, A., 2001. 'Persistence of profitability and competition in emerging markets', *Economics Letters* **72**, 247–53.

Goddard, J.A. and Wilson, J.O.S., 1996. 'Persistence of profits for UK manufacturing and service sector firms', *The Service Industries Journal* **162**, 105–17.

Goddard, J.A. and Wilson, J.O.S., 1999. 'The persistence of profit: a new empirical interpretation', *International Journal of Industrial Organization* **17**, 663–87.

Gschwandtner, A., 2009. 'Evolution of profit persistence in the US: evidence from three periods', Vienna Economics Papers 0410, University of Vienna.

Heaver, T., 1973. 'The structure of liner conference rates', *Journal of Industrial Economics* **21**, 257–65.

Im, K., Pesaran, M. and, Shin, Y. 2003. 'Testing for unit roots heterogeneous panels', *Journal of Econometrics* **115**, 53–74.

Jankowski, W.B., 1989. 'Competition, contestability and the liner shipping industry: a comment', *Journal of Transport Economics and Policy*, **23**, 199–203.

Lipczynski, J., Wilson, J. and Goddard, J., 2009. *Industrial Organization, Competition, Strategy, Policy*, Harlow: Prentice-Hall.

Martin, S., 2002. *Industrial Economics, Economic Analysis and Public Policy*, Oxford: Blackwell.

Maruyama, N. and Odagiri, H., 2002. 'Does the "persistence of profits" persist? A study of company profits in Japan, 1964–97', *International Journal of Industrial Organization* **20**, 1513–33.

Mueller, D.C., 1977. 'The persistence of profits above the norm', *Economica* **44**, 369–80.

Mueller, D.C., 1986. *Profits in the Long Run*, Cambridge: Cambridge University Press.

Mueller, D.C., 1990a. *The Dynamics of Company Profits: An International Comparison*, Cambridge: Cambridge University Press.

Mueller, D.C., 1990b. 'The persistence of profits in the United States', In: Mueller (ed.) (1990a), pp. 35–57.

Patterson, K.D., 2000. 'Bias reduction in autoregressive models', *Economics Letters* **68**, 135–41.

Pearson, R., 1987. 'Some doubts on the contestability of liner shipping markets', *Maritime Policy and Management* **14**, 71–8.

Stephan, A. and Tsapin, A., 2008. 'Persistence and determinants of firm profit in emerging markets', CESIS Electronic Working Paper Series, Paper No. 151.

Sys, C., 2009. 'Is the container liner shipping industry an oligopoly?', *Transport Policy* **165**, 259–70.

Sys, C., Meersman, H. and Van de Voorde, E., 2011. 'A non-structural test for competition in the container liner shipping industry', *Maritime Policy and Management* **38**, 219–34.

Waring, G.F., 1996. 'Industry differences in the persistence of firm-specific returns', *American Economic Review* **865**, 1253–65.

Yurtoglu, B., 2004. 'Persistence of firm-level profitability in Turkey', *Applied Economics* **36**, 615–25.

APPENDIX 6A

Table 6A.1 Evolution of operational results at container division level

	2000	2001	2002	2003	2004	2005	2006	2007	2008
EBITDA									
APL	284	189	134	406	892	845	567	766	299
CCNI	–	–	–	–5	19	38	–20	–14	5
CSCL	–	131	–27	225	629	695	366	764	–
CMA CGM	109	36	110	328	620	820	823	1284	1260
COSCO Container L.	–	–	–18	329	610	1114	1912	3835	–
CSAV	–	–	35	67	145	189	–197	93	–
Hanjin Shipping	317	193	9	362	793	616	326	482	–
Hapag Lloyd	87	288	238	456	393	538	267	851	–
K-Line	–	–	–	273	649	1,100	992	1,023	1,838
Maersk	1,092	1,356	1,481	2,082	2,806	3,420	1,540	2,408	2,262
Matson	–	–	–	145	166	189	164	190	–
MISC Berhad	–	455	435	380	662	1681	1,320	1,394	774
Mitsui-OSK L. (MOL)	–	–	–	173	555	383	75	150	–
NYK	–	–	–	215	445	188	–	211	–
OOCL	–	–	91	359	729	745	805	868	610
RCL	–	–	61	57	128	160	117	107	57
UASC	–	–	0	56	118	136	79	–	–
Wan Hai Lines	–	–	21	48	187	202	153	252	–
Yang Ming Line	–	–	460	232	497	455	50	187	–
ZIM	–	–	28	99	251	261	189	142	–

	2000	2001	2002	2003	2004	2005	2006	2007	2008
Δ EBITDA %									
APL		**-33.5**	**-29.1**	203.0	119.7	**-5.3**	**-32.9**	35.1	**-61.0**
CCNI					480.0	100.0	**-152.6**	**-30.0**	133.6
CSCL			**-120.9**	922.7	179.7	10.5	**-47.3**	108.8	
CMA CGM		**-66.8**	202.8	198.2	89.0	32.2	0.4	56.0	**-1.9**
COSCO Container L				1966.5	85.6	82.6	71.6	100.5	
CSAV				91.8	118.5	29.8	**-204.4**	147.2	
Hanjin Shipping		**-39.0**	**-95.3**	3922.2	119.0	**-22.3**	**-47.1**	47.9	
Hapag Lloyd		232.2	**-17.3**	91.6	**-13.8**	36.9	**-50.3**	218.5	
K-Line					137.6	69.4	**-9.8**	3.2	79.6
Maersk		24.2	9.2	40.6	34.8	21.9	**-55.0**	56.4	**-6.1**
Matson					14.5	13.9	**-13.2**	15.9	
MISC Berhad			**-4.3**	**-12.7**	74.1	154.1	**-21.4**	5.5	**-44.4**
Mitsui-OSK L. (MOL)					220.8	**-31.0**	**-80.4**	99.5	
NYK					107.0	**-57.8**			
OOCL				295.6	102.8	2.2	8.1	7.7	**-29.7**
RCL				**-6.6**	124.6	25.0	**-27.1**	**-8.3**	**-46.7**
UASC				19962.1	109.4	16.0	**-41.9**		
Wan Hai Lines				128.6	289.6	8.0	**-24.3**	64.7	
Yang Ming Line				**-49.6**	114.2	**-8.5**	**-89.0**	274.0	
ZIM				253.6	153.5	4.0	-27.6	**-24.9**	

Note: Negative numbers in bold.

Table 6A.2 Evolution of return on sales at container division level

	2000	2001	2002	2003	2004	2005	2006	2007	2008
ROS									
APL	0.075	0.053	0.039	0.097	0.168	0.142	0.095	0.115	0.038
CCNI	–	–	–	**-0.013**	0.036	0.063	**-0.047**	**-0.019**	0.005
CSCL	–	–	**-0.021**	0.122	0.269	0.198	0.094	0.144	–
CMA CGM	0.057	0.018	0.042	0.086	0.113	0.137	0.098	0.109	0.083
COSCO Container L.	–	–	**-0.007**	0.105	0.157	0.187	0.189	0.259	–
CSAV	–	–	0.021	0.031	0.054	0.048	**-0.051**	0.022	–
Evergreen	0.094	0.074	0.058	0.026	0.047	0.096	0.091	0.012	0.104
Hanjin Shipping	0.092	0.055	0.002	0.077	0.164	0.127	0.058	0.065	–
Hapag Lloyd	–	0.084	0.060	0.151	0.107	0.118	0.034	0.100	0.073
Hyundai M.M.	0.086	0.056	**-0.007**	0.086	0.105	0.096	0.021	0.062	0.125
K-Line	–	–	–	0.046	0.097	0.160	0.124	0.086	0.079
Maersk	0.115	0.133	0.127	0.154	0.178	0.159	0.061	0.090	–
Matson	–	–	–	0.187	0.195	0.215	0.173	0.189	0.208
MISC Berhad	–	0.295	0.300	0.265	0.330	0.597	0.433	0.412	

	2000	2001	2002	2003	2004	2005	2006	2007	2008
Mitsui-OSK L. (MOL)	–	–	0.050	0.149	0.092	0.016	0.022	–	–
NYK	–	–	–	0.055	0.105	0.041	**-0.005**	0.032	–
OOCL	–	–	0.037	0.111	0.176	0.159	0.175	0.154	0.093
RCL	–	–	0.202	0.169	0.278	0.297	0.211	0.187	0.103
UASC	–	–	0.000	0.069	0.120	0.131	0.077	–	–
Wan Hai Lines	–	–	0.023	0.043	0.130	0.134	0.095	0.134	–
Yang Ming Line	–	–	0.351	0.109	0.179	0.153	0.015	0.045	–
ZIM	–	–	0.017	0.049	0.099	0.089	0.062	0.037	–
Average	0.085	0.094	0.071	0.091	0.148	0.153	0.084	0.108	0.090

Note: Negative numbers in bold. By way of comparison, the A.P. Møller-Maersk Group improved its financial performance between 2007 and 2008 increasing its ROS from 23.3 to 269 % while it gained only 18.94 US cents out of every dollar in 2009. Drilling down towards two other of its business segments the annual reports reveal that the ROS of the business segment A.P.M. terminal grew continuously (2007: 16.27%, 2008: 18.37% and 2009: 24.09%) (cross-subsidisation?) while the business segment Maersk Tankers saw its ROS drop to 25.76% after maintaining its at about 30% for the 2007–08 period. As a benchmark, a look at other industries shows that Audi achieved a ROS of 8.1% in 2008 and 5.4 % in 2009. The ROS of Nippon Steel diminished continuously (2006: 13.9%, 2007: 11.7% and 2008: 7%) while that of Proctor & Gamble increased slightly (2006: 19.42%, 2007: 20.20% and 2008: 20.46%).

Table 6A.3   Evolution of net profit at container division level

	2000	2001	2002	2003	2004	2005	2006	2007	2008
Net profit									
APL	284	19	**-73**	406	892	845	344	523	83
CCNI	–	–	–	9	17	35	**-20**	**-14**	1
CSCL	–	162	**-72**	167	486	444	111	441	–
CMA CGM	101	25	49	255	566	553	611	966	111
COSCO Container L.	–	–	**-145**	211	600	861	1,215	2,907	–
CSAV	–	–	–	72	206	132	**-58**	–	–
Hanjin Shipping	**-59**	**-60**	16	248	502	390	404	156	–
Hapag Lloyd	73	204	150	455	386	328	107	269	–
K-Line	–	–	–	97	305	620	382	562	919
Maersk	518	152	59	586	1,512	1,278	2,249	106	205
Matson	–	–	–	93	–	–	–	–	–
MISC Berhad	–	444	354	346	604	1259	814	875	730
Mitsui-OSK Line	–	–	–	56	517	965	27	69	–
NYK	–	–	–	44	–	149	**-82**	114	–
OOCL	–	–	52	329	671	651	581	2,548	276
RCL	–	–	28	20	95	119	80	100	**-24**
UASC	–	–	4	70	135	115	54	–	–
Wan Hai Lines	–	–	98	130	212	165	96	193	–
Yang Ming Line	–	–	32	195	307	282	36	187	–
ZIM	–	–	**-9**	47	172	187	80	28	–
Average	–	–	42.89	183.18	449.13	483.26	341.26	555.63	276.68

	2000	2001	2002	2003	2004	2005	2006	2007	2008
Δ Net profit %									
APL		-93	-484	-656	120	-5	-59	52	-84
CCNI		–	–	–	89	106	-156	-29	104
CSCL		–	-145	332	191	-9	-75	298	–
CMA CGM		-75	98	420	122	-2	10	58	-89
COSCO Container L.		–	–	246	185	44	41	139	–
CSAV		–	–	–	186	-36	-144	–	–
Hanjin Shipping		-1	126	1494	103	-22	3	-61	–
Hapag Lloyd		177	-26	203	-15	-15	-67	151	–
K-Line		–	–	–	215	103	-38	47	64
Maersk		-71	-61	891	158	-15	76	-95	93
Matson		–	–	–	–	–	–	–	–
MISC Berhad		–	-20	-2	75	109	-35	7	-17
Mitsui-OSK Line		–	–	–	823	87	-97	160	–
NYK		–	–	–	–	–	-155	239	–
OOCL		–	–	535	104	-3	-11	339	-89
RCL		–	–	-29	375	25	-33	25	-124
UASC		–	–	1650	93	-15	-53	–	–
Wan Hai Lines		–	–	33	63	-22	-42	102	–
Yang Ming Line		–	–	509	57	-8	-87	420	–
ZIM		–	–	622	266	9	-57	-65	–

Note: Negative numbers in bold.

7. Modal accessibility disparity to terminals and its effect on the competitiveness of HST versus air transport

Juan Carlos García-Palomares, Javier Gutiérrez, Juan Carlos Martín and Concepción Román

7.1 INTRODUCTION

Spain has become a paradigmatic example of how to expand the European high-speed train (HST) network to become a high-density network that will interconnect the main Spanish cities. It has been much trumpeted that this expansion will increase the competitiveness of this mode versus other transport modes, such as coaches, private cars or air transport, and that a better modal share could be obtained for interurban transport in Spain. Nevertheless, little attention has been paid to an important issue, that is, how access to terminals plays an important role in promoting this so-called 'competitiveness'.

In Spain, one of the most important developed routes is the Madrid–Zaragoza–Barcelona corridor. This link is interesting to analyze because it joins the two most important economic poles of Spain, Madrid and Barcelona, and HST is in direct competition with the domestic airline market. This has resulted in an increased interest in the analysis of how different factors affect the modal competition in interurban corridors. Thereby, special attention is given to the different components that affect passengers' behavior in interurban corridors, particularly the effects of access to terminals, train stations, and airports. For example, Román and Martín (2011), find that modal competition between rail and plane for interurban travel passengers in the Madrid–Barcelona corridor is highly affected by the as yet neglected effect of access time to terminals. This strengthens the case for studying the spatial effects of the location of train stations and airports within the context of HST and air transport competitiveness.

However, empirical research that studies modal competition between HST and air transport at an aggregate level often deals with the problem generally, by only considering the presence of an HST station and airport in the same location. Adler et al. (2010) use a game-theoretic setting to analyze the modal competition with and without HST investment. The authors use a social welfare function that can analyze the potential effects of the investments on producers (privatized companies providing transportation services), consumers (the traveling public, split into business and leisure categories), government authorities (local or federal) and the infrastructure manager, accounting for the effects of infrastructure modifications on taxes and subsidies as well as the environment. Passenger choice among alternatives is based on the discrete choice theory of product differentiation (Anderson et al., 1996). A representative consumer is assumed to choose the travel alternative (mode and route) that yields the highest utility. The utility depends on the various characteristics of the alternative, including fare, travel time, distance and routing.

We argue that not only the presence of an HST station but also the level of service provided by the station is of importance. The term 'level of service' comprises many aspects that affect modal competitiveness, one of which is the focus of this chapter: the accessibility of the HST station. Furthermore, most quantitative empirical research has given little attention to this important issue and typically modal competitiveness has been centrally focused on the basis of travel time and price, as the main components of the total generalized costs. However, other components might be just as important for passengers, and policy makers should be aware of this. For example, it would be interesting to observe the different spatial patterns of terminals' hinterland (the spatial distribution of areas where the probability of choosing a transport mode is higher due to the access component of each transport terminal).

This chapter focuses on this up-to-now neglected aspect of transport mode competitiveness. Whether and how the level of service of transport terminals affects modal competition between HST and air transport will be studied, and, in particular, the level of competitiveness that can be accrued by the access times provided by private cars and transit in different market segments. The chapter addresses this question by linking together the results of a stated choice experiment that includes respondent heterogeneity and interaction effects, and a geographical information system (GIS) that takes into account different areas of Madrid that analyze the access time to Atocha (Madrid HST station) and Barajas (Madrid airport). An innovative element included in the chapter is that both mandatory and leisure trips are analyzed using private car and public transport as access modes. As a result, it was possible to study how modal competitiveness is affected for each of these segments. The study area of the research is the province of Madrid in Spain.

The rest of this chapter is organized as follows. The next section describes briefly the dataset, the questionnaire and the experimental design. Section 7.3 describes the model estimated to analyze the modal competition in the Madrid–Barcelona corridor. The results of the GIS are then presented in Section 7.4, focusing on the spatial analysis of the relative competitiveness of air transport versus HST. In this section we also discuss how the relative access times to terminals influence the modal competitiveness for different types of trips and access modes. Finally, Section 7.5 concludes.

7.2 COLLECTING THE DATASET

A stated choice experiment for air transport passengers was carried out in order to analyze the effects of HST in the Madrid–Barcelona corridor. Bliemer and Rose (2011) maintain that a discrete choice experiment (DCE) is a popular and adequate technique that allows researchers to construct databases for modeling transport behavior preferences that can be used to estimate willingness to pay (WTP) measures for important attributes which influence the selection of transport modes. In a DCE, respondents are asked in one or multiple choice tasks to select their most preferred alternative from a given set of alternatives that are characterized by different levels of attributes. In our case, respondents are asked to comment on modal competition between air transport and HST. The experiment complements the revealed preference data gathered for conventional train passengers, air transport passengers, coach passengers, car drivers and car passengers.[1] The purpose of the experiment was to gain insight into passengers' preferences with regard to transport mode choice and to study whether access time to the train station is an important attribute determining the relative competitiveness of HST versus air transport.

The revealed preference (RP) data are based on a survey administered during April and May 2004 that gathered information about travel behavior in the principal modes: car driver, car passenger, bus, conventional train and plane. Bus users were interviewed in the Avenida de America bus station; air passengers were approached at the corresponding boarding gates at Barajas Airport, people traveling by train were interviewed at the train station, and car users were interviewed in the petrol stations strategically located on the national road A-II. RP data were complemented with stated preference (SP) data for plane users. Thus, passengers also participated in a stated choice experiment regarding the plane (the dominant mode) and the new HST alternative. As all the participants in the exercise were actually traveling in the corridor, the no-traveling option was not considered.

It is beyond the scope of this chapter to analyze other significant changes that can be produced as a result of the HST such as the new potential pattern of economic activity, total number of offices and jobs, in the Atocha area. Other important issues, such as to what extent higher prices for real estate due to the increased attractiveness of this hinterland area near the HST station, are not considered. However, a decrease in car accessibility will affect the modal competitiveness of HST and this will be analyzed under a perspective based on the spatial analysis of all the areas included in the province of Madrid.

The questionnaire was divided into four sections: identification data, trip information, and household and personal socioeconomic information. Trip information included questions related not only to the actual mode but also to those available alternatives that were not chosen by the individual for the reference trip. The DCE deals specifically with air travel choice entering into competition with the new HST service and included the typical level-of-service attributes such as travel time, access/egress time, travel cost, and frequency. We also included two latent variables: reliability and comfort. The former was included to account for the negative effect of delays over the scheduled departure time, and the latter to determine the effect of having more space in plane seats.

Respondents were asked to complete a computer-aided DCE involving the choice of transport mode from among two possible alternatives, based on the plane they were ready to board and the new HST. The two alternatives were labeled 'air transport' and 'HST'. To capture the trade-offs between the six attributes included in the experiment,[2] the two alternatives displayed the different level of services for all of them with the exception of comfort for HST which was considered as good as the large-pitch seat offered in the air transport (high comfort). Given that for some attributes the level of service was known, this was the reference point for the hypothetical scenario.

Each respondent faced nine choice tasks in which the attributes shown were varied according to the selected experimental design.[3] Note that depending on the attributes, the levels were adapted according to the experience of the present trip of the passenger. Code levels were associated with plausible values of the corresponding attributes. For greater realism, the levels assigned to some attributes in the SP exercise were customized to each respondent's experience pivoting the information provided by some questions included in the questionnaire about the reference alternative (the plane, in this case). Thus, the levels of travel cost and access time were defined in terms of the values experienced by the sample respondents; plausible percentage variations according to the available information about future fares and access time for the HST were also considered. The service frequency was also customized to the departure time declared by the respondent. This information is presented in Table 7.1. Note that passengers on package tours were excluded from the sample.

The mixed or joint estimation method proposed by Bradley and Daly (1997), combining RP and SP data, allowed us to estimate the utility of the new alternative, in our case the HST, and of those that already existed. The main interest of our model lies in analyzing the principal factors that influence the modal choice in the corridor after the introduction of the HST. In the analysis, taking into consideration the aim of the chapter, special attention was given to the perception of access and egress time to the train stations and airports. Thus, total travel time was divided into its principal components: access/egress time, waiting time, and in-vehicle time.

Thus, the RP data were complemented with a dataset consisting in choices made by plane users that provided information about their travel preferences in nine different choice situations.[4] A summary of the descriptive analysis of the sample is shown in Table 7.2.

In the Madrid–Barcelona corridor, total travel time by plane is substantially less than in the other modes but, in this case, the proportion of access and waiting time (over the total duration of the journey) is very high (nearly 70 percent). The car is the second-fastest mode with a total travel time of 70 minutes less than by train[5]

Nearly 56 percent of the trips were mandatory (work and education) and 54 percent of the travelers were men. We also observed differences in per capita weekly income, ranging from €167 for car passengers to €351 for plane users. And finally, the expenditure rate[6] goes from 1.23 for car passengers to 2.86 for car drivers.

Figures 7.1 and 7.2 show the differences in access time to terminals for plane and train users, respectively. It can be seen that the access time to airports was less than the access time to train stations for only 54 percent of the travelers who chose to travel by plane (Figure 7.1), which means that 46 percent of the individuals who traveled by plane considered this alternative more competitive in other level-of-service attributes. It can be inferred that, for these passengers, it is possible that in-vehicle travel time and frequency are more highly valued attributes. However, for the

Table 7.1 *Attributes and levels*

Attributes	Levels	Plane		HST	
		Departure before 9:00	Departure after 9:00	Departure before 9:00	Departure after 9:00
Travel cost (c_v)	−1	$c_v*1.10$		c_v	
	0	c_v		$c_v*0.90$	
	+1	$c_v*0.90$		$c_v*0.80$	
Travel time (t_v)	−1	1h 20 min		2h 45 min	
	0	1h 10 min		2h 30 min	
	+1	1h		2h 15 min	
Access + egress time (t_a)	−1	$t_a*1.20$		t_a	
	0	t_a		$t_a*0.90$	
	+1	$t_a*0.80$		$t_a*0.80$	
Frequency (headway) (f)	−1	Every 30 min	Every 60 min	Every 60 min	Every 90 min
	+1	Every 15 min	Every 30 min	Every 30 min	Every 60 min
Reliability (r)	−1	30 min delay (Inside the plane)		10 min delay	
	0	15 min delay (in the boarding gate)		5 min delay	
	+1	Departure on time		Departure on time	
Comfort (C)	−1	Low / Small leg room / Narrow seats			
	+1	High / Ample leg room / Wide seats		High / Ample leg room / Wide seats	

Note: c_v = Travel cost in plane; t_a = Access + egress time in plane.

Table 7.2   Main characteristics of the sample, Madrid–Barcelona corridor, 2004

	Chosen mode					
	Car driver	Car passenger	Bus	Train	Plane	Total
Choice	38	18	39	51	295	441
Availability[+]	165	92	165	288	435	–
Level-of-service attributes (average per available alternative)						
Access time (minutes)	–	–	27	29	36	–
Waiting time (minutes)	–	–	40	28	58	–
In-vehicle time (minutes)	357	369	477	332	59	–
Egress time (minutes)	–	–	33	39	37	–
Travel cost/fuel (€)	46.07	22.70	25.13	62.33	95.19	–
Toll (€)	18.32	4.45	–	–	–	–
Access cost (€)	–	–	2.66	5.47	7.31	–
Egress cost (€)	–	–	3.50	7.07	7.91	–
Headway (minutes)	–	–	46	150	33	–
Socioeconomic characteristics (classification per chosen mode)						
Trip motive						
Work or education	16	3	10	31	187	247
	(42%)	(17%)	(26%)	(61%)	(63%)	(56%)
Other	22	15	29	20	108	194
	(58%)	(83%)	(74%)	(39%)	(37%)	(44%)
Men	26	8	15	28	160	237
	(68%)	(44%)	(38%)	(55%)	(54%)	(54%)
Women	12	10	24	23	135	204
	(32%)	(56%)	(62%)	(45%)	(46%)	(46%)
Age (average)	41	31	28	39	36	36
Per capita weekly income (average €)	355.93	166.89	188.25	341.57	350.68	328.88
Expenditure rate* (average)	2.86	1.23	1.41	2.68	2.81	2.62

Notes:
* Per capita family income/available time.
+ It can be seen that not all types of public transport are available to passengers. When passengers consider that under no circumstance would they travel by some specific mode, then this transport mode is not available in the choice set.

majority of the train travelers (91 percent), access time to train stations was significantly lower than it was to airports. So, at first glance, this attribute may be quite sensitive in determining the overall attractiveness of the new HST (Figure 7.2).[7]

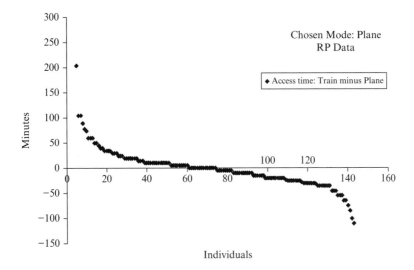

Figure 7.1   Differences in access time to terminals for plane travelers

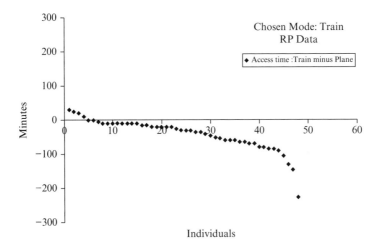

Figure 7.2   Differences in access time to terminals for train travelers

7.3   MODEL AND RESULTS

Discrete choice models are derived under the assumption of utility-maximizing behavior by the decision maker. The specification of the econometric model is based on random utility theory (Domencich and

McFadden, 1975; Ortúzar and Willumsen, 2001). It states that the utility of alternative j for individual q has the expression:

$$U_{jq} = V_{jq} + \varepsilon_{jq}, \tag{7.1}$$

where V_{jq} is the representative or systematic utility,[8] and ε_{jq} is a random term that includes unobserved effects. V_{jq} depends on the observable attributes of alternative j, and on the socioeconomic characteristics of individual q. When ε_{jq} are distributed iid Gumbel, we obtain the popular multinomial logit (MNL) model. The nested logit (NL) model (Williams, 1977) is appropriate when the set of options available for a decision maker can be grouped into nests in such a way that the independence-of-irrelevant-alternatives property of the MNL holds for alternatives within the same nest, and does not hold for options belonging to different nests. This model is obtained when the vector of random terms follows the generalized extreme value distribution.

The mixed estimation combining RP and SP data is based on the hypothesis that variances of the error terms in both datasets are proportional (Ben-Akiva and Morikawa, 1990), and can be expressed as:

$$\sigma_\varepsilon^2 = \mu^2 \sigma_\eta^2, \tag{7.2}$$

where μ is an unknown scale parameter, and ε and η are the error terms of the RP and SP utilities, respectively. This leads to the following utility functions for a given alternative j:

$$U_j^{RP} = V_j^{RP} + \varepsilon_j = \theta X_j^{RP} + \alpha Y_j^{RP} + \varepsilon_j$$

$$\mu U_j^{SP} = \mu(V_j^{SP} + \eta_j) = \mu(\theta X_j^{SP} + \omega Z_j^{SP} + \eta_j), \tag{7.3}$$

where θ, α, and ω are parameters to be estimated; X_j^{RP} and X_j^{SP} are attributes common to the RP and SP datasets; and Y_j^{RP} and Z_j^{SP} are attributes that only belong to the designated dataset.

Bradley and Daly (1997) proposed an estimation method based on the construction of an artificial NL structure where RP alternatives are placed right below the root, and each SP alternative is placed in a single-alternative nest with a common scale parameter μ This procedure will ensure that μ is estimated to obtain uniform variance.[9]

Once μ is estimated, a utility function can be constructed using common and non-common RP–SP parameters (Louviere et al., 2000). If attributes are only defined for the SP case, their parameters must be scaled by μ. However, those corresponding to attributes measured in the RP base do not need to be scaled, even if they appear only in the SP utility (Cherchi and Ortúzar, 2004).

7.3.1 Model Specification

We considered a linear-in-the-parameter (but not linear-in-the-attributes) specification for the utility function that included transport costs divided by the expenditure rate (Jara-Díaz and Farah, 1987). As we obtained a significant proportion of household income spent on transport, ranging from 5 to 27 percent for the different modes, we include cost squared terms as recommended by Jara-Díaz (1998). In order to account for a richer specification of the access/egress time to train stations and airports, we defined the interaction of this variable with the travel time. We also considered the interaction of the trip motive with travel time. This allowed us to analyze the perception of travel time in terms of the trip motive. The utilities for the RP and SP alternatives were:

RP alternatives:

$$U^{RP}_{car-driver} = C_{cd} + (\theta_{t_v} + \theta_{t_v*T}T)t_v + \theta_{c/e_r}\frac{c}{e_r} + \theta_{c^2/e_rI}\frac{c^2}{e_rI}$$

$$U^{RP}_{car-passenger} = C_{cp} + (\theta_{t_v} + \theta_{t_v*T}T)t_v + \theta_{c/e_r}\frac{c}{e_r} + \theta_{c^2/e_rI}\frac{c^2}{e_rI}$$

$$U^{RP}_{bus} = C_b + \theta_{t_a}t_a + \theta_{t_w}t_w + (\theta_{t_v} + \theta_{t_v*T}T)t_v + \theta_{c/e_r}\frac{c}{e_r} + \theta_{c^2/e_rI}\frac{c^2}{e_rI}$$

$$U^{RP}_{train} = C_{train} + \theta_{t_a}t_a + \theta_{t_w}t_w + (\theta_{t_v} + \theta_{t_v*T}T)t_v + \theta^{train}_{t_v \cdot t_a}t_v t_a + \theta_{c/e_r}\frac{c}{e_r} + \theta_{c^2/e_rI}\frac{c^2}{e_rI} + \theta_f f$$

$$U^{RP}_{plane} = \theta_{t_a}t_a + \theta_{t_w}t_w + (\theta_{t_v} + \theta_{t_v*T}T)t_v + \theta^{plane}_{t_v \cdot t_a}t_v t_a + \theta_{c/e_r}\frac{c}{e_r} + \theta_{c^2/e_rI}\frac{c^2}{e_rI} + \theta_f f \tag{7.4}$$

SP alternatives:

$$U^{SP}_{HST} = \theta_{t_a}t_a + (\theta_{t_v} + \theta_{t_v*T}T)t_v + \theta^{train}_{t_v \cdot t_a}t_v \cdot t_a + \theta_{c/e_r}\frac{c}{e_r} + \theta_{c^2/e_rI}\frac{c^2}{e_rI} + \theta_f f + \theta_r r$$

$$U^{SP}_{plane} = \theta_{t_a} t_a + (\theta_{t_v} + \theta_{t_v*T} T) t_v + \theta^{plane}_{t_v \cdot t_a} t_v \cdot t_a + \theta_{c/e_r} \frac{c}{e_r} + \theta_{c^2/e_r I} \frac{c^2}{e_r I} + \theta_f f + \theta_r r$$

$$+ \theta_{COM*t_v} COM \cdot t_v \qquad (7.5)$$

where, t_v is in-vehicle travel time; t_a is access + egress time; t_w is waiting time; c is travel cost; f is service headway; r is reliability (minutes of delay); COM is equal to 1 if the level of comfort is high (more space and leg room in the plane seat); T is equal to 1 if the trip motive is work or education; e_r is the expenditure rate; I is per capita family income; and the θ_s are unknown parameters. Regarding the model structure for the transport modes whose utility is presented in equations (7.4) and (7.5), we estimate an NL model that considered the correlation between train and plane. This means that individuals perceive these alternatives as close substitutes.

7.3.2 Estimation Results

Table 7.3 shows the estimation results corresponding to the best model obtained. All parameter estimates have the expected signs, and were significant at an acceptable confidence level, with only the exceptions of headway and waiting time. We applied the likelihood ratio test (Ortúzar and Willumsen, 2001) to check the advantage of having specific rather than generic parameters in the interaction term of access time with in-vehicle time $(t_a \cdot t_v)$; in all cases analyzed, the specific models were superior. The alternative specific constants (taking the plane as the reference) turned out to be significant (except for the train),[10] and with a negative sign, indicating that plane (or train) would be preferred if the effect of the other attributes were zero.

As travel time interacts with other levels of service attributes, marginal utilities are not represented by fixed values. According to our specification, the marginal utility of travel time for the different alternatives is represented by the following expressions:

Car and bus: $\dfrac{\partial U}{\partial t_v} = \theta_{t_v} + \theta_{t_v*T} T$;

Plane: $\dfrac{\partial U}{\partial t_v} = \theta_{t_v} + \theta_{t_v*T} T + \theta_{CA*t_v} COM + \theta_1$; $\qquad (7.6)$

Train/HST: $\dfrac{\partial U}{\partial t_v} = \theta_{t_v} + \theta_{t_v*T} T + \theta^{train}_{t_v \cdot t_a} t_a$.

Table 7.3   Estimation results

Parameter		Estimates	(*t*-ratios)
Car-driver constant	C_{cd}	–3.6070	(–3.14)
Car-passenger constant	C_{cp}	–4.7140	(–3.52)
Bus constant	C_b	–2.5470	(–2.12)
Travel time (t_v)	θ_{t_v}	–0.0056	(–2.20)
Travel cost/er (c/e_r)	θ_{c/e_r}	–0.0654	(–4.99)
Headway (f)	θ_f	–0.0026	(–0.70)
Travel cost2/$e_r I$ ($c^2/e_r I$)	θ_{c^2/e_r}	0.0208	(3.75)
Access + egress time (t_a)	θ_{t_a}	–0.0129	(–2.09)
Waiting time (t_w)	θ_{t_w}	–0.0046	(–0.72)
Travel time_Work + education (t_v*T)	θ_{t_v*T}	–0.0026	(–2.02)
Travel time*Access + egress time Train ($t_v*t_{a\ Train}$)	$\theta_{t_v*t_{a\ Train}}$	–0.00006	(–1.94)
Travel time*Access + egress time Plane ($t_v*t_{a\ Plane}$)	$\theta_{t_v*t_{a\ Plane}}$	–0.00016	(–2.09)
Reliability (delay) (r)	θ_r	–0.0348	(–2.85)
Travel time * Comfort high (COM*t_v)	$\theta_{COM\_t_v}$	0.0069	(1.82)
HST–Plane nest parameter	Φ	0.4222	(3.40)
			[–4.66]*
Scale factor SP	μ	0.4145	(3.05)
			[–4.30]*
$l*(0)$		–2,124.7995	
$l*(\theta)$		–1,996.9479	
Observations		2,917	

Note: * *t*-ratio with respect to $\Phi = 1$ and $\mu = 1$.

Thus, the marginal utility of travel time varies with the trip motive, access/egress time, and the level of comfort.

Similarly, the marginal utility of access/egress time varies with the duration of the trip, and with the alternative:

Plane: $$\frac{\partial U}{\partial t_a} = \theta_{t_a} + \theta^{plane}_{t_v t_a} \ ;$$

Train/HST: $$\frac{\partial U}{\partial t_a} = \theta_{t_a} + \theta^{train}_{t_v t_a} \ . \tag{7.7}$$

The negative sign of the coefficients θ_{t_a} and $\theta_{t_v t_a}$ indicates that the disutility produced by an additional minute in access time increases with in-vehicle travel time in a given alternative. Therefore, whenever we found significant negative coefficients for the interaction term $t_a \cdot t_v$, increments in travel time could increase the negative perception of access time. On the other hand, increments in access time would increase the negative perception of travel time.

7.4   SPATIAL ANALYSIS

A Geographical Information System (ArcGIS) was used to store the population, employment, and network data. Thus, access times to terminals, Atocha HST station and Barajas airport, by private and public transport can be calculated to further analyze whether the relative position of the zones in Madrid can favor the competitiveness of HST or air transport.

The metropolitan area of Madrid was divided into 69 zones, corresponding to the 21 districts of the municipality of Madrid and the 48 suburban municipalities. The metropolitan area has been divided into four different rings, in order to present a summary of the results of our analysis: (i) the seven central districts of the municipality of Madrid, (ii) the 14 peripheral districts of the municipality of Madrid, (iii) the suburban municipalities (26 municipalities) which were already integrated in the metropolitan area in the 1960s and 1970s (larger and closer to Madrid), and (iv) the remaining suburban municipalities (22), smaller and more peripheral. It can be seen that the distribution of population and employment is very uneven (Figure 7.3 and Table 7.4). The first ring contains more employment than population. The opposite occurs in the other rings where there is more population than employment. Also, the employment is more concentrated in the NW–NE sector, while the population is more concentrated in the S–SE. Nevertheless, population distribution is more dispersed.

Access times by private car were calculated in ArcGIS, using a dense road network (Figure 7.3). All metropolitan roads were taken into account, as well as the main streets of the city of Madrid. This road network represents the situation in 2010, and the average speed for each arc was estimated taking into account the type of road and the average level of congestion. With this network, private car travel times through the network from each of the 69 centroids to Atocha HST station and Barajas airport were calculated.

Public transit times were calculated using the 'Transport Information System' from the Consorcio de Transportes de Madrid. This system contains all public transit networks in 2010 (including urban and interurban bus, Metro and Light and suburban rail). Travel times to Atocha HST station and Barajas airport were also calculated from the 69 centroids.

Population and employment data correspond to the year 2009.

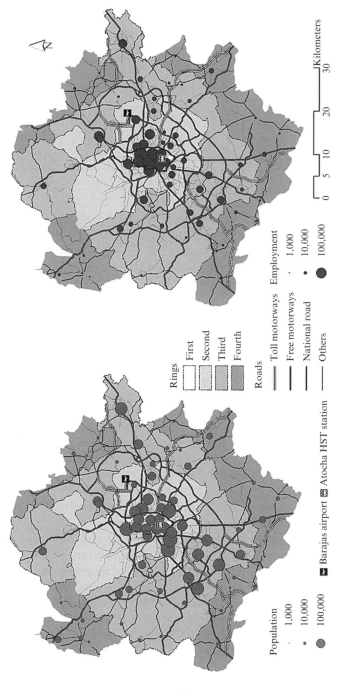

Figure 7.3   Population and employment distribution in the Madrid metropolitan area

Population
· 1,000
• 10,000
● 100,000

■ Barajas airport 🚶 Atocha HST station

Rings
First
Second
Third
Fourth

Roads
—— Toll motorways
—— Free motorways
—— National road
—— Others

Employment
· 1,000
• 10,000
● 100,000

Kilometers
0 5 10 20 30

139

Table 7.4   Population and employment distribution, according to rings, 2009

Rings	Spatial units	Employment total	Mean	Std dev.	Population total	Mean	Std dev.
First	7	886,966	126,709	35,213	821,795	117,399	53,275
Second	14	753,559	53,826	31,716	2,158,811	154,201	69,565
Third	26	768,200	29,546	23,215	2,411,249	92,740	71,047
Fourth	22	133,912	6,087	6,148	551,385	25,063	31,808
Total	69	2,542,637	36,850	41,577	5,943,240	86,134	74,978

Source: Statistics Institute of the Community of Madrid.

Population data were obtained from the 'Padrón' and employment from the 'Directorio de Unidades de Actividad Económica'. Both variables are provided by the Statistics Institute of the Community of Madrid. Population and employment data were used to calculate weighted indicators for access times and probability distribution.

7.4.1   Access Time to Terminals and Modal Competitiveness

In this section the results of our network analysis regarding the access time to terminals by public and private transport will be presented and discussed. In the analysis, the probability distribution of using air transport versus HST for the spatial analysis for mandatory and non-mandatory trips will also be highlighted.[11] It can be seen below that terminal accessibility has been calculated with no weights and weighting according the distribution of population and employment for each of the centroids considered in our analysis. The competitiveness of transport modes is analyzed with the spatial distribution of the probability of using air transport, considering the average trip for the remaining variables included in the modal competition model. In order to facilitate the interpretation of results, these have been averaged according to rings.

It can be seen that the average access time to Barajas airport by private car is 29.2 minutes, 18 percent higher than the access time to Atocha HST station which is only 24.7 minutes (Table 7.5). The same analysis for public transport shows that access time to Barajas is 55.6 minutes, 28 percent higher than the access time to Atocha (43.3 minutes). It is well known that Barajas is one of the most important European airports, enjoying a central location inside the city of Madrid. However, it is clear that the train station performs better in terms of accessibility than the airport. This fact is explained not only in terms of location but also because of transport

Table 7.5   *Access times to Atocha and Barajas by transport mode (minutes)*

	No weights				Population weights				Employment weights			
	Atocha HST station		Barajas airport		Atocha HST station		Barajas airport		Atocha HST station		Barajas airport	
	Car	Transit	Car	Transit	Car	Transit	Car	Transit	Car	Transit	Car	Transit
N	69	69	69	69	69	69	69	69	69	69	69	69
Min	3.0	11.0	7.0	7.0	3.0	11.0	7.0	7.0	3.0	11.0	7.0	7.0
Max	46.0	86.0	56.0	98.0	46.0	86.0	56.0	98.0	46.0	86.0	56.0	98.0
Average	24.7	43.3	29.2	55.6	20.7	32.3	26.8	50.7	17.6	31.3	23.7	42.6
Std dev.	10.0	21.0	10.7	21.1	9.7	15.3	8.5	16.8	9.4	14.6	7.8	17.5
CV	40.3	48.5	36.5	38.0	46.8	47.4	31.6	33.1	53.7	46.6	33.1	41.1

infrastructure. Atocha is still one of the central hub nodes in Madrid's public transport network, which is highly characterized by the dominant position of some central nodes, the station being one of them. Atocha is the central station of the suburban rail network and it is also an important intermodal node for urban and interurban buses and the underground.

Table 7.5 also shows the weighted access times to terminals and it can be seen that the concentration of employment and population in the inner rings explains why the average times decrease, thus retaining a better performance for the case of the train station. The advantage of Atocha in terms of accessibility is even more significant when the indicators are weighted by population and for the case of public transport. In this case, access times to Barajas are negatively affected due to the highly concentrated urban areas in the south of Madrid, which are well connected with the train station and poorly connected with the airport. However, as employment is more concentrated in the NW–NE arc, this performance accessibility gap is reduced. Table 7.5 also emphasizes how the dispersion of accessibility to terminals in public transport is greater than in private transport (see the coefficient of variation), which will undoubtedly have an effect on the spatial modal competitiveness under analysis. Furthermore, the dispersion of accessibility to Atocha is greater than that to Barajas.

In addition to the better performance shown by Atocha regarding access times to terminals in public and private transport, for the average trip, that is considering the average variables included in the modal competition model, the competitiveness of air transport is greater than HST in every case (Table 7.6). This is because the probability of using air transport is greater than 0.5. Also, the highest probability of using air transport is for the mandatory trips when access to terminals is by private transport (0.657). In contrast, the lowest competitiveness of air transport is for leisure trips and public transport access (0.547). In mandatory trips, the competitiveness of air transport is increased by 6.5 percent if access to terminals is by private transport; furthermore, for leisure trips the competitiveness of air transport is increased by 7 percent if access to terminals is by private transport.

If we consider that demand for interurban transport is distributed according to the population of each of the zones under analysis, and the distribution of probability of using air transport is also weighted by the population, it can be seen that this probability is decreased in every case, so the competitiveness of air transport is lessened. The probability of using air transport is still very high for mandatory trips and access by private transport (0.648); however, the competitiveness of air transport is quite similar to HST for leisure trips and public transport access (0.513). If we use employment to calculate the weighted probability distribution of using air transport, a dual phenomenon can be observed: on one

Table 7.6 Distribution of the probability of using air transport according to type of trip and terminal access mode

	No weights				Population weights				Employment weights			
	Mandatory		Leisure		Mandatory		Leisure		Mandatory		Leisure	
	Car	Transit	Car	Transit	Car	Transit	Car	Transit	Car	Transit	Car	Transit
N	69	69	69	69	69	69	69	69	69	69	69	69
Min	0.541	0.448	0.467	0.316	0.541	0.448	0.467	0.376	0.541	0.448	0.467	0.376
Max	0.762	0.851	0.704	0.810	0.762	0.851	0.704	0.810	0.762	0.851	0.704	0.810
Mean	0.657	0.614	0.588	0.547	0.648	0.583	0.579	0.513	0.647	0.618	0.578	0.550
Std dev.	0.049	0.116	0.053	0.124	0.048	0.104	0.052	0.109	0.055	0.110	0.059	0.117
CV	7.320	18.780	8.880	18.750	7.400	17.900	8.900	21.300	8.400	17.800	10.100	21.200

hand the probabilities for private transport access are quite similar to the population-weighted distribution; on the other, the competitiveness of HST is not so good as before because in the best cases, for leisure trips and public transport access, the probability of using air transport is 0.55. This can be explained by the distribution of employment in the vicinities of Atocha and Barajas. Like the case of the terminal accessibility indicator, Table 7.6 also shows how the dispersion of the distribution of the probability of using air transport is greater when access to terminals is by public transport (see the coefficient of variation).

7.4.2   Spatial Analysis of Modal Competitiveness

In Figure 7.4, it can be seen that for mandatory and leisure trips, independently of the access mode to terminals, the competitiveness of air transport is very high in the surrounding area of Barajas airport. If we move towards the city center, located in Puerta del Sol (near Atocha station), the competitiveness of air transport decreases. Similarly, in the western and southern municipalities of the province of Madrid that are well connected to Atocha, air transport competitiveness is also reduced.

Table 7.7 shows that when access to terminals is by private transport the relative competitiveness of air transport is better when the analysis is focused on the outer rings, that is, private car access makes air transport more competitive than HST. This effect is quite similar to the urban sprawl effect caused by private cars. On the other hand, public transport access tends to decrease the competitive advantage of air transport, and in the case of leisure trips it can be seen that both modes are equally competitive for the first and fourth rings.

Figures 7.4 and 7.5 present a clear picture that synthesizes the spatial competitiveness of air transport in the province of Madrid. It is not surprising that some zones in the surrounding area of Barajas can achieve a probability of using air transport of 0.85. However, for some central and southern districts of the municipality of Madrid, this probability diminishes to less than 0.50. If we focus on public transport access, it can be seen that the second ring presents the higher competitiveness of air transport, and that this situation is worse for the first and the two outer rings. In this case, it is clear that the suburban rail with a direct connection to Atocha makes an important contribution to the differences observed between the zones with and without a suburban rail network. This can also be confirmed by the higher standard deviations for the two outer rings (Table 7.7).

Finally, Figure 7.5 shows how the competitiveness of air transport is lower for the leisure trips because in all zones the probability of using air transport is lower for this type of trip. It is also evident that the competi-

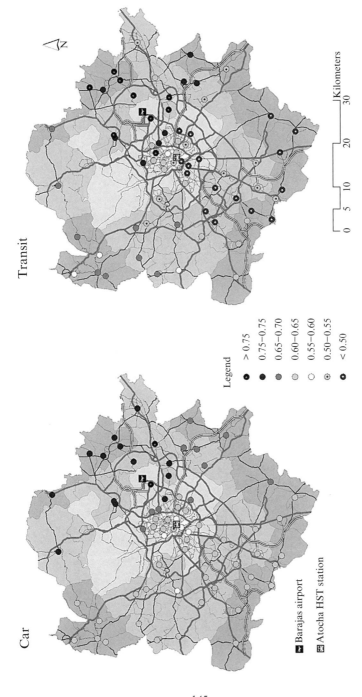

Car

Transit

N

Legend

● > 0.75
● 0.75–0.75
● 0.65–0.70
○ 0.60–0.65
○ 0.55–0.60
◉ 0.50–0.55
◉ < 0.50

Barajas airport

Atocha HST station

Kilometers

0   5   10   20   30

Figure 7.4   Spatial distribution of the probability of using air transport for mandatory trips

145

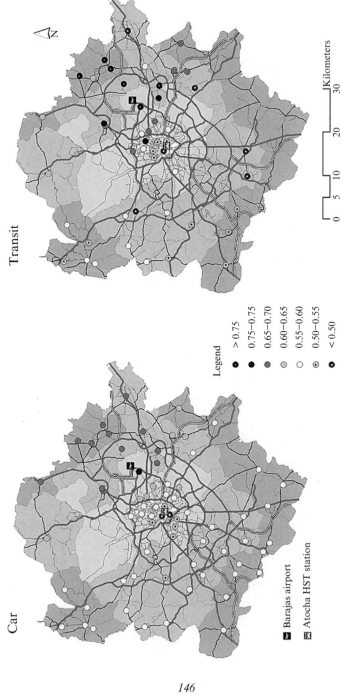

Figure 7.5   Spatial distribution of the probability of using air transport for leisure trips

146

Table 7.7   Mean and standard deviation for the probability of using air transport according to type of trip, terminal access and ring location

Rings	Mandatory trips				Leisure trips			
	Car		Transit		Car		Transit	
	Mean	Std dev.	Mean	Std dev.	Mean	Std dev.	Mean	Std dev.
Population weights								
First	0.600	0.041	0.576	0.063	0.528	0.043	0.503	0.064
Second	0.644	0.040	0.595	0.107	0.574	0.043	0.526	0.112
Third	0.667	0.047	0.577	0.112	0.599	0.052	0.508	0.118
Fourth	0.657	0.033	0.567	0.100	0.588	0.036	0.496	0.106
Total	0.648	0.048	0.583	0.104	0.579	0.052	0.513	0.109
Employment weights								
First	0.611	0.041	0.615	0.087	0.539	0.042	0.545	0.092
Second	0.662	0.053	0.647	0.113	0.593	0.057	0.581	0.120
Third	0.673	0.050	0.600	0.122	0.606	0.054	0.532	0.130
Fourth	0.659	0.036	0.578	0.113	0.590	0.039	0.508	0.122
Total	0.647	0.055	0.618	0.110	0.578	0.059	0.550	0.117

tiveness of air transport is more adversely affected in the zones of the first ring that are well connected to Atocha.

7.5   CONCLUSIONS

This chapter sheds some light on a neglected component that affects passengers' behavior in interurban corridors: access time to terminals, train stations, and airports. We have analyzed the relative spatial competitiveness of air versus HST transport in the province of Madrid for a particular corridor in Spain: Madrid–Barcelona.

We have shown that spatial competitiveness is strongly affected by the access times to terminals, and that this competitiveness depends on different characteristics, such as whether the trip is mandatory or not and the chosen access mode. Our spatial analysis has shown that private transport tends to favor the relative competitiveness of air transport in the corridor, and on the other hand public transport decreases the potential of air transport. It was also clear that some zones benefited greatly from the existence of the suburban rail network to increase the competitiveness of HST.

Therefore, the relative accessibility levels to terminals play an important role that should not be neglected in order to determine the overall mode competitiveness in interurban corridors. Thus, if private transport is disadvantaged in the vicinity of airports, this policy would increase the relative HST competitiveness.

Finally, our chapter shows that the combined use of two well-known methodologies, such as discrete choice demand analysis and GIS makes a significant contribution to analyzing the relative spatial competitiveness of transport modes in scenarios such as that examined here: interurban transport corridors.

NOTES

1. For further details of the DCE and revealed preference (RP) data, see Román and Martín (2011).
2. These six attributes were included in the experiment to characterize the relative competitiveness of both transport modes. It can be seen that the main level-of-service attributes such as price, in-vehicle travel time, access–egress time, and frequency are included. Two latent variables, reliability and comfort, are also included.
3. A main-effects fractional factorial design consisting of six attributes (four defined at three levels and two at two levels) and nine scenarios for each alternative was created using the WINMINT software, developed by Rand Europe (http://www.hpgholding. nl/; the former Hague Consulting Group: HCG).
4. The dataset is part of a research project financed by the Spanish Ministry of Transport with the main purpose of analyzing potential demand for new HST services in the Madrid–Barcelona corridor (see Román et al., 2010 for more details about the project).
5. Note that the new HST will reduce the in-vehicle travel time for the train by approximately 50 percent.
6. This variable is defined as the ratio between per capita family income and available time. It was used in the specification of the model, as we shall see below.
7. Accessibility to train stations has been analyzed in a number of studies that show how access time to terminals plays a significant role in determining the catchment area of terminals and how the relative competetiveness of each mode could also be strongly affected by the spatial location of the terminals. See, for example, Rietveld (2000), Wardman and Tyler (2000), Martens (2004), Givoni and Rietveld (2007), and Román and Martín (2011). Most of the studies analyze commuting and short-distance corridors.
8. In fact, it is the conditional indirect utility obtained when we analyze the consumer problem in a context of discrete choice (McFadden, 1981; Jara-Díaz, 1998).
9. This method is known in the literature as the Bradley and Daly nested logit trick.
10. It was not included in the final model.
11. The probability distribution of using air transport versus HST is calculated according to the air transport and HST nodes, that is, buses and private cars are not considered as alternatives.

REFERENCES

Adler, N., Pels, E. and Nash, C., 2010. 'High-speed rail and air transport competition: game engineering as tool for cost–benefit analysis', *Transportation Research B* **44**, 812–33.

Anderson, S.P., de Palma, A. and Thisse, J.-F., 1996. *Discrete Choice Theory of Product Differentiation*, Boston, MA: MIT Press.

Ben-Akiva, M.E. and Morikawa, T., 1990. 'Estimation of travel demand models from multiple data sources', Proceedings of the 11th International Symposium on Transportation and Traffic Theory, Yokohama July.

Bliemer, M.C.J. and Rose, J.M., 2011. 'Experimental design influences on stated choice outputs: an empirical study in air travel choice', *Transportation Research A* **45**, 63–79.

Bradley, M.A. and Daly, A.J., 1997. 'Estimation of logit choice models using mixed stated preference and revealed preference information', in: Stopher, P.R. and Lee-Gosselin, M. (eds), *Understanding Travel Behavior in an Era of Change*, Oxford: Pergamon, pp. 209–32.

Cherchi, E. and Ortúzar, J. de D., 2004. 'On fitting mode-specific constants in the presence of new options in RP/SP models', *Transportation Research A*, **40** 1–18.

Domencich, T.A. and McFadden, D., 1975. *Urban Travel Demand: A Behavioural Analysis*, Amsterdam: North-Holland.

Givoni, M. and Rietveld, P., 2007. 'The access journey to the railway station and its role in passengers' satisfaction with rail travel', *Transport Policy* **14**, 357–65.

Jara-Díaz, S.R., 1998. 'Time and income in travel choice: towards a microeconomic activity-based theoretical framework', in: Garling, T. Laitila, T. and Westin, K. (eds), *Theoretical Foundations of Travel Choice Modeling*, New York: Elsevier Science, pp. 51–74.

Jara-Díaz, S.R. and Farah, M., 1987. 'Transport demand and users' benefits with fixed income: the goods/leisure trade-off revisited', *Transportation Research B* **21**, 165–70.

Louviere, J.J., Hensher, D.A. and Swait, J.D., 2000. *Stated Choice Methods: Analysis and Application*, Cambridge: Cambridge University Press.

Martens, K., 2004. 'The bicycle as a feedering mode: experiences from three European countries', *Transportation Research D* **9**, 281–94.

McFadden, D., 1981. 'Econometric models of probabilistic choice', in: Manski, C. and McFadden, D. (eds), *Structural Analysis of Discrete Choice Data with Econometric Applications*, Cambridge, MA: MIT Press, pp. 198–272.

Ortúzar, J. de D. and Willumsen, L.G., 2001. *Modelling Transport* (3rd edn), Chichester: John Wiley & Sons.

Rietveld, P., 2000. 'The accessibility of railway stations: the role of the bicycle in the Netherlands', *Transportation Research D* **5**, 71–5.

Román, C., Espino, R. and Martín, J.C., 2010. 'Analyzing competition between the high speed train and alternative modes: the case of the Madrid–Zaragoza–Barcelona corridor', *Journal of Choice Modelling* **3**, 84–108.

Román, C. and Martín, J. C., 2011. 'The effect of access time on modal competition for interurban trips: the case of the Madrid–Barcelona corridor in Spain', *Networks and Spatial Economics* **11**, 661–75.

Wardman, M. and Tyler, J., 2000. 'Rail network accessibility and the demand for inter-urban rail travel', *Transport Reviews*, **20**, 3–24.

Williams, H.C.W.L., 1977. 'On the formation of travel demand models and economic valuation measures of user benefit', *Environment and Planning A* **9**, 285–344.

8. Modelling the extended gateway concept in port hinterland container logistics

Fedele Iannone

8.1 INTRODUCTION

Port hinterland container logistics is the process of planning, organizing and controlling the multimodal flows of maritime containers and their related information between gateway seaports and inland locations. It also includes the planning, design, implementation and organization of public and private infrastructure, as well as regulatory issues affecting the competitiveness and sustainability of distribution operations.

Optimization of port hinterland container logistics is crucial to meet rising international trade demand and the challenges related to sustainable development. Inefficient hinterland connections undermine the competitiveness both of seaports and of the wider regional logistics and productive systems the seaports belong to, while leading to increased internal and external costs of supply chains.

The steady growth in container traffic worldwide is putting great pressure on maritime terminals and port hinterland networks, particularly road networks surrounding the major port cities. A critical challenge many container ports are currently facing is the congestion due to insufficient storage space, long dwell times and poor inland transport. This generates a need for innovative landside intermodal distribution solutions essentially based on the combination of different transport modes and interchange nodes. The overall aim is to achieve benefits from quick container release operations in seaports, and from the efficient forwarding of loading units via high capacity connections towards optimal inland multimodal facilities. At these facilities, further distribution over short and long distances can then be arranged.

The multimodal interchange nodes in the hinterland network of seaports are described differently in different countries, such as for example 'inland ports' or 'inland terminals' in the United States and Canada, 'strategic rail freight interchanges' in the United Kingdom, 'dry ports' in Sweden and other European countries, and 'interports' in Italy as an abbreviation of 'interior ports' (see, for instance, UNCTAD, 1982, 1991; Leitner and Harrison, 2001; Iannone et al., 2007; Rodrigue and Notteboom, 2009; Roso and Lumsden, 2010; Cullinane and Wilmsmeier, 2011). In some cases, these facilities all have the same functions: modal interchange, temporary storage and distribution of intermodal loading units, customs clearance and inspection services, semi-manufacturing and other value-added supply-chain logistics services, and even wholesale and retail trade. Within the container logistics industry, dry ports have become an increasingly popular means for boosting seaport capacity, facilitating intermodal transport and expanding port hinterlands.

The customs dimension is particularly relevant to discriminate among dry port facilities by qualifying the so-called 'extended gateways'. The *extended gateway concept* has for years indicated a particular type of 'trade facilitation' providing the possibility of relying on a regime of customs continuity between seaports and dry ports. Under extended gateway systems, customs authorities qualify dry ports as an integral part (that is an extension) of specific seaports. The containers can be transported between the seaports and dry ports without the need for customs transit documentation. Transport organization can be done by shipping lines and/or maritime terminal companies, respectively, in the cases of *carrier haulage* and *terminal operator haulage*. This saves a great deal of time and money for the release operations in seaports and is the basis for sustainable transport. Merchants can delay the compliance of all customs formalities, while obtaining the release of their containerized cargoes nearer to their customer base and possibly at a more precisely defined time; maritime terminal companies face less pressure on their facilities thanks to shorter port dwell times; inland intermodal connections can be better planned and utilized; and governments can increase their revenue from taxes due to the positive link between trade facilitation and freight flows.

Dry ports represent a significant innovation changing the layout, flows and scope of inland logistics networks. Yet, research on the modelling of dry ports is only just beginning, and many issues still need to be more comprehensively considered. Indeed, new types of quantitative models need to be developed to address the extended gateway role of dry ports in both supply-chain management and port hinterland intermodal infrastructure and service networks. In addition, these models should be formulated based on the so-called 'triple bottom line' or 'sustainable' perspective, by simultaneously incorporating economic, environmental and social performance measures of port hinterland container logistics.

The extended gateway concept incorporates some of the natural consequences of the dry port concept, but it puts more emphasis on the coordination and control of the flows in the multimodal hinterland network
(Veenstra and Zuidwijk, 2010). Therefore, dry port development according to the extended gateway perspective faces a number of challenges:
new partnerships have to be established, new business models have to be
developed, and transparency of goods and information flows has to be
achieved.

Motivated by these reasons, in this chapter a capacitated network programming model – called the 'interport model' – is described as a tool for
the economic analysis and strategic planning of port hinterland container
logistics systems according to the extended gateway concept. The model
optimizes the costs of the inland multimodal distribution of full and empty
containers imported through a regional seaport cluster (inward interport
model). The loading units can also transit through one or more regional
dry port facilities acting as extended gateways (the so-called 'interports'),
as well as through extra-regional inland locations featuring a railway terminal, before reaching their final destinations.

The major novelty of this analytical tool consists of the detailed modelling of the container release operations at seaports and interports, including the possibility for shippers to postpone storage and customs operations
to the interports. More specifically, the interport model allows the measurement of the economic, environmental and social benefits arising from
the employment of extended gateways and intermodal transport in port
hinterland container distribution. It can simulate long-term alternative
scenarios in terms of supply of infrastructure and services, demand characteristics, and government and industrial policies. In this respect, the model
enables an examination of possible public and private policy initiatives in
the field of port hinterland intermodal logistics.

Two empirical applications of the model based on real data are also
presented in the chapter. In particular, for the purpose of this work,
the observed real situation concerning the inland container distribution
through the port–interport logistics system of the Campania region in
Italy has been compared with two different policy scenarios simulated
by the interport model. These represent 'ideal' scenarios assuming a fully
operational customs status of the regional interports as well as improved
rail connections from the regional seaports and interports. A first modelled scenario also internalizes in the objective function the external costs
of inland transport (in terms of climate change, air pollution, noise, accidents and congestion), while the second takes no account of transport
externalities. These modelling applications have been formulated and
solved by means of a high-level computer programming language.

8.1.1   Plan for this Research

The rest of the chapter is organized as follows. Section 8.2 provides a conceptual description of the primal and dual programs of the interport model. Section 8.3 presents the sea–land intermodal logistics system of the Campania region; in addition, it illustrates and discusses the general features and main results of the application of the interport model to the simulation of the two ideal policy scenarios concerning the inland distribution of import containers through the Campanian seaports and interports. Section 8.4 addresses conclusions, while also envisaging further research developments.

8.2   METHODOLOGY

The interport model is an inventory theoretic and capacitated linear programming model optimizing the road and rail distribution of full and empty containers over an inland network encompassing seaports, interports and other locations. As presented here, the model is a novel extension of the homonym transhipment model developed by Iannone and Thore (2010) for investigating the port hinterland distribution of import containers (inward interport model). The primal objective function now also internalizes the external costs in terms of greenhouse gas emissions, air pollution, noise, accidents and congestion deriving from inland transport operations.

This section proposes a stylized illustration of a typical port hinterland container distribution network as represented by the interport model. Such a small-scale theoretical example covers all the features of the large-scale networks that can be investigated by means of the model. Finally, a general description of the primal and dual programs of the interport model is provided.

A comprehensive mathematical formulation of the inward interport model incorporating transport external costs is available in Iannone (2011), and a detailed illustration of the relationships existing between primal and dual programs in the linear programming model can be found, for instance, in Thompson and Thore (1992), Jensen and Bard (2003) and Thore and Iannone (2005).

8.2.1   Stylized Port Hinterland Container Distribution Network and Problem Description

Figure 8.1 illustrates a hypothetical first-tier regional node infrastructure system for container traffic. This system comprises a single seaport

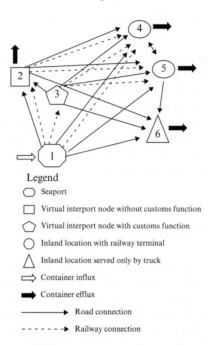

Figure 8.1   Stylized multimodal port hinterland logistics network with virtual interport nodes

represented by node 1, and a single interport featuring the two 'virtual nodes' 2 and 3 that are supposed to have an identical geographical location but involve in part different interport processing activities. Finally, there are three other regional and extra-regional inland locations, nodes 4, 5, 6, of which only 4 and 5 have a railway terminal.

Seaport node 1 is the origin node of this small network, while nodes 2, 4, 5 and 6 are the destination nodes. There is one influx into the network: the supply of imported containers at node 1. There are four effluxes: the demands at nodes 2, 4, 5 and 6 for containers discharged at the seaport. Nodes 2, 4 and 5 are also intermediate nodes enabling the multimodal transhipment of containers transported from the seaport to destination. Node 3 is a pure intermediate multimodal transhipment node because it does not feature a container demand; it is also supposed to perform a customs function and is connected to the seaport by rail only for container transfers under the responsibility of shipping lines (carrier haulage) and with no accompanying inland customs transit document.[1] In general, node 3 is employed only for the handling of full containers. Both virtual nodes 2 and 3 have the same outbound multimodal connections.

With regard to the rail links represented in Figure 8.1, seaport node 1 is connected to node 4 and to nodes 2 and 3. Node 3 is reachable from the seaport node by rail carrier haulage only and exclusively for the forwarding of customs bonded full containers. Nodes 2 and 3 are also linked to nodes 4 and 5.

Each rail service available in real life at the interport is represented by the corresponding specific rail connections simultaneously available at each virtual interport node. In particular, the rail service from the seaport to the interport is supposed to carry containers simultaneously from node 1 to node 2 and from node 1 to node 3. In the same way, the rail service from the interport to node 4 carries containers simultaneously from node 2 to node 4 and from node 3 to node 4. And so on.

With regard to the road links, node 1 is connected to all the other nodes of the network, excluding virtual node 3. Both virtual nodes 2 and 3 are linked by road to all the other inland locations of the network; furthermore, road transport at a zero generalized cost is admitted from virtual node 3 to virtual node 2 to meet the container demand of importing operators located in the interport. Finally, other inland nodes that have a rail terminal are connected by truck to some inland locations that are directly linked to the regional seaport–interport system. In particular, node 4 can also be employed as an intermediate node to serve node 5, while node 5 can also be employed as an intermediate node to serve nodes 4 and 6.

In practice, at the inland nodes served by rail it is assumed that multimodal transhipment operations for various origin destination (O/D) combinations can take place, that is for traffic relations from the supplying seaport to the inland final demanding nodes. More specifically, at the extra-regional nodes served by rail it is assumed that only rail-to-truck and truck-to-truck transhipment operations will take place, while at the interport it is also assumed that there will be rail-to-rail and truck-to-rail transhipment operations.

The stylized network in Figure 8.1 is assumed to be typified by relatively small inland locations featuring a railway terminal (including the interport location). Like the other nodes of the network, the inland locations served by rail are also assumed to be centroid areas in which container traffic terminates. Given this configuration of the network, intra-zonal post-haulage activities at these locations are assumed to serve negligible (very short) distances. Consequently, such activities have been omitted from the modelling entirely.

To sum up, once an imported full container has been cleared by customs at node 1, it can be sent directly to one of the demand locations 2, 4, 5 and 6. Alternatively, it can be sent to its destination by transiting through one or more intermediate transhipment nodes (excluding the virtual interport node 3 which has a customs function). A similar forwarding scheme applies to empty containers.

But there is also another possibility for the distribution of full containers. Rather than being cleared by customs at node 1, a full container may be shipped by bonded and sealed rail transportation from node 1 to node 3, which virtually represents the customs-clearing facility located at the interport in the hinterland. Once cleared here, the container may be transferred to its final location. Of course, empty containers do not require customs clearance before being released from intermodal nodes.

The splitting of a single interport facility into two separate virtual nodes enables the formulation of a standard linear programming model for the entire network, thus avoiding explicit 0–1 programming features to handle the decisions concerning where to carry out the customs clearance and storage operations for full containers.

8.2.2   The Primal Interport Model

As proposed here, the primal program of the interport model minimizes the total social generalized logistic cost for port hinterland distribution of imported full and empty containers (inward interport model). It solves the problem of the optimal inland routing of standardized loading units discharged at one or more seaports. This task includes clarifying the quantity of containers to be shipped from seaports, the transportation modal choice along each inland link, and the detailed pathway through the system chosen, including the possibility of multimodal transhipment operations at one or more regional interports and at other intermediate inland nodes featuring a railway terminal. The model also determines whether shippers will choose to have their containerized consignments controlled and cleared by customs directly at the seaports, or whether they will prefer to comply with customs formalities at the interports.

The problem is subjected to flow-balance constraints at all nodes, nonnegativity constraints on endogenous variables, and capacity constraints on all rail connections. Flow conservation at origin nodes requires that the supply at each node must suffice to cover the flows leaving the same node. For intermediate nodes the balancing conditions state that the flow entering each node must suffice to cover the flows leaving it. Finally, for each destination node, the deliveries forthcoming at the node must suffice to cover demand.

The critical direct and indirect internal cost items explicitly taken into account by the model are: (i) container handling costs, (ii) container storage costs at seaports and interports, (iii) costs for physical inspection and X-ray scanner control by customs at seaports and interports,

(iv) in-transit inventory holding costs, (v) container leasing costs, and (vi) container transport costs. The external transport costs included in the model are: (i) climate change, (ii) air pollution, (iii) noise, (iv) accidents, and (v) congestion. The model also features a road supply submodel for the quantification of road transport times on a national scale according to the road regulations.[2] The total travel times by rail over admitted connections are exogenous.

By means of parameters representing dwell times, free of charge storage times, handling charges, demurrage charges, probabilities and costs of customs controls, the interport model simulates in detail the container release operations and their associated pricing mechanisms at seaport and interport terminals, including the possibility of relocating storage and customs operations from the seaports to the interports (that is, the extended gateway concept). In this respect, the model allows for spelling out various arrangements of customs checks on full containers (automated computerized controls, documentary control, X-ray scanning controls and physical inspections).

The primal equilibrium solution of the model can be broken down into merchant flows and carrier flows, representing the optimum of a hypothetical shipper operating the entire network. Generally, the overall solution for this economic agent can be shown to coincide with the decentralized solutions of individual programs for each participating logistic agent who ships containers through the network.

All the model's elements are for one planning period (which in the empirical applications has corresponded to an operational year), and are assumed not to vary during the planning horizon.

8.2.3 The Dual Interport Model

When a direct programming problem is one of cost minimization, the dual program is one of maximizing value. The dual program of the interport model maximizes the total net appreciation of container flows' shadow value cumulating in the network, while also including the shadow value of rail services' capacity constraints. The problem is subject to the conditions that the value appreciation created along each and every link be 'exhausted' by its costs; in addition, there are both non-negativity and non-positivity constraints on endogenous variables.

In the primal interport problem there is a given supply of full and empty containers at each seaport, and a given demand at each inland location (excluding the virtual interport nodes that have a customs function); furthermore, there are intermediate transhipment nodes (also including all virtual interport nodes) and capacity limits of rail services. Accordingly, in the dual interport problem, there are shadow prices for each type of traffic flow (that is, flows of full and empty containers) implied at the nodes of the network. These dual variables measure the value or worth of relaxing the corresponding flow conservation constraints by one unit. The dual problem also features shadow prices associated with primal constraints of rail connections. These parameters can be interpreted as imputed costs assessed on container shipments along the concerned rail connections.

The shadow prices of the traffic flows implied at the nodes of the network have to be non-negative. What this means is that the shipped container at some nodes may be 'scarce', that is, commands a positive shadow price. Or the container may be a 'free good', in which case the shadow price is zero. This happens if there is a build-up of unwanted container inventory at the node, so that an excess availability is created. The shadow prices of rail capacity constraints have to be non-positive.

Furthermore, there are dual constraints. There is one dual constraint for each and every modal link in the network. This expresses an important principle that is referred to as 'exhaustion of value'. Along any positive road flow in the network, the increase in shadow value (that is the difference between the shadow price at destination and the shadow cost at origin) must be exhausted by the total social unit logistic cost of the shipment. In contrast, along any positive rail flow in the network, the imputed appreciation along the rail link plus the shadow price of the capacity limit must be exhausted by the total social unit logistic cost of the shipment. That is, all cumulating values must have a source that can be accounted for. No free value can arise. In general, optimality requires non-negative shipments' reduced costs equalling the slack values in exhaustion of value constraints.

Finally, the optimal value of the dual objective function is unique and equals the optimal value of the primal function. Here one encounters the exhaustion of value principle again. The total increase in shadow value over the network equals the total social logistic cost of port hinterland container distribution. This is the 'fundamental theorem of duality' in linear programming: the optimal value of the direct problem equals the optimal value of the dual problem.

8.3   EMPIRICAL ANALYSIS

This section presents the current features and policy orientations concerning the port–interport logistics system of the Campania region. Furthermore, it illustrates the general features and main results of the application of the interport model to the simulation of two ideal policy scenarios optimizing the inland distribution of import containers through the Campanian sea–land intermodal load centres, while also including a topological and functional description of the large-scale real port hinterland network under consideration. The output data in terms of modal split and total costs resulting from primal optimizations are also compared with the observed real-life situation. Finally, optimal dual results from the modelled scenario incorporating transport external diseconomies in objective function are shown in detail.

8.3.1 The Sea-Land Intermodal Logistics System in the Campania Region: Current Features and Policy Orientations

Campania is a region located in southern Italy. The network system of first-tier sea–land intermodal load centres in Campania encompasses the Mediterranean seaports of Naples and Salerno, and the interports of Nola and Marcianise (Figure 8.2). Both interports are located approximately 30 km from the port of Naples; furthermore, Nola is situated 57 km from the port of Salerno, while Marcianise 80 km. The distance between the two interports is just 32 km.

The main characteristics and difficulties of the Campanian regional logistics system for intermodal traffic and particularly for inland distribution of maritime containers can be summarized as follows: (i) port

Figure 8.2   The Campania region and its first-tier sea–land intermodal logistic system

hinterland still limited exclusively to the national scale; (ii) low rates of utilization of the existing rail transport capacity from seaports and interports; (iii) suspension of rail connections at the Salerno port due to safety reasons (since 2005); (iv) congestion on the road system throughout the region; (v) port capacity saturation; (vi) severe congestion and high container dwell times at the port of Naples also deriving from slow customs procedures; and (vii) legal and technical barriers to fair and non-discriminatory competition in rail traction services between seaports and interports.

In 2010 the intermodal terminal company of the Marcianise interport was authorized to operate a customs bonded area for international container operations. In 2011 an X-ray scanner was installed within this interport. Nevertheless, neither Nola nor Marcianise is currently employed as an extended gateway supporting the inland traffic of containers transiting through the seaports of Naples and Salerno.

On the other hand, by virtue of an ancient customs regime still in force in Italy, the port–interport rail connections in Campania can be employed for merchant traffic only if operated by private rail traction providers. Port–interport container forwarding solutions arranged by shipping lines according to the extended gateway concept (that is, without the need for customs transit documentation) are possible only where rail services provided by the Italian state-owned rail carrier are available. In particular, 'Trenitalia' is the incumbent rail traction provider belonging to the state-owned rail holding FS Group ('Gruppo Ferrovie dello Stato') and the sole company authorized to operate rail services under facilitated conditions for customs bonded containers travelling under steamship bills of lading from and to the Italian seaports.

At the end of 2007, for the first time, a number of containers were carried under an extended gateway regime between the port of Naples and the interport of Nola by Trenitalia under the responsibility of a major shipping line. The port dwell time for these containers was only 1.7 days. Unfortunately, for some years Trenitalia has ceased to operate container rail services between the Campanian seaports and interports due to severe financial problems that are necessitating a reorganization of the cargo division of the company.

A prospective solution identified by the Campanian policy makers to improve the competitiveness of inland container logistics operations in the region provides for a grant scheme for funding the shuttle trains operated by a private company between Naples and Nola. The hypothesized incentives would take account of the reduction of negative externalities arising from transferring the movement of containers from road to rail between the seaport and the interport.

8.3.2   General Features of Empirical Applications of the Interport Model to the Campania Region

For the purpose of this work, two empirical applications of the *interport model* to the inland distribution operations which can be carried out over a 12-month period for containers imported into Italy through the Campania region have been devised based on real industry data.[3] In particular, two ideal scenarios different from the real-life situation have been simulated to investigate the optimization potential arising from specific policies addressing the improvement of competitiveness and sustainability of inland container distribution operations through the region.

In both modelled scenarios we have assumed a fully operational customs status of both the Campanian interports of Nola and Marcianise. This has permitted a simulation whereby shipping lines can arrange the customs bonded rail transfer of full containers between the regional seaports and interports according to the extended gateway concept. Also, we have assumed the availability of all container rail services operated from the Campanian regional logistics system during 2005–07 (hence, also including the services operated from the port of Salerno). The annual capacity assumed for each of these services corresponds to the maximum capacity surveyed from 2005 to 2007.

A first modelled ideal scenario does not take into account transport external costs and minimizes a total internal generalized logistic cost of port hinterland distribution of imported full and empty containers. The other application features the internalization of transport externalities in the objective function; accordingly, in this case the model minimizes a total social generalized logistic cost of port hinterland container distribution.

The results in terms of logistic flows and total internal, external and social costs deriving from these two ideal policy scenarios simulated by means of the interport model have been compared with the observed real-life scenario in 2007.[4] Finally, optimal dual results from the policy scenario incorporating transport externalities in its primal objective function have been analysed.

As in Iannone and Thore (2010), the real port hinterland container network under consideration features 24 nodes and 163 road and rail links (Figure 8.3). It consists of the following seaports, interports and other inland locations in Italy:[5]

1.   Seaports: Naples (NAP) and Salerno (SAL).
2.   Interports: Nola (NOL/NCC) and Marcianise (MAR/MCC).[6]
3.   Inland locations accessible both by road and by rail: Bari city/rail

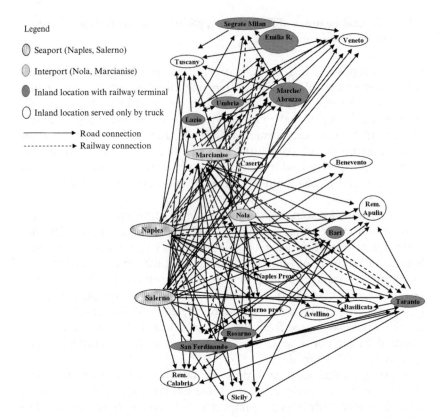

Figure 8.3   The real port hinterland container network under consideration

terminal (BAR); Taranto city/rail terminal (TAR), San Ferdinando city/rail terminal (SAN), Rosarno city/rail terminal (ROS), Lazio region/Civitavecchia rail terminal (LAZ), Abruzzo and Marche region/Ancona rail terminal (ABR), Umbria region/Foligno rail terminal (UMB), Emilia Romagna region/Rubiera rail terminal (EMI), Lombardia region/Segrate Milan rail terminal (MIL).

4. Inland locations accessible by road only: Naples province (NAP2), Salerno province (SAL2), Caserta province (CAS), Avellino province (AVE), Benevento province (BEN), remaining part of Puglia region (PUG), Basilicata region (BAS), remaining part of Calabria region (CAL), Sicily region (SIC), Tuscany region (TOS), Veneto region (VEN).

The two regional interports and the other 20 regional and extra-regional inland nodes indicated represent the existing network of locations actually involved in the inland traffic of maritime containers handled at the Campanian seaports.

The seaports at Naples and Salerno are connected by truck to all the inland locations of the network. Naples is connected by rail to the regional interports at Nola and Marcianise and to some (but not all) final destinations with a rail terminal; Salerno is connected by rail to the Nola interport and to the Bari city/terminal. There is no rail connection between Salerno and Marcianise. Thus, the customs clearance of containers discharged at the port of Naples may take place either in the seaport itself or at the interports of Nola and Marcianise. The customs clearance of containers discharged at the port of Salerno may take place either in the seaport itself or at the interport of Nola.

The interports are connected by road to all the other inland locations of the network, and by rail to some final destinations that possess a rail terminal. The network under consideration also includes the following rail connections available in the years preceding 2007: Naples–Foligno, Naples–Ancona, Nola–Foligno, Nola–Rubiera, Marcianise–Taranto and Marcianise–Civitavecchia.

The extra-regional destinations reachable by rail from the nodes of the Campanian regional logistic system can also serve by road some other destinations which could be alternatively served directly from Campania. In practice, all inland nodes of the network served by rail are assumed to also perform a multimodal transhipment function for various O/D combinations.

Ultimately, each empirical model features 26 nodes and 219 admitted road and rail links (including two virtual nodes at each regional interport and their related connections), 866 unknowns and 124 constraints. The models have been programmed and solved with the GAMS (General Algebraic Modelling System) computer language, using the solver CPLEX (Brooke et al., 1998).

The external cost parameters employed in the analysis of real-life and modelled scenarios (Table 8.1) have been calculated using specific figures released by the 'Amici della Terra' association in collaboration with 'Ferrovie dello Stato', the Italian state-owned railway holding (AdT and FS, 2005).[7] An average weight of containerized goods equalling 14 tonnes/TEU and a container tare of 2.3 tonnes/TEU have been assumed for these computations. Clearly, the longer the transport distance, the greater will be the total external cost saving due to the modal shift from road to rail for any given transport volume.

Table 8.1   Marginal external costs of container transport in Italy (€/TEU-km)

	Road transport		Rail transport	
	Full containers	Empty containers	Full containers	Empty containers
Greenhouse gases	0.037	0.005	0.012	0.0017
Air pollution	0.142	0.020	0.020	0.0029
Noise	0.108	0.015	0.067	0.0095
Accidents	0.021	0.003	0.002	0.0002
Congestion	0.264	0.037	0.000	0.0000
Total	0.572	0.081	0.101	0.0140

8.3.3   Main Results from Empirical Models and Their Interpretation

Results from primal optimizations and comparison with real-life situation
Table 8.2 gives evidence of annual container shipments and capacity utilization on all rail services originating at the Campanian seaports and interports in real-life situations and modelled ideal scenarios. The observed real figures on traffic to the interports of Nola and Marcianise also include possible transit of containers shipped from the Campanian seaports to extra-regional inland locations, whereas the observed real traffic from the interports also includes containers not discharged from the Campanian seaports but originating elsewhere. The observed real figures on traffic to extra-regional locations also include possible transits. The modelling solutions' figures exclusively refer to the shipments of containers discharged from the regional seaports, including transits.

Table 8.3 compares the railway transport's shares on the annual inland traffic of containers imported through the seaports of Naples and Salerno in the different scenarios. Table 8.4 compares the annual rail traffic volumes from/to the interports of Nola and Marcianise for import containers handled at the regional seaport cluster. Table 8.4 also shows the rail transport's shares on the total annual inland traffic of containers imported through the Campanian seaports and leaving the interports in the different cases of analysis. Table 8.5 lists the total internal, external and social logistic costs in the different scenarios.

Note that the modelled ideal scenarios, compared with the existing situation, feature greater overall rail transport volumes and rail capacity utilization (Table 8.2). This is a remarkable result that mainly derives from the total internal generalized logistic cost reductions permitted by the employment of both the interports of Nola and Marcianise as

Table 8.2 Observed real data and modelled ideal scenario data on traffic of full and empty containers, capacity constraints and capacity utilization on rail connections from/to the Campanian seaports and interports

One-way railway service	Maximum weekly trains, 2005–07	Annual maximum capacity, 2005–07 (TEU)	Shipments in the last observed year, 2005–07 (TEU)	Capacity utilization in the last observed year, 2005–07 (%)	Annual shipments resulting from the modelled ideal scenario without externalities (TEU)	Annual capacity utilization resulting from the modelled ideal scenario without externalities (%)	Annual shipments resulting from the modelled ideal scenario with externalities (TEU)	Annual capacity utilization resulting from the modelled ideal scenario with externalities (%)
Naples–Nola	5	15,000	6,707	44.7	15,000	100.0	15,000	100.0
Naples–Marcianise	1	3,000	481	16.0	3,000	100.0	3,000	100.0
Naples–Bari	5	12,500	6,054	48.4	9,408	75.3	9,408	75.3
Naples–Rosarno	3	7,500	2,408	32.1	7,500	100.0	7,500	100.0
Naples–S. Ferdinando	1	2,500	2,410	96.4	2,500	100.0	2,500	100.0
Naples–Ancona	1	2,500	44	1.8	1,114	44.6	1,114	44.6
Naples–Foligno	1	2,500	30	1.2	1,272	50.9	1,272	50.9
Naples–Rubiera	1	2,500	129	5.2	155	6.2	155	6.2
Nola–Taranto	3	7,500	1,618	21.6	0	0.0	334	4.5
Nola–Rosarno	2	5,000	1,078	21.6	0	0.0	59	1.2
Nola–S. Ferdinando	5	12,000	475	4.0	0	0.0	618	5.2
Nola–Foligno	1	2,500	51	2.0	0	0.0	14	0.6
Nola–Rubiera	1	2,500	66	2.6	0	0.0	0	0.0
Nola–Segrate Milan	5	3,000	750	25.0	114	3.8	122	4.1
Marcianise–Taranto	1	2,500	24	1.0	0	0.0	2,500	100.0
Marcianise–Rosarno	1	2,500	0	0.0	0	0.0	0	0.0
Marcianise–Civitavecchia	1	2,500	0	0.0	0	0.0	0	0.0
Salerno–Nola	1	2,500	395	15.8	2,500	100.0	2,500	100.0
Salerno–Bari	1	2,500	2,081	83.2	2,500	100.0	2,500	100.0
Total	40	93,000	24,801	26.7	45,063	48.5	48,596	52.3

*Table 8.3   Market share of rail transport in inland container traffic from
             the Campanian seaports (real situation and modelled ideal
             scenarios) (%)*

Market share of railway transport	From Naples	From Salerno	From Naples and Salerno
Total inland traffic			
Observed real situation	8.83	0.00	4.85
Modelled ideal scenario without transport externalities	19.40	2.96	11.99
Modelled ideal scenario with transport externalities	19.40	2.96	11.99
Inland traffic to the Campanian interports			
Observed real situation	9.1%	0.0%	8.8%
Modelled ideal scenario without transport externalities	23.81%	79.37%	26.04%
Modelled ideal scenario with transport externalities	22.78%	76.88%	24.92%
Inland traffic to other inland locations			
Observed real situation	8.67%	0.00%	3.76%
Modelled ideal scenario without transport externalities	16.85%	1.51%	8.25%
Modelled ideal scenario with transport externalities	17.30%	1.51%	8.35%

extended gateways of the regional seaport system. Of course, the ideal
scenario internalizing the externalities in objective function presents
the greatest level of total rail flows from the Campanian logistic nodes
(48,596 TEU) and hence the greatest level of overall rail demand/supply
balance (52.3 per cent). More specifically, both modelled ideal scenarios feature the same volume of containers shipped by rail from the
Campanian seaports (44,949 TEU), which is approximately equivalent to
a 117 per cent increase compared with the real-life situation. In addition,
the internalizing scenario presents greater rail flows from the Campanian
interports (3,647 TEU) than those resulting from the solution of the non-
internalizing scenario (114 TEU).

On the whole, as reported in Table 8.2, the rail container flows from
the Campanian interports generated by the optimization models are
lower than those of the real-life scenario (4,062 TEU). This is because
the observed figures on traffic from the interports in Table 8.2 also incorporate traffic of containers not originating at the seaports of Naples and
Salerno and that are not included in this study. Indeed, the containers

Table 8.4   Market share of rail transport in inland traffic from the Campanian interports for containers discharged at the Campanian seaports (real situation and modelled ideal scenarios)

	Observed real situation	Modelled ideal scenario without transport externalities	Modelled ideal scenario with transport externalities
Containers discharged at Naples			
Rail traffic leaving Nola and Marcianise (full and empty TEU)	134	0	3,431
Rail transport's share of total inland traffic leaving Nola and Marcianise (%)	3.6	0.0	19.1
Containers discharged at Salerno			
Rail traffic leaving Nola and Marcianise (full and empty TEU)	0	114	216
Rail transport's share of total inland traffic leaving Nola and Marcianise (%)	0.0	100.0	100.0
Containers discharged at Naples and Salerno			
Rail traffic leaving Nola and Marcianise (full and empty TEU)	134	114	3,647
Rail transport's share of total inland traffic leaving Nola and Marcianise (%)	3.6	0.6	20.0

discharged at the Campanian seaports and shipped from the interports by rail in 2007 amounted to just 134 TEU (Table 8.4).

In light of the above results, the market shares of rail transport on the annual inland traffic of containers discharged in the seaports of Naples and Salerno are bigger in the simulated ideal scenarios than in the real situation (Table 8.3). In particular, with regard to the inland container traffic from the seaports to the interports, the ideal scenario internalizing the externalities in objective function presents a lower market share of rail transport than that obtained from the solution of the non-internalizing ideal scenario. This result may in the first instance seem odd but can be explained by considering both the capacity

Table 8.5 Total internal, external and social logistic costs for inland distribution of import containers handled at the Campanian seaports (real situation and modelled ideal scenarios)

	Observed real situation	Modelled ideal scenario without transport externalities	Modelled ideal scenario with transport externalities
Total internal generalized logistic cost for inland distribution of full and empty containers discharged in Naples (€m)	180.67	170.89	170.93
Total internal generalized logistic cost for inland distribution of full and empty containers discharged in Salerno (€m)	50.54	50.36	50.37
Total internal generalized logistic cost for inland distribution of full and empty containers discharged in Naples and Salerno (€m)	231.21	221.25	221.31
Total external cost for road and railway transport of full and empty containers discharged in Naples and Salerno (€m)	11.84	9.70	9.32
Total social generalized logistic cost for inland distribution of full containers discharged in Naples and Salerno (€m)	243.05	230.95	230.63

saturation on seaport–interport rail connections under both simulated scenarios (Table 8.2) and the fact that, under the internalizing scenario, most of the containers carried by road from the seaports to the interports are only in transit through the interports. Indeed, the internalization of transport external costs favours a greater use of the railway by interports for transferring the containers discharged at the Campanian seaports to other extra-regional locations (Tables 8.2 and 8.4). Hence, rail transport's share of total inland traffic from the regional interports to the extra-regional nodes in the internalizing scenario is greater than that resulting from the optimal solution of the non-internalizing scenario (Table 8.4).

In general, the possibility of arranging the transfer of containers by railway carrier haulage under customs bond between seaports and interports dramatically reduces the generalized cost of release operations at the seaports, favouring a full utilization of the rail capacity connecting seaports and extended gateways in both optimized scenarios. In addition, as already argued by Iannone and Thore (2010), an extended gateway logistics system based on a regime of customs continuity between seaports and interports, and backed up by an efficient railway system, could prove to be an effective trade facilitation to expand the hinterland of the Campanian seaports.

Nevertheless, shippers have failed to seize even the customs clearance opportunities that have been available at Nola in the past. In 2007, their behaviour was far from being optimal, and the strategic rail connection from Naples to Nola was used at less than half of its full capacity (Table 8.2). Such a finding confirms that, in the field of intermodal logistics, a number of specific factors, including opportunistic behaviour, inertia and bounded rationality, can often result in choices actually diverging from a hypothetical optimum.

As for total costs (Table 8.5), the ideal scenarios present lower levels of internal and external logistic costs compared with the real situation. The total internal cost saving resulting from the simulated scenarios ranges between 4.28 per cent and 4.31 per cent, whereas the total external cost saving ranges between 18.1 per cent and 21.3 per cent. The negative impact of transport operations – in terms of greenhouse gases, air pollution, noise, accidents and congestion – have therefore also been monetized with regard to both the existing situation and the modelled ideal scenario which does not incorporate the externalities in its objective function.

When comparing only the two ideal scenarios, the trade-off between total internal costs and total external costs is obvious. The internalization of transport external costs in the objective function stimulates rail-based container distribution solutions, thus determining slightly higher internal generalized logistic costs and lower external costs compared with the scenario without externalities. The total internal cost for road and rail distribution of full and empty containers discharged in the Campanian seaports would amount to €221.25 million and €221.31 million in the non-internalizing and the internalizing scenarios, respectively. The total transport external cost in the two different case studies would amount to €9.70 million and €9.32 million. To sum up, the scenario incorporating externalities in the objective function would feature the lowest total social generalized inland logistics cost. Compared with the real-life situation, the overall cost reduction is more than 5 per cent, amounting to €12.42 million.

Table 8.6　Shadow price (€/TEU) of full and empty container flows implied at the nodes of the network (modelled ideal scenario with transport externalities)

Node	Full containers		Empty containers	
	Containers discharged at NAP	Containers discharged at SAL	Containers discharged at NAP	Containers discharged at SAL
NAP	0.00	37.60	0.00	15.80
SAL	631.00	0.00	426.70	0.00
NOL	915.60	448.30	702.80	398.70
NCC	748.80	386.20	775.90	529.30
MAR	915.60	486.30	702.80	400.60
MCC	748.80	395.20	775.00	364.70
NAP2	782.40	358.90	597.10	299.50
SAL2	886.20	255.20	661.60	235.00
CAS	795.50	365.40	605.30	303.50
AVE	836.70	279.10	630.90	249.90
BEN	918.30	356.80	681.60	298.10
PUG	1,089.50	528.70	787.30	404.50
TAR	1,257.30	740.00	955.40	534.00
BAR	1,112.90	611.20	840.90	514.00
BAS	1,049.70	418.80	762.80	336.60
CAL	1,383.90	1,006.50	1,114.60	703.60
ROS	1,362.00	984.60	1,100.90	690.60
SAN	1,376.30	985.60	1,109.80	696.50
SIC	0.00	1,572.10	0.00	1,031.20
LAZ	1,203.50	768.10	857.30	551.40
ABR	1,175.70	896.00	879.10	627.90
UMB	1,160.40	963.30	873.90	706.00
TOS	0.00	1,245.90	0.00	839.20
EMI	1,365.40	1,270.40	1,015.40	1,031.30
MIL	1,508.90	1,126.90	1,104.80	941.90
VEN	0.00	1,484.90	0.00	1,088.70

Dual results in the internalizing scenario

The computer solutions of the modelling applications have also provided marginal values corresponding to the shadow prices for primal constraints and to the reduced costs for primal variables. Table 8.6 lists the optimal dual variables corresponding to each flow-balance condition of the primal problem incorporating externalities in objective function. There are shadow prices associated with flow conservations for full and empty containers discharged at the ports of Naples and Salerno. Every dual variable represents the change in the optimal primal objective function's value per unit increase of the right-hand-side coefficient of its corresponding primal constraint. For instance, the dual price of €915.60 corresponding to the balancing condition at the NOL node in the second column of the table means that by raising by 1 TEU the demand at the Nola interport for full containers discharged at Naples (NAP), the optimal total social logistic cost of port hinterland distribution would increase by €915.60. This monetary amount is given as the sum of the total generalized unit cost of release operations for full containers cleared by customs at the port of Naples and leaving by truck (€716.90) and the total social unit cost of road transport from the port of Naples to the interport of Nola (€198.70). In general, the marginal value of unit increase in demand at final destinations in the *interport model* equals the total social unit logistic cost of distribution to that location.

For the purpose of illustration of the exhaustion of value along the links of the network, Tables 8.7 and 8.8 list: (i) the increases of shadow price occurring along all permitted rail links for the traffic of full containers discharged at the Campanian seaports, (ii) the shadow prices of rail capacity constraints, (iii) the total social generalized unit logistic costs of distribution operations, and (iv) the unit reduced costs of all rail shipments. The optimal rail traffic patterns feature a reduced cost equal to zero. In particular, along each used link, a hypothetical logistic agent forwarding containers breaks exactly even: the dual price appreciation along the link plus the dual price of the capacity limit is exactly exhausted by the total social unit logistic cost of the shipment. Slack values in non-binding exhaustion of value constraints represent the reduced costs. Optimal shipments are therefore associated with zero reduced costs, whereas positive reduced costs represent the unit costs of including a non-basic variable in the optimal solution. For instance, as indicated in Table 8.7, it is not optimal to send by train from Marcianise (MAR) to Taranto (TAR) any full loading unit discharged at the port of Naples (NAP) and already cleared by customs. If one insists on sending a unit between those two inland nodes the optimal value of the objective function would increase by €131.90. This amount corresponds to the difference between the imputed cost (€473.70) and the increase in the shadow price (€341.80). In particular, the imputed cost is calculated as the sum of the total social logistic unit cost (€469.80) and the absolute value of the capacity limit's dual price (€3.90); the increase in shadow price is calculated as the difference between the dual price at destination (€1,257.30) and the dual price at origin (€915.60).

The dual prices of rail capacity constraints in Tables 8.7 and 8.8 indicate the imputed value of the objective function that would arise from an improvement in rail infrastructure and/or services. They confirm

Table 8.7 *Exhaustion of value along rail links and the rail shipments'*
reduced costs for full containers imported through the port of
Naples (modelled ideal scenario with transport externalities)
(€/TEU)

Rail link	Traffic of full containers discharged at NAP			
	Difference between the shadow price at destination and the shadow cost at origin	Shadow price of capacity constraint	Total social generalized logistic cost of port hinterland distribution operations	Reduced cost
NAP-NOL	915.60	−388.70	895.20	368.40
NAP-NCC	748.80	−388.70	360.10	0.00
NAP-MAR	915.60	−391.20	892.80	368.40
NAP-MCC	748.80	−391.20	357.60	0.00
NAP-BAR	1,112.90	0.00	1,112.90	0.00
NAP-ROS	1,362.00	−334.70	1,027.30	0.00
NAP-SAN	1,376.30	−357.30	1,019.00	0.00
NAP-ABR	1,175.70	0.00	1,175.70	0.00
NAP-UMB	1,160.40	0.00	1,160.40	0.00
NAP-EMI	1,365.40	0.00	1,365.40	0.00
NOL-TAR	341.80	0.00	473.70	131.90
NOL-ROS	446.50	0.00	591.70	145.20
NOL-SAN	460.70	0.00	592.70	131.90
NOL-UMB	244.80	0.00	570.40	325.50
NOL-EMI	449.80	0.00	901.10	451.20
NOL-MIL	593.40	0.00	734.00	140.70
NCC-TAR	508.50	0.00	508.50	0.00
NCC-ROS	613.20	0.00	626.50	13.30
NCC-SAN	627.50	0.00	627.50	0.00
NCC-UMB	411.60	0.00	605.20	193.60
NCC-EMI	616.60	0.00	935.90	319.30
NCC-MIL	760.10	0.00	768.90	8.70
MAR-TAR	341.80	−3.90	469.80	131.90
MAR-ROS	446.50	0.00	582.70	136.20
MAR-LAZ	287.90	0.00	474.50	186.60
MCC-TAR	508.50	−3.90	504.70	0.00
MCC-ROS	613.20	0.00	617.50	4.30
MCC-LAZ	454.70	0.00	509.30	54.60

the importance of the Campanian interport logistics system to support
the inland traffic of containers handled at the regional seaports. With
reference to imports, an increase in the capacity over the rail connections of Naples–Nola (NAP–NOL, NAP–NCC), Naples–Marcianise

*Table 8.8   Exhaustion of value along rail links and the rail shipments'
reduced costs for full containers imported through the port of
Salerno (modelled ideal scenario with transport externalities)
(€/TEU)*

Rail link	Traffic of full containers discharged at SAL			
	Difference between the shadow price at destination and the shadow cost at origin	Shadow price of capacity constraint	Total social generalized logistic cost of port hinterland distribution operations	Reduced cost
SAL-NOL	448.30	−46.50	401.80	0.00
SAL-NCC	386.20	−46.50	339.70	0.00
SAL-BAR	611.20	−51.40	559.70	0.00
NOL-TAR	291.60	0.00	473.70	182.10
NOL-ROS	536.20	0.00	591.70	55.40
NOL-SAN	537.20	0.00	592.70	55.40
NOL-UMB	514.90	0.00	570.40	55.40
NOL-EMI	822.10	0.00	901.10	79.00
NOL-MIL	678.60	0.00	734.00	55.40
NCC-TAR	353.80	0.00	480.40	126.60
NCC-ROS	598.40	0.00	598.40	0.00
NCC-SAN	599.40	0.00	599.40	0.00
NCC-UMB	577.10	0.00	577.10	0.00
NCC-EMI	884.20	0.00	907.80	23.50
NCC-MIL	740.70	0.00	740.70	0.00
MAR-TAR	253.70	−3.90	469.80	220.00
MAR-ROS	498.30	0.00	582.70	84.40
MAR-LAZ	281.90	0.00	474.50	192.60

(NAP–MAR, NAP–MCC), Naples–Rosarno (NAP–ROS), Naples–San Ferdinando (NAP–SAN), Salerno–Nola (SAL–NOL, SAL–NCC), Salerno–Bari (SAL–BAR) and Marcianise–Taranto (MAR–TAR, MCC–TAR) would generate benefits. For instance, as reported in Table 8.8, the total social generalized logistic cost reduction due to a unit relaxation of the capacity constraint of the railway connection from Salerno (SAL) to Bari (BAR) would equal €51.40.

8.4   DISCUSSION AND CONCLUSIONS

The extended gateway concept is gaining more and more momentum as a business network innovation based on the possibility of duplicating and/or complementing some container seaport activities at hinterland intermodal facilities called 'dry ports' (or 'interports'). If properly implemented in port hinterland network systems, extended gateways can relieve seaport congestion phenomena and promote the shift of standardized loading units from road-only transport to alternative and more sustainable inland transport solutions, thus reducing the internal and external costs of supply chains.

This chapter has described the interport model as a mathematical programming tool for the economic analysis and strategic planning of such kind of innovation. A conceptual explanation of the primal and dual formulations of the model optimizing the distribution of import containers (inward interport model) under a sustainable logistics perspective (that is, by also taking account of transport externalities in total logistic costs) has been provided. The inland multimodal container network and flows of the seaports of Naples and Salerno located in the Campania region of southern Italy have served as the basis for the two empirical applications presented. The full and empty loading units imported into Italy through the regional seaport cluster can transit through the regional interports at Nola and Marcianise, as well as through extra-regional railway terminals, before reaching their final destinations. Finally, main modelling results have been shown and these have also been compared with the real-life situation.

The practical implementation of the extended gateway concept within a regional logistics system first requires cooperation and integration among a number of public and private actors, including seaports, interports, shipping lines, inland intermodal carriers, customs and so on. In Campania, some maritime terminal companies and freight forwarders are still reluctant to engage in a clear long-term partnership with interports for fear of a core activities shift to other operators. In addition, there are no examples of shipping lines investing in interports. Possible future successful implementations of extended gateway systems in Italy should also imply greater liberalization and further regulatory changes for rail traction service provision in port hinterland container markets.

The proposed case studies have highlighted the economic, environmental and social benefits arising from more advanced intermodal and customs procedures for inland distribution of import containers through the Campanian seaport–interport logistics system. The empirical models have allowed us to measure the advantages arising both from an interport-based extended gateway system (providing the arrangement of port hinterland container transport operations by shipping lines), and from the improvement of the rail connections available at the regional seaports and interports. In particular, the availability of customs facilitation at the interports will be of little help as long as the rail connections between seaports and interports remain inadequate. This has essentially been demonstrated by the full capacity utilization of the seaport–interport rail connections resulting from both the modelled scenarios.

Taking into account the customs regime currently in force in Italy, the recent port hinterland logistics policy orientations of the Campanian regional government, and the existing situation in the regional market of inland container transport services, it is certainly possible to increase the utilization of the rail capacity of the short-distance port–interport connections in Campania. This can be achieved by introducing new policy measures that should include, *inter alia*:

1. also allowing private rail traction companies to provide transit services under facilitated conditions between seaports and interports; and
2. supporting and promoting the interports of Nola and Marcianise in an equitable manner.

The results obtained from the simulated scenarios can (also) be used as a reference for public policy makers to adopt rational decisions on internalization and to promote port hinterland intermodal transport solutions for sustainable development. As demonstrated in this chapter, the internalization of external diseconomies in transport prices can only lead to a greater use of rail services between the regional interports and extra-regional locations. Such a finding thus suggests a possible policy measure of providing a grant scheme for funding container shuttle trains on these routes, based only on the internalization of external transport costs. Through the provision of incentives based on the total external cost saving deriving from transferring the movement of containers from road-only to rail transport, it might be possible to implement a reasonable pricing system that would generate a better spread of traffic and a fairer division between the different modes of transport connecting the interports of Nola and Marcianise to other locations outside the Campania region for the forwarding of cargoes and loading units transiting through the Campanian seaports. This policy measure could resolve, at least in part, the current bottlenecks in some connections of the seaports of Naples and Salerno with their hinterland.

With regard to some limitations of the *interport model*, a major abstraction in linear programming is that the objective function and the constraints are formulated by summing individual terms that are proportional to the values of variables. There are many real-world problems, however, in which non-linearities are present. For instance, there might be economies of scale that allow one to reduce costs as the volume of activities increases. Piecewise linear functions often need to be used to represent economies of scale in logistic costs associated with concentrated flows.

Furthermore, the deterministic assumption in the interport model has been designed to keep the analysis at a basic level, recognizing that most real problems contain deterministic elements as well as random parameters with accompanying probability distributions. For instance, terminal and customs operations and delays could be modelled by using queuing theory, dynamic programming and stochastic programming.

A specific aspect that would deserve attention is the modelling of reliability, including safety stocks and their associated costs. Business logistics literature indicates that buffer inventories can be calculated based essentially on: (i) the customer service level, (ii) the uncertainty in shipment lead time, and (iii) the demand forecast error. The transit time of transport services is only a part of the total lead time of shipments. The main challenge in port hinterland container logistics modelling seems to be that of calculating the unit safety stock costs at destination in relation to the movements of full containers transported simultaneously by different and alternative transport solutions featuring different lead times. In the currently available literature on container network optimization, safety stock costs are calculated only with relation to the deliveries of total batches of containers by single transport solutions (Leachman, 2008; Jula and Leachman, 2011); this means that each destination is supposed to be served by a single transport solution only. In our opinion, a good starting point for more realistic approximations of safety inventories are the analytical results achieved by Boute and Van Mieghem (2011) and Combes (2011). These contributions show how to estimate the safety stock for a single good that is sourced from two locations ('dual sourcing') or by using simultaneously different transport solutions.

Future extensions of the interport model could also be applied to other container network systems in Europe, including barge transport and taking account of other modern industrial practices such as the cross-border extended gateway logistics and the port hinterland distribution arranged by maritime terminal operators.

NOTES

1. In compliance with the customs regulations currently in force in Italy, only railway transport permits the necessary conditions of fiscal safety relating to inland haulage with no

accompanying inland transit document for containerized cargoes that have not yet been cleared through customs.

2. In empirical applications of the model, total travel times by road over admitted links are equal to the driving time both on motorways and on other roads plus the time for rests and stops prescribed by Italian road regulations under the '1 driver on board' hypothesis. Road driving times are computed by assuming the average speed for two different admitted trucks over motorways and other roads. The number and duration of rests and stops to be observed in transportation by truck are calculated as a function of the driving time.

3. Empirical data have largely been collected through questionnaires and interviews with public bodies and private firms. The main data are available in Iannone and Thore (2010), but in this chapter, the definitive figure on the average customs declared value of containerized imports in the Campania region during 2007 (equal to 18,589 €/full TEU) has been employed for the applications presented. Further details can be obtained from the author.

4. For the purpose of this work, a calibration of the interport model against real data has not been necessary. That task has already been carried out by Iannone and Thore (2010) through the optimization of a 'baseline scenario' to reproduce the existing situation concerning the inland traffic of containers discharged at the Campanian seaports in 2007. In that scenario, there are no rail connections available at the port of Salerno and customs clearance of containers is not allowed at the interport of Marcianise. Hence, only the interport of Nola can be used as an extended gateway and exclusively for containers discharged at the port of Naples. The objective function minimizes the total internal generalized logistic cost of port hinterland container distribution. The model proved to be calibrated quite well; the differences between optimized results and observed real-life situations can be attributed to the fact that it is not easy and sometimes not even possible to include in the model a number of specific factors characterizing the real world. For instance, some services and procedures were initiated in Campania only in the final months of 2007, whereas in the model they are assumed to have been available and operational since the beginning of the planning horizon. In addition, as also noted by Notteboom (2001), there are a number of historical, psychological, political and personal factors, including opportunistic behaviour, inertia and bounded rationality of economic agents, that influence intermodal logistics choices. Such factors often result in practical choices that can diverge even from the theoretical optimum.

5. In the empirical applications of the model, the nodes are coded as indicated in brackets.

6. Figure 8.3 represents only real nodes and real links. Indeed, the number of nodes and links actually included in the formulation of the empirical models is higher due to the representation of each real interport facility by means of two virtual nodes. The virtual nodes without a customs function corresponding to the interport facilities at Nola and Marcianise are respectively coded NOL and MAR, whereas their associated virtual nodes with customs function are coded NCC and MCC.

7. AdT and FS (2005) did not estimate congestion costs associated with rail freight transport. Hence, as shown in Table 8.1, it has not been possible to calculate the marginal congestion costs of container transport by rail in Italy.

REFERENCES

AdT and FS, 2005. 'The Environmental and Social Costs of Transport in Italy – Fifth Report', Rome.

Boute, R.N. and Van Mieghem, J.A., 2011. 'Global dual sourcing and order smoothing', mimeo, available at: http://www.kellogg.northwestern.edu/faculty/vanmieghem/articles.htm (accessed September 10, 2011).

Brooke, A., Kendrick, D., Meeraus, A. and Raman, R., 1998. *GAMS: A User's Guide*, Washington, DC: GAMS Development Corporation.

Combes, F., 2011. 'Inventory theory and mode choice in freight transport: the case of the simultaneous use of two transport modes on one shipper–receiver relationship', European Transport Conference 2011 Proceedings, Glasgow, Scotland, UK, 10–12 October.

Cullinane, K. and Wilmsmeier, G., 2011. 'The contribution of the dry port concept to the extension of port life cycles', in: Böse, J.W. (ed.), *Handbook of Terminal Planning*, New York: Springer, pp. 359–79.

Iannone, F., 2011. 'The extended gateway concept in port hinterland container logistics: a theoretical network programming formulation', Working Papers SIET 2011, available at: http://www.sietitalia.org/wpsiet/F.%20Iannone_WPSIET2011.pdf.

Iannone, F. and Thore, S., 2010. 'An economic logistics model for the multimodal inland distribution of maritime containers', *International Journal of Transport Economics* **37**, 281–326.

Iannone, F., Thore, S. and Forte, E., 2007. 'Inland container logistics and interports: goals and features of an ongoing applied research', in: Borruso, G., Forte, E. and Musso, E. (eds), *Economia dei trasporti e Logistica economica: ricerca per l'innovazione e politiche di governance*, Naples: Giordano Editore, pp. 385–414.

Jensen, P.A. and Bard, J.F., 2003. *Operations Research: Models and Methods*, New York: John Wiley & Sons.

Jula, P. and Leachman, R.C., 2011. 'A supply-chain optimization model of the allocation of containerized imports from Asia to the United States', *Transportation Research E* **47**, 609–22.

Leachman, R., 2008. 'Port and modal allocation of waterborne containerized imports from Asia to the United States', *Transportation Research E* **44**, 313–31.

Leitner, S.J. and Harrison, R., 2001. 'The identification and classification of inland ports', Research Report Number 0-4083-1, Center for Transportation Research, Bureau of Engineering Research, University of Texas at Austin.

Notteboom, T., 2001. 'Spatial and functional integration of container port systems and hinterland networks in Europe', in: ECMT (ed.), *Land access to Seaports*, Round Table 113, Paris: Economic Research Centre ECMT-OECD, pp. 5–55.

Rodrigue, J.-P. and Notteboom, T., 2009. 'The terminalization of supply chains: reassessing the role of terminals in port/hinterland logistical relationships', *Maritime Policy & Management* **36**, 165–83.

Roso, V. and Lumsden, K., 2010. 'A review of dry ports', *Maritime Economics & Logistics* **12**, 196–213.

Thompson, G.L. and Thore, S., 1992. *Computational Economics: Economic Modelling with Optimization Software*, San Francisco, CA: The Scientific Press.

Thore, S. and Iannone, F., 2005. 'The hub-and-spoke model a tutorial', mimeo, Carvoeiro, Portugal, August, available at: http://www.stenthore.info/computational.htm.

UNCTAD, 1982. 'Multimodal Transport and Containerisation', (TD/B/C.4/238/ Supplement 1, Part Five: Ports and Container Depots), Geneva.

UNCTAD, 1991. *Handbook on the Management and Operation of Dry Ports*, Geneva: United Nations.

Veenstra, A. and Zuidwijk, R., 2010. 'The future of seaport hinterland networks', in: Kroon, L., Zuidwijk, R. and Li, T. (Eds), *Liber Amicorum Jo van Nunen*, Breda: Dinalog and RSM-Erasmus University of Rotterdam, pp. 205–15.

9. Rising car user costs: comparing aggregated and geo-spatial impacts on travel demand and air pollutant emissions

Benjamin Kickhöfer, Friederike Hülsmann, Regine Gerike and Kai Nagel*

9.1 INTRODUCTION

Our chapter starts from the assumption that car user costs are about to increase in the forthcoming decades. This is likely to have impacts on aggregated air pollutant emissions and on the spatial distribution of emissions. The concentration of some air pollutants still exceeds the limiting values prescribed by the European Union, especially in urban areas. Thus, the main focus of this chapter is the question whether a decrease in car travel demand due to higher user costs would result in an overproportional reduction of air pollutant emissions. When it comes to the discussion of cost-related transport policies, large-scale transport models are needed. However, for the analysis of air pollutant emissions, a detailed investigation of the micro level is also necessary. In order to combine both objectives, we use a multi-agent transport model for our simulations. The multi-agent transport simulation MATSim[1] is able to simulate large-scale scenarios. It is also particularly suitable for calculating air pollutant emissions on a detailed level as complete daily plans are modeled and the traveler's identity is kept throughout the simulation process. For illustration purposes of the impacts on air pollutant emissions, nitrogen dioxide (NO_2) is chosen. Furthermore, the transport sector is the main source of NO_2 emissions and NO_2 concentration limits are still often exceeded.

Section 9.2 describes the methodology. It starts with a presentation of the transport model in Subsection 9.2.1, followed by a description of the emission modeling tool in Subsection 9.2.2. Section 9.3 consists of three Subsections: first, a presentation of the Munich base scenario; second, a description of the simulation approach and a definition of four policy scenarios; and third, the validation of the base scenario with respect to modal split and traffic volumes. In Section 9.4 aggregated car-user price elasticities of different subpopulations (inner-urban traffic, commuter, and inverse commuter) are calculated and discussed. Furthermore, car travel demand as well as NO_2 emissions are analyzed on a spatially disaggregated level for all scenarios. The chapter ends with a conclusion in Section 9.5.

9.2 METHODOLOGY

This section (i) gives a brief overview of the general simulation approach of MATSim and (ii) shortly describes the emission modeling tool that is developed by the authors. In this present chapter, only general ideas will be presented. For further information, see Raney and Nagel (2006) and Appendix 9A or Hülsmann et al. (2011).

9.2.1 Transport Simulation with MATSim

In MATSim, each traveler of the real system is modeled as an individual agent. The approach consists of an iterative loop that has the following steps:

1. *Plan generation* All agents independently generate daily plans that encode among other things their desired activities during a typical day as well as the transport mode for every intervening trip.
2. *Traffic flow simulation* All selected plans are simultaneously executed in the simulation of the physical system.
3. *Evaluating plans* All executed plans are evaluated by a utility function which encodes in this chapter the perception of travel time and monetary costs for the available transport modes.
4. *Learning* Some agents obtain new plans for the next iteration by modifying copies of existing plans. This modification is done by several modules that correspond to the available choice dimensions. In this chapter, agents adapt their routes only for car trips. Furthermore, they can switch between the car and public transport modes. The choice between plans is performed with respect to a random utility model.

The repetition of the iteration cycle coupled with the agent database enables the agents to improve their plans over many iterations. This is why it is also called a learning mechanism (see Appendix 9A). The iteration cycle continues until the system has reached a relaxed state. At this point, there is no quantitative measure of when the system is 'relaxed'; we just allow the cycle to continue until the outcome is stable.

9.2.2   Emission Modeling Tool

There are several sources of air pollution that can be assigned to road traffic: warm emissions are emitted when the vehicle's engine is already warmed up, whereas cold-start emissions occur during the warm-up phase. Warm emissions differ with respect to driving speed, acceleration, and stop duration as well as vehicle characteristics including vehicle type, fuel type, cubic capacity, and euro class (André and Rapone, 2009). Cold emissions differ with respect to distance traveled, parking time, average speed, ambient temperature, and vehicle characteristics (Weilenmann et al., 2009). Furthermore, emissions also result from evaporation and air conditioning. Due to their small contribution to the overall emission level, this last source is not considered in this present chapter.

The calculation of warm emissions is composed of two steps: first, kinematic characteristics and vehicle attributes are deduced from the MATSim simulation output; then, this information is used in order to extract emission factors from a database. MATSim exhibits activity chains for every agent over the entire day. Whenever an agent enters or leaves a road segment a time stamp is created. Thereby, it is possible to calculate the free-flow travel time and the travel time in a loaded network for every agent and road segment. As MATSim keeps demographic information until the system is relaxed, information about each agent's vehicle is available at any time. Vehicle attributes are derived from survey data (see Subsection 9.3.1) and comprise vehicle type, age, cubic capacity, and fuel type. They can, therefore, be used for very differentiated emission calculations. Where no detailed information about vehicle type is available, fleet averages for Germany are used.

Having identified the above kinematic characteristics for a road segment, specific travel behavior resulting from such data is assigned by using the detailed handbook of emission factors called (HBEFA).[2] For some European countries including Germany, the handbook contains country-specific emission factors that can vary by vehicle characteristics, road category, gradient, and speed limit. The handbook provides further disaggregated emission factors depending on four traffic situations: free flow, heavy, saturated, and stop&go. Such traffic situations are described by kinematic characteristics, which are deduced from driving cycles, that is, time – velocity profiles. Typical driving cycles form the basis for calculating traffic situations and, thus, typical emission factors in HBEFA.

In order to assign emission factors to the traffic flows generated by

MATSim, the driving behavior of an agent on a certain road segment in the MATSim simulation is linked to the respective HBEFA driving cycle. Therefore, each road segment is divided into two parts representing stop&go and free-flow traffic situations. A similar methodology was developed by Hatzopoulou and Miller (2010) who, in a simpler approach, assume fixed exhaust emissions per time unit. This chapter uses a more detailed calculation based on different traffic situations: it is based on the assumption that cars role in free flow until they have to wait in the queue where a stop&go traffic situation applies. The length of the queue depends on the traffic demand on the road. If demand is higher than the capacity of a road segment, a queue emerges where stop&go is assumed. Another reason for the segmentation of a road segment into free-flow and stop&go parts is due to the marginal difference between the emission factors of free flow, heavy and saturated. In contrast to these three traffic situations, the emission factors of stop&go are around twice as high. The difference between actual travel time and free-flow travel time per road segment corresponds to travel time spent in stop&go. The average speed of stop&go that represents a kinematic characteristic of the typical stop&go driving behavior can be obtained from the HBEFA database. The stop&go average speed and travel time are used to calculate the queue length. The respective emission factors can be assigned to the resulting stop&go and free-flow fractions. The implementation of the approach has been evaluated in a test scenario, which compared real traffic data with MATSim simulations for a single road segment. For a more detailed description of the emission modeling tool, see Hülsmann et al. (2011).

Regarding cold-start emissions, HBEFA provides the relevant factors for passenger cars only. The application of the relevant cold-start emission factor depends on two attributes: distance traveled and parking time. The latter is calculated by subtracting the time stamp when the activity starts from the time stamp when the activity ends. The subsequent distance traveled is determined by aggregating the lengths of all road segments the agent drives along until the next activity is reached. The longer the parking time and the accumulated distance, the higher the cold-start emission factor.

In order to further process the warm- and cold-start emissions, so-called 'emission events' are generated and further segmented into a warm pollution and cold-start pollution emission event. The former describes the warm emissions for each person and road segment and adds a time stamp. Cold-start pollution is given for each person and the road segment on which the trip starts. The definition of emission events follows the MATSim framework that uses events for storing disaggregated information in XML format (see Appendix 9A).

9.3 SCENARIO: MUNICH, GERMANY

The methodology described in Section 9.2 is now applied to a large-scale scenario of the Munich metropolitan area with about two million individuals. For this purpose, a scenario needs to be set up based on network and survey data. The process is described in Subsection 9.3.1, followed by a specification of the simulation procedure in Subsection 9.3.2 and a validation in Subsection 9.3.3 where we discuss to what extent the simulation reproduces reality.

9.3.1   Setting up the Scenario

Network (supply side)
Network data were provided by the municipality of Munich (RSB, 2005). The data match the format of the aggregated static transport planning tool VISUM.[3] It represents the road network of the federal state of Bavaria, being more detailed in and around the city of Munich and less detailed further away. It consists of 92,259 nodes and 222,502 connecting edges (= links). Most road attributes, such as free speed, capacity, number of lanes, and so on. are defined by the road type. Only geographical position and length are attributes of each single link. These data are converted to MATSim format by taking length, free speed, capacity, number of lanes, and road type from VISUM data. VISUM road capacities are meant for 24-hour origin–destination matrices. Since the network is almost empty during night hours, peak-hour capacity is set to VISUM capacity divided by 16 (not 24). This results in an hourly capacity of about 2,000 vehicles per lane on an urban motorway. In order to speed up computation, some road categories corresponding to small local roads are removed from the network. Furthermore, nodes with only one ingoing and one outgoing link are removed. The two resulting links are then merged, bringing the size of the network down to 17,888 nodes and 41,942 links. When merging, the two link lengths are summed up; free speed is calculated based on the minimal time needed for passing the original links; capacity is set to the minimum of the two links; the number of lanes is calculated based on the number of vehicles that fit on the two original links; and finally the road type – important input for emission calculations – is set to the one of the outgoing link.

Population (demand side)
In order to obtain a realistic time-dependent travel demand, several data sources are converted into the MATSim population format. The level of detail of the resulting individual daily plans naturally depends on the

information available from either disaggregated stated preference data or aggregated population statistics. Therefore, *three subpopulations* are created, each corresponding to one of the three different data sources:

1. *Inner-urban traffic* (based on Follmer et al., 2004) The synthetic population of Munich is created on the basis of very detailed survey data provided by the municipality of Munich RSB (2005), called 'Mobility in Germany' (MiD 2002). In the area of the Munich municipality, 3,612 households (with 7,206 individuals) were interviewed. The data consist of different datasets such as household data, person-specific data, and trip data. A detailed description of survey methods and data structure can be found in Follmer et al. Individuals were asked to report their activities during a complete day including activity locations, activity start and end times as well as the transport mode for the intervening trips. Due to privacy protection, the exact coordinates of activity locations are not available, but only the corresponding traffic analysis zones (1,066 zones in total). For the generation of the synthetic MATSim population, individual activity locations are distributed randomly within these zones. Furthermore, all incomplete datasets are removed, for example, when the location or the starting time of one activity are missing in the survey. The train and bus transport modes are treated as public transport trips, motorbikes and mopeds are treated as car trips. The ride (= in car as passenger), bike and other (= unknown) transport modes are kept for the initial MATSim population. Overall, the data cleaning results in 3,957 individuals, the representative sample for demand generation. Finally, these agents are 'cloned' while holding activity transport analysis zones constant but finding new random locations within these zones for every clone. This process is performed until the population reaches the real-world size of 1.4 million inhabitants. Thus, for this study the synthetic population living inside the Munich municipality boundaries consists of 1,424,520 individuals.

   MiD 2002 also provides detailed vehicle information for every household. Linking this data with individuals makes it possible to assign a vehicle to a person's car trip and thus, to calculate emissions based on this detailed information. As of now there is, however, no vehicle assignment module which models intra-household decision making. It is, therefore, possible that a vehicle is assigned to more than one person at the same time.

2. *Commuter traffic* (based on Böhme and Eigenmüller, 2006) Unfortunately, the detailed data for the municipality of Munich contain information neither about commuters living outside of Munich and

working in Munich nor about people living in Munich and working outside of Munich. The data analyzed by Böhme and Eigenmüller provide information about workers who are subject to the social insurance contribution with the base year 2004. Origin and destination zones are classified corresponding to the European 'Nomenclature of Statistical Territorial Units' (NUTS),[4] level 3. Thus, the origin–destination flows between Munich and all other municipalities in Germany are available. However, neither departure time nor transportation mode is provided. The total number of commuters tends to be under-estimated since public servants and education trips are not included in this statistic. Therefore, every origin–destination relation is increased by a factor of 1.29 (Guth et al., 2010). Initially, car trips are assumed to be 67 percent of the total commuter trips, public transport 33 percent (MVV, 2007). Departure times are set so that people arrive at their workplace, according to a normal distribution with N (8 a.m., 2 hours) when routed on an empty network. Work end times are set to nine hours after the arrival at the working place. This results overall in 510,150 commuters from which 306,160 people have their work-place in Munich. All these MATSim agents perform a daily plan that encodes two trips: from their home location to work and back. Due to this simplification, they are the first contribution to 'background traffic', as it will be called from here on.

3. *Commercial traffic* (based on ITP/BVU, 2005)   The second contribution to 'background traffic' is given by commercial traffic with the base year 2004. On behalf of the German Ministry of Transport, ITP/BVU (2005) published the origin–destination commodity flows throughout Germany differentiated by mode and 10 groups of commodities. Origin and destination zones inside Germany are classified corresponding to NUTS 2 level, and outside Germany to NUTS 3 level, respectively. The number of trucks (> 3.5 tons) between two zones or within a zone is calculated based on the commodity flow in tons and the average loading of trucks.[5] The starting and ending points of the trips are – due to the lack of more detailed data – randomly distributed inside the origin and destination zones, respectively. The resulting MATSim agents obtain a plan that consists of only two activities with one intervening trip. Departure times are set so that the number of 'en-route vehicles' in the simulation matches a standard daily trend for freight vehicles.[6] For this scenario, trips are considered only if they are carried out at least once in Bavaria during the day. This results in 158,860 agents with one single commercial traffic trip.

Overall, the synthetic population now consists of 2,093,530 agents.

To speed up computations, a 10 percent sample is used in the subsequent simulations; other studies indicate that this seems to be an appropriate percentage in order to achieve results close enough to reality (see, for example, Chen et al., 2008). For background traffic, no detailed vehicle information is available. Emissions are, therefore, calculated with the help of fleet averages for cars and trucks from HBEFA.

9.3.2 Simulation Approach

Choice dimensions
For the mental layer within MATSim which describes the behavioral learning of agents, a simple utility-based approach is used in this chapter. When choosing between different options with respect to a random utility model, agents are allowed to adjust their behavior between two choice dimensions: route choice and mode choice. The former allows individuals to adapt their routes on the road network when going by car. The latter makes it possible to change the transport mode for a subtour (see Appendix 9A) within the agent's daily plan. Only a switch from car to public transport or the other way around is possible. Trips that are initially done by any other mode remain fixed within the learning cycle. From a research point of view, this approach can be seen as defining a system where public transport is a placeholder for all substitutes of the car mode.

Utility functions
In the calculations for the travel-related part of utility (see equation (9A.1) in the appendix), travel time and monetary distance costs are considered as attributes of every car and public transport (pt) trip. Due to the lack of data of the municipality of Munich, the utility parameters are taken from Kickhöfer (2009) who based the estimations on data from Switzerland provided by Vrtic et al. (2008). The initial formulation of the utility functions for these estimations is as follows:

$$V_{car,i,j} = \beta_0 + \beta_{tr,car} \cdot t_{i,car} + \beta_{cost,car} \cdot c_{i,car} \tag{9.1}$$

$$V_{pt,i,j} = \beta_{tr,pt} \cdot t_{i,pt} + \beta_{cost,pt} \cdot c_{i,pt},$$

where t_i is the travel time of the trip to activity i and c_i is the corresponding monetary cost. Travel times and monetary costs are mode dependent, indicated by the indices. The utilities $V_{car,i,j}$ and $V_{pt,i,j}$ for person j are computed in 'utils'. Estimating the parameters[7] $\hat{\beta}_{tr,car} = -2.26/h$,

$\hat{\beta}_{tr,pt} = -2.36/h$, $\hat{\beta}_{cost,car} = -0.2/mU$ and $\hat{\beta}_{cost,pt} = -0.0535/mU$, and splitting the time-related parameters into opportunity costs of time and additional disutility caused by traveling (see, for example, Kickhöfer et al., 2011), leads to the functional form[8] for the overall utility of an activity:

$$V_{car,i,j} = \frac{2.26}{h} t_{*,i} \cdot \ln\left(\frac{t_{perf,i}}{t_{0,i}}\right) - \frac{0.2}{mU} \cdot c_{i,car} \tag{9.2}$$

$$V_{pt,i,j} = \frac{2.26}{h} t_{*,i} \cdot \ln\left(\frac{t_{perf,i}}{t_{0,i}}\right) - \frac{0.0535}{mU} \cdot c_{i,pt} - \frac{0.1}{h} \cdot t_{i,pt}.$$

In this chapter, $c_{i,car}$ and $c_{i,pt}$ are calculated for every trip by multiplying the distance between activity locations $i - 1$ and i by a specific out-of-pocket distance cost rate for car and public transit (see below). For the functional form of the positive utility earned by performing an activity, see equation (9A.2) in the appendix. Because of the argument regarding the opportunity cost of forgone activity time when arriving early (see Appendix 9A), the *effective* marginal disutility of early arrival is $\hat{\beta}_{early,eff} = -\hat{\beta}_{perf} \cdot t_{*,i}/t_{perf,i} \approx -\hat{\beta}_{perf} = -2.26/h$ which is equal to the effective marginal disutility of traveling by car $-\hat{\beta}_{tr,car,eff}$. The effective marginal disutility of traveling by pt is, by the same argument,

$$\hat{\beta}_{tr,pt,eff} = -\hat{\beta}_{perf} \cdot t_{*,i}/t_{perf,i} - |\hat{\beta}_{tr,pt}| \approx -\hat{\beta}_{perf} - |\hat{\beta}_{tr,pt}| = -2.36/h.$$

As a result of this simulation approach, it is possible to observe mode reactions to price increases and to derive price elasticities of demand.

Simulation procedure
For 800 iterations, 15 percent of the agents perform route adaption (discovering new routes), 15 percent change the transport mode for a car or pt subtour in their daily plan and 70 percent switch between their existing plans. Between iteration 801 and 1,000 route and mode adaption is switched off; in consequence, agents only switch between existing options. The output of iteration 1,000 is then used as input for the continuation of the base case and the four different policy cases:

1. Base case: car user costs remain constant at 10 ct/km.
2. Policy case 1: increasing car user costs by 25% to 12.5 ct/km.
3. Policy case 2: increasing car user costs by 50% to 15 ct/km.

4. Policy case 3: increasing car user costs by 75% to 17.5 ct/km.
5. Policy case 4: increasing car user costs by 100% to 20 ct/km.

User costs for public transport are assumed to be constant at 17 ct/km for all policy cases. Note that the term 'user costs' is referred to as out-of-pocket costs for the users. All simulation runs are continued for another 500 iterations. Again, during the first 400 iterations 15 percent of the agents perform route adaption while another 15 percent choose between car and public transport for one of their subtours. The remaining agents switch between existing plans. For the final 100 iterations only a fixed choice set is available for all agents. When evaluating the impact of the car user cost increases, the final iteration 1,500 of every policy case is compared to iteration 1,500 of the base case.

9.3.3 Verification of the Base Case

Modal split
While converting the input data described by Follmer et al. (2004) into the MATSim synthetic population (see Subsection 9.3.1), some individuals were omitted due to a lack of coordinates or activity times. Therefore, Table 9.1 shows differences in the modal split over all trips comparing the input data with the synthetic subpopulation at iterations 0 and 1,500. Note that only the mode share of the subpopulation traveling within Munich is shown. As one can see, the initial synthetic population overestimates the percentage of walk trips by 2.55 percent and of bike trips by 2.05 percent, while underestimating the percentage of car trips by 3.52 percent and of ride trips by 1.61 percent. Public transport trips remain

Table 9.1   *Trips per transport mode as percentage of total trips: comparison between input data (Follmer et al., 2004) and the MATSim synthetic subpopulation*

Mode	Follmer et al. (2004)	Synthetic population it. 0	Synthetic population it. 1,500	Difference it. 0	Difference it. 1,500
Bike	10	12.05	12.05	+2.05	+2.05
Car	26	22.48	20.88	−3.52	−5.12
Pt	22	21.98	23.59	−0.02	+1.59
Ride	13	11.39	11.39	−1.61	−1.61
Undefined	0	0.55	0.55	+0.55	+0.55
Walk	29	31.55	31.55	+2.55	+2.55

almost unchanged and the unknown mode is not discussed further due to the small number of trips. The error seems to be acceptable since no major differences occur.

When the system is in a relaxed state, car trips are even more under-estimated, whereas pt trips are overestimated compared to iteration 0. Reasons might be the missing location choice module and the assumptions regarding the specification of the utility function. Overall, the additional increase in public transport and decrease in car trips amounts only to 1.6 percent Thus, the synthetic MATSim population seems to be a good starting point for analyzing the change in travel demand and air pollutant emissions due to rising car user costs.

Comparison to counting stations
Before analyzing demand and emission reductions, the realism of the executed plans in the simulation is verified. The interaction of individuals on the physical representation of the road network is simulated over 1,500 iterations as described in Subsection 9.2.1. After reaching a stable outcome, some kind of measurement must exist to determine the quality of the simu-lation output. For the Munich region, data from 166 traffic counting sta-tions is available and aggregated for every hour over time of day.

The best quality of these data is available for Thursday, January 10, 2008. It is now used to compare simulated traffic volumes to real-world values. Different statistical values can be calculated, such as mean relative error or mean absolute bias. Figure 9.1 shows two examples of standard reports that MATSim automatically generates: Figure 9.1a depicts the comparison for one hour and all counting stations. If all data points were on a 45 degree line, the simulation would nicely reproduce reality. However, as one can see, there are errors between simulated and real values. The mean relative error for every sensor is a good indicator for the overall fit of the simulation. It is calculated as:

$$MRE = |\frac{Q_{sim} - Q_{real}}{Q_{sim}}|, \tag{9.3}$$

where Q_{sim} indicates the simulated and Q_{real} the real-world vehicle flow over the corresponding counting station in the corresponding hour. Averages for a given hour are obtained by averaging over all sensors. In the example shown in Figure 9.1b, the simulation deviates strongly from reality during night hours, that is, from midnight until 7 a.m. During daytime, that is, from 7 a.m. until the evening, the hourly mean relative error is between 30 percent and 50 percent with better values in the afternoon.

In order to reach this accuracy, some adjustments were done, for

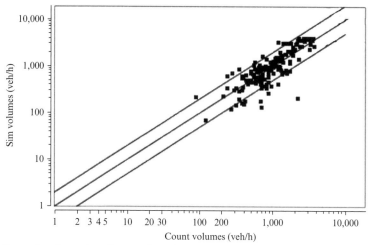

(a) Comparison for one hour (2 p.m. to 3 p.m.)

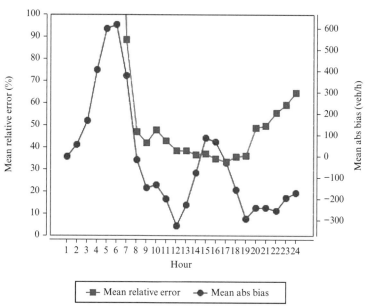

(b) Hourly analysis over time of day

*Figure 9.1   Realism of the simulation results at iteration 1500; 166 traffic
             counting stations provide real-world traffic counts for the
             Munich municipality area*

example, varying the parameters of the normal distribution that describe work arrival time peak and variance for commuters (see Subsection 9.3.1). For now, since this is meant to be a research scenario, the quality of the simulations seems to be adequate. However, by further optimizing travel demand and network information, better values for the mean relative error can be obtained as Chen et al. (2008) or Flötteröd et al. (2011) showed for a scenario of Zurich, Switzerland.

9.4 THE RELATIONSHIP BETWEEN CAR TRAVEL DEMAND AND AIR POLLUTANT EMISSIONS

This section aims at investigating two research questions: (i) 'Are price elasticities of emissions higher than those for car travel demand?', and if yes, (ii) 'Can a spatial effect be observed?'. In Subsection 9.4.1, we derive overall price elasticities of car travel demand from the simulation and then compare these to price elasticities of NO_2 emissions. In Subsection 9.4.2, we first identify areas with high travel demand in the city of Munich using a more disaggregated approach. In a second step, we present a spatial analysis of absolute changes in demand and NO_2 emissions due to policy case 4. Then, we investigate the role of absolute changes in emissions per vehicle kilometer following the same spatial analysis.

9.4.1 Aggregated Price Elasticities

In this chapter, possible reactions of car users to increasing distance costs comprise either choosing shorter but eventually more time consuming routes or changing the transport mode to public transport, the placeholder for all substitutes to car.

Figure 9.2 shows the daily demand for vehicle kilometers traveled (vkm) over different distance cost factors (from 10 ct/km for the base case up to 20 ct/km for the highest policy case). The reduction in demand is presented for three different subpopulations (see Subsection 9.3.1): circles correspond to inner-urban traffic, triangles and plus signs to inverse commuter and commuter, respectively. The inner-urban demand for vehicle kilometers traveled drops from about 400,000 vkm in the base case by 18 percent to roughly 333,000 vkm in the highest policy case. Much larger reductions in car travel demand are observed for the other subpopulations: car travel demand of inverse commuters drops from 1,650,000 vkm by 54 percent to 754,000 vkm, and for commuters from 4,624,000 vkm by 72 percent to 1,290,000 vkm. The big difference

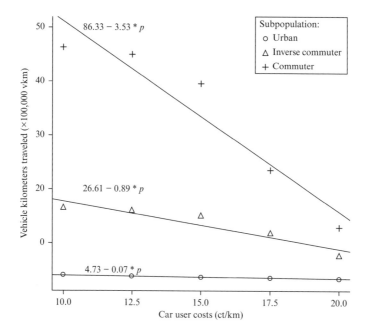

*Figure 9.2 Overall daily vehicle kilometers traveled for the base case
and the four policy cases by subpopulation: simulated values
and estimations as linear regression functions (values for a
representative 10% sample)*

between inner-urban demand and (inverse) commuters is due to the much
longer distances traveled by the last two groups where the car mode gets
extremely unattractive. Travel demand reactions for freight traffic is not
shown since this subpopulation is not allowed to change from car (or
truck) to public transport. The figure also provides linear regression lines
including their functional forms for every subpopulation. Even though,
especially for commuter traffic, a linear regression obviously does not
lead to the best fit (one can see the 'inverse-S-shape' produced by the
logit model), it is still quite appropriate in order to derive constant price
elasticities.

Choosing $p_0 = 10$ as the operating point, price elasticities of demand can
directly be derived for every policy case i, using:

$$\eta_{q,p} = \frac{(q_i - q_0)/q_0}{(p_i - p_0)/p_0}, \tag{9.4}$$

where q_i is the travel demand at price level p_i. In order to describe the overall relationship between user costs and car travel demand, a constant price elasticity can be derived using the regression functions:

$$\eta_{q,p} = \frac{dq}{dp} \cdot \frac{p_0}{\hat{q}_0}, \tag{9.5}$$

where d_q/d_p is the gradient of the corresponding regression function and $\hat{q}_0$ is the estimated initial demand for car trips at $p_0 = 10$ ct/km. Applying equation (9.5) to the three subpopulations leads to the following estimated constant price elasticities of car travel demand:

$$\hat{\eta}_{p,q}^{Urban} = -0.173, \quad \hat{\eta}_{p,q}^{Inverse\,Commuter} = -0.502, \quad \hat{\eta}_{p,q}^{Commuter} = -0.692.$$

These estimations indicate that, for example, a car user cost increase of 10 percent (at the operating point $p_0 = 10$ ct/km) leads to a reduction in car trips by 1.73 percent for inner-urban traffic, by 5.02 percent for inverse commuter and by 6.92 percent for commuter. Graham and Glaister (2002) present a wide range of fuel price elasticities collected from different studies. When summarizing the different studies, the authors find short-term fuel price elasticities in the range from –0.2 to –0.5, for Germany around –0.45. However, the range within Germany goes from –0.25 to –0.86. The fuel price elasticities found in this chapter are somewhat smaller for inner-urban traffic and within the range for inverse commuter and commuter. Obviously, introducing more choice dimensions into the model, such as location choice or the possibility of dropping activities, is likely to influence the results. At this point, it can be stated that, overall, the model produces reasonable behavioral reactions to car user price increases.

Similarly to Figure 9.2, overall NO_2 emissions are shown in Figure 9.3, again for the base case and the four policy cases. Linear regression lines and functional form are also provided. In this figure, freight traffic emissions are indicated by crosses in order to show the big impact of freight traffic emissions on overall emission levels. Since freight demand is not allowed to change the mode to public transport, its emissions stay more or less stable for all policy cases. Only a small reduction can be observed, probably resulting from shorter distances chosen by the router module. Equally to the price elasticities of demand, price elasticities of NO_2 emissions are calculated:

$$\hat{\varepsilon}_{p,q}^{Urban} = -0.219, \quad \hat{\varepsilon}_{p,q}^{Inverse,\,Commuter} = -0.608, \quad \hat{\varepsilon}_{p,q}^{Commuter} = -0.792.$$

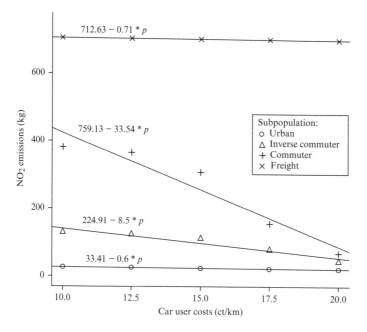

Figure 9.3   *Overall daily NO_2 emissions in kilograms for the base case and the four policy cases by subpopulation: simulated values and estimations as linear regression functions (values for a representative 10% sample)*

The price elasticities are found to be roughly the same for other exhaust emission types under consideration (PM and SO_2). When comparing them to the price elasticities of car travel demand from above, one can notice a higher elasticity of emissions than of demand for all subpopulations. Thus, an increase in car-user costs leads to a higher reduction in emissions than in demand. Two explanations come to mind:

1. An overproportional fraction of travelers who performed long car trips with high speed levels now change from car to public transport ('biased mode switch effect').
2. Travelers are driving faster on formerly congested roads ('congestion relief effect').

Both explanations are based on the fact that emission levels are usually the lowest for speed levels around 60 km/h (see, for example, Maibach et al., 2008, p. 58). Emissions per vehicle kilometer increase for lower but also for higher speed levels, forming a 'U-shaped' function with its minimum around 60 km/h. That is, when mainly trips with high speed levels are reduced (in this case by changing to another mode), overall emissions drop more than demand. The same is true when traffic flow becomes more fluid on formerly congested roads. It seems that the second effect can be observed since our model includes spillback effects, different traffic states, and individual vehicle characteristics. The following subsection will address this hypothesis by looking at spatial patterns of changes in travel demand and in air pollutant emissions.

9.4.2   Spatial Analysis of Changes in Car Travel Demand and Air Pollutant Emissions

This subsection analyzes car travel demand and NO_2 emissions on a spatially disaggregated level. Using the features of the emission modeling tool, demand and NO_2 emissions can be aggregated per road segment and for any desired time interval. For visual presentation of the spatial effect within the urban area of Munich, emissions are spatially smoothed using a Gaussian distance weighting function with a radius of 500 m. Starting with the base case shown in Figure 9.4, one notices a high level travel demand (in vehicle kilometers traveled) for the inner ring road, the middle ring road, the main arterial motorways, and the tangential motorway in the northwest of Munich (see Figure 9.4a). Travel demand is highly correlated with the level of exhaust emissions (see Figure 9.4b).[9] The population exposure of NO_2 emissions near these road sections is critical; this is also found in the air pollutant concentration levels at monitoring stations, for example, at Landshuter Allee (LFU, 2011). Figure 9.5 shows the absolute change in NO_2 emissions between the base case and the 100 percent price increase (policy case 4). As already presented in Subsection 9.4.1, the increase in car user costs leads to an important reduction in emission levels. This finding is now confirmed by Figure 9.5a which decomposes the overall effect in a spatial distribution. The lesson learned when comparing that picture to Figure 9.4 is that roads with the highest potential for emission reductions are located along the corridors with the highest travel demand (and therefore the highest emissions). Figure 9.5a also shows that potential gains are considerably larger at the medium- and high-speed roads than, for example, in the inner urban area. Our approach allows us to show such effects on a detailed single-street level while still being applicable to large-scale scenarios. This allows both the identification of relevant corridors ('hot spots') and the spatially disaggregated analysis of the consequences of policy measures.

In order to answer the question whether spatial patterns of higher emission elasticities compared to demand elasticities can be observed,

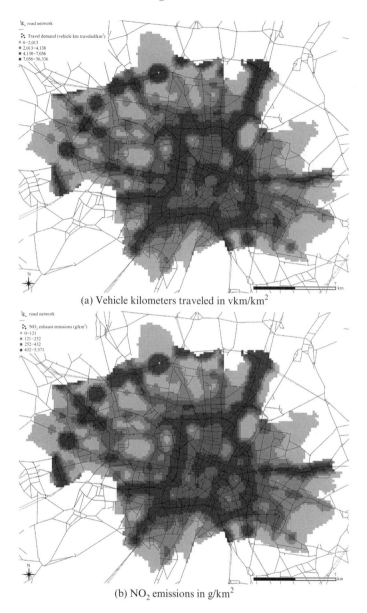

(a) Vehicle kilometers traveled in vkm/km^2

(b) NO$_2$ emissions in g/km^2

Note: Plots based on spatial averaging for all road segments. Values for a representative 10% sample.

Figure 9.4 *Base case: areas with high car travel demand and areas with high NO$_2$ emissions*

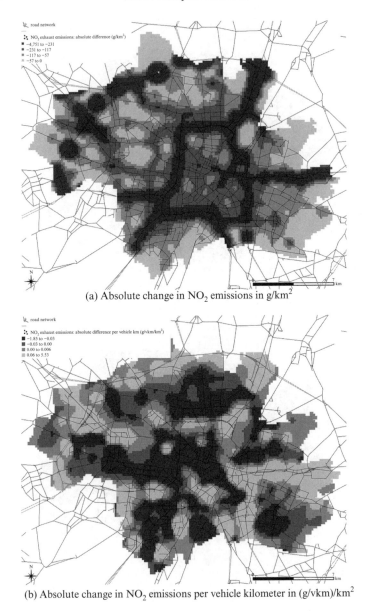

(a) Absolute change in NO$_2$ emissions in g/km^2

(b) Absolute change in NO$_2$ emissions per vehicle kilometer in (g/vkm)/km^2

Note: Plots based on spatial averaging for all road segments. Values for a representative 10% sample.

Figure 9.5   Absolute changes in NO$_2$ emissions between the base case and the 100% price increase (policy case 4)

Figure 9.5b is analyzed. Similar to Figure 9.5a, it depicts the absolute difference in emission levels between the base case and the 100 percent price increase (policy case 4), but now the absolute change in *emissions per vehicle kilometer traveled*. Values above zero imply that vehicles produce more emissions per km traveled, whereas values below zero indicate that vehicles emit fewer emissions for the same distance. Again, two effects can be observed that correspond with those presented in Subsection 9.4.1:

1. The 'biased mode switch effect' is most important for the main arterial motorways and the tangential motorway in the northwest of Munich: Figure 9.5a indicates that overall emissions (and demand) go down on these road segments. But following Figure 9.5b, average emissions per vehicle kilometer go up (light gray areas).
2. The 'congestion relief effect' seems to be less coherent in Figure 9.5b than the first effect. However, dark gray areas indicate that average emissions per vehicle kilometer go down. This means that a reduction in travel demand leads to lower emissions per vehicle kilometer.

The first effect can be interpreted as follows: in the base case, average speeds on motorways were closer to the (emission) optimal speed of 60 km/h. Fewer vehicles on these roads lead to higher emissions per vehicle kilometer, since travelers drive faster. That is, congestion relief leads to higher emissions per vehicle kilometer. A similar finding was obtained by Newman and Kenworthy (1989), who state that the average traffic speed is correlated positively, and not negatively, with gasoline consumption per capita. The second effect might be interpreted as follows when combining the aggregated and the disaggregated observations: it is likely that due to the reduction in demand, average travel speeds in the corresponding areas get closer to the (emission) optimal speed of 60 km/h. Emissions along a congested urban road are about twice as high as when traffic is flowing. When car travel demand is reduced and, thereby, the traffic situation on the road segment changes from stop&go to saturated or even heavy, emissions are more reduced than the flow on that road segment. That is, congestion relief leads to lower emissions per vehicle kilometer especially in urban contexts.

9.5   CONCLUSION

In this chapter, we set up a real-world scenario of the Munich metropolitan area and simulated travel demand of a 10 percent sample (around 200,000 individuals) with a large-scale multi-agent simulation. We coupled the simulation with detailed emission factors from the 'Handbook Emission Factors for Road Transport', considering the kinematic characteristics derived from the simulation and vehicle attributes obtained from survey data. Since the simulation keeps track of the approximate position and attributes of every traveler's vehicle during every time step, it was possible to map the kinematic characteristics to different traffic situations such as free flow or stop&go. Thereby, emissions were calculated every time a traveler leaves a road segment, or starts his/her engine. The mapping of demand (in vehicle kilometers) or emissions back to the road segments was therefore quite straightforward.

We then introduced four policy cases, where user costs for cars are rising from 10 ct/km in four steps up to 20 ct/km. Aggregated price elasticities of demand were found to be in a reasonable range for all sub-populations. Commuters reacted more sensitively to the price increase than inner-urban travelers, for example, by changing from car to public transport. Price elasticities of NO_2 emissions turned out to be higher than those of demand. Two possible explanations were given: first, it might happen that an overproportional fraction of travelers who performed long car trips with high speed levels changed from car to public transport. We called this the 'biased mode switch effect'. Second, it seems that travelers are driving faster on formerly congested roads, referred to as the 'congestion relief effect'.

A spatially more disaggregated analysis allowed us to identify so-called 'hot spots' that have a high potential for emission reduction: absolute emissions dropped most in many, but not all, areas where travel demand was high. Furthermore, the spatial analysis showed that the biased mode switch effect was most important for high-speed arterials and tangential motorways since absolute emissions (and demand) go down on these road segments, but average emissions per vehicle kilometer go up. Due to higher speeds, fewer vehicles – in this case – lead to higher emissions per vehicle kilometer. The congestion relief effect was found to be less coherent in terms of the type of road segment. Nonetheless, some areas showed a reduction in emissions per vehicle kilometer caused by a reduction in demand. Due to higher speeds, fewer vehicles – in this case – lead to lower emissions per vehicle kilometer. Possibly, both effects stem from the fact that the emission optimal speed is usually around 60 km/h. Measures that allow travelers to drive faster than that will result in higher emissions per vehicle kilometer. However, the relief of congestion seems to bear some potential to reduce emissions on urban roads.

This chapter can add valuable information to the transport planning and policy-making process by providing insights into a new emission calculation model for large-scale scenarios. In future studies, we plan to account for more choice dimensions than just route and mode choice. This is likely to influence the results. Also, the robustness of the results needs to be tested by performing sensitivity analysis. A possible extension would be the modeling of air pollutant concentration which could be used to validate simulation results with measured concentration values.

NOTES

* This work was funded in part by the German Research Foundation (DFG) within the research project 'Detailed evaluation of transport policies using microsimulation'. Important data were provided by the Municipality of Munich, more precisely by 'Kreisverwaltungsreferat München' and 'Referat für Stadtplanung und Bauordnung München'. Our computer cluster is maintained by the Department of Mathematics at Technische Universität Berlin. The authors would like to thank two anonymous reviewers for their valuable comments.
1. 'Multi-Agent Transport Simulation', see www.matsim.org (accessed April 9, 2013).
2. 'Handbook of Emission Factors for Road Transport', Version 3.1, see www.hbefa.net (accessed April 9, 2013).
3. 'Verkehr In Städten UMlegung' developed by PTV AG, see www.ptv.de (accessed April 9, 2013).
4. See http://epp.eurostat.ec.europa.eu/portal/page/portal/nuts_nomenclature/introduction (accessed February 18, 2011).
5. Estimations are based on personal correspondence with Dr Gernot Liedke from Karlsruhe Institute of Technology (October 2010).
6. Estimations are based on personal correspondence with Dr Gernot Liedke from Karlsruhe Institute of Technology (October 2010).
7. Estimated parameters are in this chapter flagged by a hat. h is one hour and mU is a unit of money.
8. The alternative specific constant β_0 (see, for example, Train, 2003), is estimated not significantly different from zero and is, therefore, not considered in the functional form of the utility functions. This essentially means that no general a priori preference for one of the transport modes can be found in the data.
9. Our method currently localizes all emissions on a road segment at the center coordinate. This explains why the tangential motorway in the northwest of Munich is shown as a sequence of circles rather than an uninterrupted line.

REFERENCES

André, M. and Rapone, M., 2009. 'Analysis and modelling of the pollutant emissions from European cars regarding the driving characteristics and test cycles', *Atmospheric Environment* **43**, 986–95.
Böhme, S. and Eigenmüller, L., 2006. 'Pendlerbericht Bayern', Technical report, IAB.
Chen, Y., Rieser, M., Grether, D. and Nagel, K., 2008. 'Improving a large-scale

agent-based simulation scenario', VSP Working Paper 08-15 Transport Systems Planning and Transport Telematics, TU Berlin, see www.vsp.tu-berlin.de/publications.

Flötteröd, G., Chen, Y. and Nagel, K., 2011. 'Behavioral calibration and analysis of a large-scale travel microsimulation', *Networks and Spatial Economics* **12**, 481–502.

Follmer, R., Kunert, U., Kloas, J. and Kuhfeld, H., 2004. 'Mobilität in Deutschland – Ergebnisbericht', Technical report, infas/DIW. See www.kontiv2002.de (accessed April 9, 2013).

Graham, D.J. and Glaister, S., 2002. 'The demand for automobile fuel: a survey of elasticities', *Journal of Transport Economics and Policy* **36**, 1–25.

Guth, D., Holz-Rau, C., Killer, V. and Axhausen, K.W., 2010. Räumliche Dynamik des Pendelverkehrs in Deutschland und der Schweiz: Das Beispiel München und Zürich, *disP – The Planning Review* **47**, 12–28.

Hatzopoulou, M. and Miller, E., 2010. 'Linking an activity-based travel demand model with traffic emission and dispersion models: transport's contribution to air pollution in Toronto', *Transportation Research D* **15**, 315–25.

Hülsmann, F., Gerike, R., Kickhöfer, B., Nagel, K. and Luz, R., 2011. 'Towards a multi-agent based modeling approach for air pollutants in urban regions', in: *Proceedings of the Conference on 'Luftqualität an Straßen'*, Bundesanstalt für Straßenwesen, FGSV Verlag GmbH, May, pp. 144–66. Also VSP WP 10-15, see www.vsp.tu-berlin.de/publications.

ITP/BVU, 2005. 'Prognose der deutschlandweiten Verkehrsverflechtungen 2025', Technical report, URL http://daten.clearingstelle-verkehr.de/220/ (accessed April 9, 2013).

Kickhöfer, B., 2009. 'Die Methodik der ökonomischen Bewertung von Verkehrsmaßnahmen in Multiagentensimulationen', Diplomarbeit (Diploma Thesis), TU Berlin, Institute for Land and Sea Transport Systems, Berlin, June. Also VSP WP 09-10, see www.vsp.tu-berlin.de/publications.

Kickhöfer, B., Grether, D. and Nagel, K., 2011. 'Income-contingent user preferences in policy evaluation: application and discussion based on multi-agent transport simulations', *Transportation* **38**, 849–70.

LFU, 2011. 'Überschreitungshäufigkeit für Feinstaub – PM10, Stickstoffdioxid und Schwefeldioxid', Technical report, Bayerisches Landesamt für Umwelt. URL http://www.lfu.bayern.de/luft/lueb/ueberschreitung\s\do5(p)m10\s\do5(s)o2\s\do5(n)o2/index.htm (accessed August 30 2011).

Maibach, M., Schreyer, D., Sutter, D., van Essen, H., Boon, B., Smokers, R., Schroten, A., Doll, C., Pawlowska, B. and Bak, M., 2008. 'Handbook on estimation of external costs in the transport sector,' Technical report, CE Delft.

MVV, 2007. 'Regionaler Nahverkehrsplan für das Gebiet des Münchner Verkehrs- und Tarifverbundes', Technical report, Munich Local Transport Provider.

Newman, P.W.G. and Kenworthy, J.R., 1989. 'Gasoline consumption and cities', *Journal of the American Planning Association* **55**, 24–37.

Raney, B. and Nagel, K., 2006. 'An improved framework for large-scale multi-agent simulations of travel behaviour', in: Rietveld, P., Jourquin, B. and Westin, K. (eds), *Towards Better Performing European Transportation Systems*, London: Routledge, pp. 305–47.

RSB, 2005. Municipality of Munich: Referat für Stadtplanung und Bauordnung.

Train, K., 2003. *Discrete Choice Methods with Simulation*, Cambridge: Cambridge University Press.

Vrtic, M., Schüssler, N., Erath, A., Bürgle, M., Axhausen, K., Frejinger, E., Bierlaire, M., Rudel, R., Scagnolari, S. and Maggi, R., 2008. 'Einbezug der Reisekosten bei der Modellierung des Mobilitätsverhaltens', Schriftenreihe 1191, Bundesamt für Strassen, UVEK, Bern, CH. Final Report for Project SVI 2005/004.

Weilenmann, M., Favez, J.-Y. and Alvarez, R., 2009. 'Cold-start emissions of modern passenger cars at different low ambient temperatures and their evolution over vehicle legislation categories', *Atmospheric Environment* **43**, 2419–29.

APPENDIX 9A   SIMULATION DETAILS

This appendix presents more information about the MATSim simulation approach that is used in this chapter. Every step of the iterative loop in Section 9.2.1 is illustrated in more detail in the following.

Plan Generation

An agent's daily plan contains information about his/her planned activity types and locations, about duration and other time constraints of every activity, as well as the mode, route, the desired departure time, and the expected travel time of every intervening trip (= leg). Initial plans are usually generated based on microcensus information and/or other surveys. The plan that was reported by an individual is marked as 'selected' in the first step.

Traffic Flow Simulation

The traffic flow simulation executes all selected plans simultaneously in the physical environment and provides output describing what happened to each individual agent during the execution of its plan. The *car traffic flow simulation* is implemented as a queue simulation, where each road (= link) is represented as a first-in first-out queue with two restrictions (Gawron, 1998; Cetin et al., 2003). First, each agent has to remain for a certain time on the link, corresponding to the free speed travel time. Second, a link storage capacity is defined which limits the number of agents on the link; if it is filled up, no more agents can enter this link. The *public transport simulation* simply assumes that traveling takes twice as long as traveling by car on the fastest route in an empty network[1] and that the travel distance is 1.5 times the beeline distance between the activity locations. public transport is assumed to run continuously and without capacity restrictions (Grether et al., 2009; Rieser et al., 2009).

All other modes are modeled similar to public transport: travel times are calculated based on mode-specific travel speed and the distance estimated for public transport. However, the attributes of these modes are not relevant for the present chapter since agents are only allowed to switch from car to public transport and the other way around. Trips from the survey that are no car or public transport trips, are held fixed during the learning cycle, thus not changing mode share in any direction.

Output of the traffic flow simulation is a list that describes for every agent different *events*, for example, entering or leaving a link, arriving or leaving an activity. These events are written in XML-format and include agent ID, time, and location (link or node ID). It is, therefore, quite straightforward to use this disaggregated information for the calculation of link travel times or costs (which is used by the router module), trip travel times, trip lengths, and many more.

Evaluating Plans

In order to compare plans, it is necessary to assign a quantitative measure to the performance of each plan. In this work, a simple utility-based approach is used. The elements of our approach are as follows.

First, the total utility of a plan is computed as the sum of individual contributions:

$$V_{total} = \sum_{i=1}^{n} (V_{perf,i} + V_{tr,i}), \tag{9A.1}$$

where V_{total} is the total utility for a given plan; n is the number of activities; $V_{perf,i}$ is the (positive) utility earned for performing activity i; and $V_{tr,i}$ is the (usually negative) utility earned for traveling during trip i. Activities are assumed to wrap around the 24-hour period, that is, the first and the last activity are stitched together. In consequence, there are as many trips between activities as there are activities.

Second, a logarithmic form is used for the positive utility earned by performing an activity:

$$V_{perf,i}(t_{perf,i}) = \beta_{perf} \cdot t_{*,i} \cdot \ln\left(\frac{t_{perf,i}}{t_{0,i}}\right), \tag{9A.2}$$

where $t_{perf,i}$ is the actual performed duration of the activity, $t_{*,i}$ is the 'typical' duration of an activity, and β_{perf} is the marginal utility of an activity at its typical duration. β_{perf} is the same for all activities, since in equilibrium all activities at their typical duration need to have the same marginal utility. $t_{0,i}$ is a scaling parameter that is related both to the minimum duration and to the importance of an activity. As long as dropping activities from the plan is not allowed, $t_{0,i}$ has essentially no effect.

Third, the disutility of traveling used for simulations is estimated from survey data which is explained in Section 9.3.2.

In principle, arriving early or late could also be punished. For the present chapter, there is, however, no need to do so, since agents are not allowed to reschedule their day by changing departure times. Arriving early is already implicitly punished by foregoing the reward that could be accumulated by doing an activity instead (opportunity cost). In consequence, the effective (dis)utility of waiting is already $-\hat{\beta}_{perf} \cdot t_{*,i}/t_{perf,i} \approx -\hat{\beta}_{perf}$. Similarly, that opportunity cost has to be added to the time spent traveling.

Learning

After evaluating daily plans in every iteration, a certain number of randomly chosen agents are forced to re-plan their day for the next iteration. This learning process is, in the present chapter, done by two modules corresponding to the two choice dimensions available: a module called 'router' for choosing new routes on the road network and a module called 'subtour mode choice' for choosing a new transport mode for a car or public transport trip. The router module bases its decision for new routes on the output of the car traffic flow simulation and the knowledge of congestion in the network. It is implemented as a time-dependent best path algorithm (Lefebvre and Balmer, 2007), using generalized costs (= disutility of traveling) as input. The subtour mode choice module changes the transport mode of a car subtour to public transport or from a public transport subtour to car. A subtour is basically a sequence of trips between activity locations. However, the simulation needs to make sure that a car can only be used if it is parked at the current activity location. Thus, a subtour is defined as a sequence of trips where the transport mode can be changed while still being consistent with the rest of the trips. For example, it is assured that a car which is used to go from home to work in the morning needs to be back at the home location in the evening. If the car remains, for example, at the work location in order to use it to go for lunch, then the whole subtour of going to work and back needs to be changed to public transport.

Note

1. This is based on the (informally stated) goal of the Berlin public transport company to generally achieve door-to-door travel times that are no longer than twice as long as car travel times. This, in turn, is based on the observation that non-captive travelers can be recruited into public transport when it is faster than this benchmark (Reinhold, 2006).

References

Cetin, N., Burri, A. and Nagel, K., 2003. 'A large-scale agent-based traffic microsimulation based on queue model', in: *Proceedings of the Swiss Transport Research Conference* (STRC), Monte Verita. CH Earlier version, with inferior performance values: Transportation Research Board Annual Meeting 2003, paper number 03-4272.

Gawron, C., 1998. 'An iterative algorithm to determine the dynamic user equilibrium in a traffic simulation model', *International Journal of Modern Physics C* **9**, 393–407.

Grether, D., Chen, Y., Rieser, M. and Nagel, K., 2009. 'Effects of a simple mode choice model in a large-scale agent-based transport simulation', in: Reggiani, A. and Nijkamp, P. (eds), *Complexity and Spatial Networks: In Search of Simplicity, Advances in Spatial Science*, New York: Springer, pp. 167–86.

Lefebvre, N. and Balmer, M., 2007. 'Fast shortest path computation in time-dependent traffic networks', in: *Proceedings of the Swiss Transport Research Conference* (STRC), Monte Verita, CH, September.

Reinhold, T., 2006. *Konzept zur integrierten Optimierung des Berliner Nahverkehrs. In Öffentlicher Personennahverkehr*, Berlin, Heidelberg: Springer.

Rieser, M., Grether, D. and Nagel, K., 2009. 'Adding mode choice to a multi-agent transport simulation', *Transportation Research Record: Travel Demand Forecasting*, **2132**, 50–58.

10. Mixture–amount experiments for measuring consumer preferences of energy-saving adaptation strategies: principles and illustration

Dujuan Yang, Gamze Dane and Harry J.P. Timmermans*

10.1 INTRODUCTION

Predicting the likely impacts of new policies, plans or projects has been the core of transportation research for decades. In general, two different modeling approaches can be distinguished. Foremost, transportation researchers have collected cross-sectional data about the dependent variable (preferences, choices, and so on) and about the set of person, household, spatial, and transport variables that are assumed to influence the dependent variable of interest. The quintessence of this revealed preference approach is then choosing the right statistical or econometric approach, dependent on: (i) the nature of the dependent variable, (ii) the assumed functional relationship between the dependent variable and set of independent variables, and (iii) assumptions with regard to the unobserved variables, reflected in the variance–covariance matrix of the error terms. Rather than collecting cross-sectional data, panel data have been collected in a more limited number of cases, and dynamic models have been formulated. By assuming that the estimated parameters are invariant over time, prediction implies translating policies into the independent variables of the model, keeping the parameters fixed and then applying the model equation to calculate new values for the dependent variable.

It does not require much argumentation to realize that this approach will lose its appeal and relevance/validity once the policies have dramatically changed the estimated relationship between the dependent and independent variables or in situations where no historical data of actual behavior can be collected because the phenomenon is new. Under such circumstances, transportation researchers have found a solution by constructing experimental designs and asking subjects to express their preferences or choices for hypothetical alternatives. By assuming that such stated behavior under hypothetical situations bears some systematic relationship with choices in the real world, predictions can be made. This so-called 'stated preference' or 'choice' approach is also not error free, but it has been shown that in some cases it produces better estimates than the revealed preference approach.

Consequently, the transportation research literature witnesses a great number of studies adopting this experimental design approach (for example, Hensher, 1994; Doherty and Miller, 2000; Louviere et al., 2000; Arentze et al., 2004; Caussade et al., 2005; Hess et al., 2006; Van der Waerden et al., 2006). Subjects have typically been asked to rate hypothetical profiles (preference), to choose between systematically varied alternatives (choice) or to indicate if and how they would change their behavior (adaptation).

Although in reality, many choices are influenced by budget constraints, the construction of the experimental design in these and many similar studies does not take such constraints into account. Implicitly or explicitly researchers have assumed that the impact of any such constraints can be ignored or was not relevant. In this chapter, we shall argue that so-called 'mixture–amount' designs may be a highly relevant class of designs to study such budget-constrained phenomena. The principles underlying this approach, the construction of the design and the formulation and estimation of relevant models will be discussed, using the case of energy-saving strategies as an example. In addition, it will be shown how these standard designs can be extended to include context dependency.

The topic of energy conservation has drawn some attention in the transportation research literature. Phifer et al. (1980) developed a game to study how families deal with energy constraints, related to the 1979 gasoline shortage. Only 12 households participated in this game. Lee-Gosselin (1989) also used a game to better understand private car use in relation to potential fuel shortage. He pointed out that the CUPIG (Car Use Patterns Interview Game) methodology could be useful to calibrate existing choices and explore trade-offs. However, it used a non-monetary budget which increased respondents' burden of understanding the hypothetical situation. Doherty et al. (2002) conducted two small experiments to study car travel reduction. One was an in-depth experiment to explore household rescheduling and adaptation processes to a fuel price increase. The experiment included two main components: a week long activity scheduling CHASE (Computerized Household Activity Scheduling Elicitor) survey and a follow-up interactive stated adaptation interview. Thus, based on this review, it seems that none of the limited number studies on energy saving adaptation has adopted a stated adaptation approach based on experimental designs that include both budget constraints and context dependencies.

This chapter is organized as follows. Section 10.2 will discuss the basic principles of mixture–amount models and the corresponding design of experiments. This is followed by an explanation of how these models can be extended to include context dependency (Section 10.3). Section 10.4 will discuss an illustration of the model. The chapter is completed with a summary and conclusions (Section 10.5).

10.2   MIXTURE–AMOUNT MODELS

Stated preference models, commonly used in transportation research, systematically vary the levels of a set of attributes, according to an orthogonal fractional factorial design and ask respondents to rate the resulting attribute profiles on some preference scale. Typically, these attribute profiles are placed into choice sets and the choices are usually not constrained to satisfy any budget constraint. However, if the choice model should satisfy budget constraints, this complicates the design of the experiment as the choice percentages must sum to 100 percent. When the attribute levels are subject to this, standard mixture designs for fitting standard models, such as *simplex-lattice* designs and *simplex-centroid* designs can be used. When mixture components are subject to additional constraints, such as a maximum and/or minimum value for each component, designs other than the standard mixture designs, referred to as constrained mixture designs or *extreme-vertices* designs, are appropriate. The mixture components are non-negative proportionate amounts of the mixture. It is also possible that the allocation only concerns a fraction. In this case, the variable proportions can be rewritten as scaled fractions so that the scaled fractions sum to one.

For example, suppose there are q independent variables that are constrained to a q-dimensional dependent space. If we present the proportion of the ith component in the mixture by x_i, then:

$$x_i \geq 0 \ (1 \leq i \leq q), \ \sum_{i=1}^{q} x_i = 1. \tag{10.1}$$

Since the proportion x_i could be equal to unity, a mixture may be considered comprising only one component. Hence the factor space containing the q components may be geometrically represented by the interior and boundaries of a regular $(q - 1)$ dimensional simplex. The vertices will

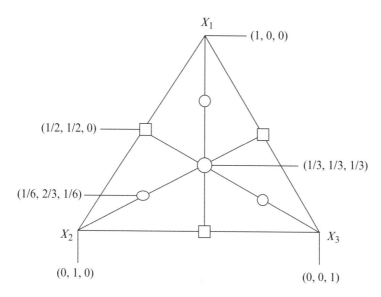

Figure 10.1 Q-dimensional simplex space for three experimental variables

represent mixtures consisting of single components, and interior points will be the result of combining all the components. Corresponding to the points in a $\{q, m\}$ lattice, the proportions used for each of the q components have $m + 1$ equally spaced values from 0 to 1. The 10 mixtures of $\{3, 2\}$ lattice are displayed in Figure 10.1 (Cornell, 1973). All points on the surface or in the interior of the simplex sum to one. It shows the typical simplex coordinates of the three vertices; (1, 0, 0), (0, 1, 0), and (0, 0, 1), and the center point; with coordinates (1/3, 1/3, 1/3). In addition, it shows the three edge midpoints; with coordinates (1/2, 1/2, 0), (1/2, 0, 1/2), and (0, 1/2, 1/2), and three interior points; with coordinates (2/3, 1/6, 1/6), (1/6, 2/3, 1/6), and (1/6, 1/6, 2/3).

In mixture experiments, the measured response is assumed to depend only on the relative proportions of the components in the mixture and not on the amount of the mixture. However, the amount of the mixture (that is, the total available budget) can also be varied as an additional factor in the experiment. These are so-called 'mixture–amount' experiments.

In the standard mixture formulation, the response is said to depend only on the proportions of mixture components. In a cost-based mixture approach to conjoint analyses, alternatives consist of profiles in which the costs of the mixture components satisfy the inequalities and the combined cost of the mixture components is the same for all profiles. That is,

$$\sum_{i=1}^{q} (c_i/A) = 1.$$

Where c_i is the cost of mixture component i, A is the total amount to be spent $c_i/A = x_i$. Simplex lattice designs $\{q, m\}$ are a class of mixture designs in which the proportion taken by each component is $m + 1$ equally spaced values from 0 to 1, $x_i = 0, 1/m, 2/m, \ldots, 1; i = 1,2,\ldots, q$ (Cornell, 1973). All possible combinations of these are used such that:

$$\sum_{i=1}^{q} x_i = 1.$$

To illustrate, the general first-degree polynomial for expressing a dependent variable U in terms of the i variables $x_1, x_2, \ldots, x_i$ is:

$$U = \sum_{i=1}^{q} \beta_i x_i, \tag{10.2}$$

and the second-degree model is:

$$U = \sum_{i=1}^{q} \beta_i x_i + \sum_{\substack{i,j=1 \\ i<j}}^{q} \beta_{ij} x_i x_j. \tag{10.3}$$

As the total amount of cost and their allocation can affect the response, different amount levels could be considered in a mixture–amount experiment (Raghavarao and Wiley, 2009). The total amount of cost or saving is denoted by A, and the r different levels of A by $a_1, a_2, \ldots, a_r$ $(r \geq 2)$. The utility function can then be expressed as:

$$U = \alpha a + \gamma a^2 + \sum_{i=1}^{q-1} \beta_i a x_i + \sum_{i=1}^{q} \beta_i x_i + \sum_{\substack{i,j=1 \\ i<j}}^{q} \beta_{ij} x_i x_j \tag{10.4}$$

In addition, the function can also be extended with terms that represent the effects of context variables on the dependent variable such as equation (10.5) in step 5 of Section 10.3. To that effect, the mixture–amount design needs to be embedded or combined with a design varying the context conditions. This process comes down to the completion of a series of mixture–amount experiments, one for each of the conditions of the context.

10.3 CONTEXT-DEPENDENT MIXTURE–AMOUNT EXPERIMENTAL DESIGNS

The design of these extended mixture–amount experiments involves the following steps. We shall explain these steps using consumer adaptation to increasing energy prices as an example. In the Netherlands, between 1996 and 2001, gas prices increased by 72 percent for domestic use, while electricity prices increased almost 50 percent. Thus, to make the illustration realistic, we assume the scenario that consumers will face the situation that their total energy expenditure has dramatically increased by around 25 percent. As a result, their energy bill will increase by €55 per month. The aim of the study is to analyze if (how much) and how consumers will save on their expenditures to compensate for this increase. More specifically, we want to estimate their preference for alternative (combinations of) saving strategies.

10.3.1 Step 1: Identify Mixture Components

Similar to the design of any stated preference design, we should start with the selection and definition of the mixture components that are of policy interest and/or assumed to influence consumer preferences and choices. According to the literature, household energy conservation behavior can be divided into two categories: efficiency and curtailment behaviors (Gardner and Stern, 2002). Considering transportation and residential sectors, there would be four basic energy-saving options: efficiency and curtailment behaviors for transportation, such as buying an energy-efficiency car or using more slow transport modes, and efficiency and curtailment behaviors for residential sectors, such as purchase of energy-efficient equipment for home or lowering thermostat settings. It should be noted that although the energy-saving potential of efficiency behavior is considered greater than that of curtailment behaviors, energy-efficient appliances do not necessarily result in a reduction of total energy consumption when people use these applications more often (for example, Berkhout et al., 2000). The importance of the interplay between efficiency and curtailment behaviors becomes apparent. Thus, let us assume that consumers can choose between (a combination of) three alternative strategies: (i) invest in an energy-efficient car; (ii) adjust their activity travel patterns to reduce their fuel consumption and/or (iii) change their behavior at home – invest in energy-saving home appliances.

10.3.2 Step 2: Create Design to Vary the Mixtures

Thus, assume that we have these three mixture components. The mixture of the attributes is denoted by x_1, x_2 and x_3 ($0 \le x_1, x_2, x_3 \le 1$ and $x_1 + x_2 + x_3 = 1$). That is, subjects can choose to save on energy either by choosing one of these options or by some combination (mixture). Consequently, the sum of these mixtures is equal to 1. We then need to construct a design that systematically varies these mixtures. The simplex lattice design {3, 3} creates 10 mixtures:

{1, 0, 0},   {1/3, 0, 2/3},
{0, 1, 0},   {1/3, 1/3, 1/3},
{0, 0, 1},   {1/3, 2/3, 0},
{2/3, 1/3, 0},   {2/3, 0, 1/3},
{0, 2/3, 1/3},   {0, 1/3, 2/3}.

Alternatively, as suggested by Raghavarao and Padgett (2005), a good design of block size 3 is a balanced incomplete block design. This design is shown in Table 10.1.

10.3.3 Step 3: Create Design to Vary the Amounts

Further, we assume that there are three amounts: a_1, a_2, and a_3. If these amounts are varied in the experiment, it allows one to analyze whether preferences for or choice of a certain mixture, depend on the amount (in our example, savings). Assume that there are three amounts of savings: a_1 (€55), a_2 (€40), and a_3 (€25). We can nest the design in Table 10.1 under these different savings, and produce a set of mixture–amount combinations. It involves 21 combinations as shown in Table 10.2. Respondents may be asked to rate these combinations on a scale from 1 to 10, 10 indicating the

Table 10.1   Three components mixture design

Mixture	Component 1	Component 2	Component 3
1	1	0	0
2	0	1	0
3	0	0	1
4	2/3	1/3	0
5	0	2/3	1/3
6	1/3	0	2/3
7	1/3	1/3	1/3

Table 10.2   Rating task design

Mixture–amount combination	Mixture component 1	Mixture component 2	Mixture component 3	Energy saving amount
1	25.00	0.00	0.00	25.00
2	0.00	25.00	0.00	25.00
3	0.00	0.00	25.00	25.00
4	16.67	8.33	0.00	25.00
5	0.00	16.67	8.33	25.00
6	8.33	0.00	16.67	25.00
7	8.33	8.33	8.33	25.00
8	40.00	0.00	0.00	40.00
9	0.00	40.00	0.00	40.00
10	0.00	0.00	40.00	40.00
11	26.67	13.33	0.00	40.00
12	0.00	26.67	13.33	40.00
13	13.33	0.00	26.67	40.00
14	13.33	13.33	13.33	40.00
15	55.00	0.00	0.00	55.00
16	0.00	55.00	0.00	55.00
17	0.00	0.00	55.00	55.00
18	36.67	18.33	0.00	55.00
19	0.00	36.67	18.33	55.00
20	18.33	0.00	36.67	55.00
21	18.33	18.33	18.33	55.00

highest evaluation score. These measurements will thus reflect people's preferences for different mixture–amount combinations.

10.3.4   Step 4: Identify Context Variables

If we assume that these preferences depend on context, in the next step context variables and their conditions should be identified. The approach, suggested by Oppewal and Timmermans (1991), can then also be applied to these mixture–amount experiments. Assuming that we have two context variables w_1 (season) and w_2 (amount of luggage if any to carry), each with two levels: w_{11} (late autumn or winter), w_{12} (other season), w_{21} (heavy luggage) and w_{22} (no heavy luggage). We thus have four possible combinations of context: {1, 1}, {1, –1}, {–1, 1} and {–1, –1}. Note that one condition for each context variable is coded as –1. The total design would thus contain four context profiles and 21 mixture–amounts for each of the four context profiles. For each profile, respondents may be asked to rate their preference for a mixture–amount combination. It should be noted that less demanding designs may be constructed, but that is beyond the present chapter.

10.3.5   Step 5: Specify Context-dependent Mixture–Amount Model

As discussed before, equation (10.4) represents the core equation of the mixture–amount model. As assumed before, we have two context variables w_1 ($l = 2$). The differentiating effects of these context conditions can be measured by estimating the interactions of the elements of equation (10.4) and the context variables. The result is equation (10.5):

$$U(E) = \alpha a_r + \gamma a_r^2 + \sum_{i=1}^{2} \beta_i a_r x_i + \sum_{i=1}^{3} \beta_i x_i + \sum_{\substack{i,j=1 \\ i<j}}^{3} \beta_{ij} x_i x_j + \sum_{l=1}^{2} w_l \times$$

$$(\alpha a_r + \gamma a_r^2 + \sum_{i=1}^{2} \beta_i a_r x_i + \sum_{i=1}^{3} \beta_i x_i + \sum_{\substack{i,j=1 \\ i<j}}^{3} \beta_{ij} x_i x_j). \tag{10.5}$$

In this equation, as we assumed before, there are three amounts and three mixture components, and hence $q = r = 3$. Let $U(E)$ be the rating response for a context-dependent combination of a mixture–amount E, and a_r ($r = 3$) represent the amount of energy savings. In equation (10.5), we assume that the relationship between utility and amount of savings is potentially non-linear as represented by the first two terms of equation (10.5). The next term depicts the interaction effects of amounts and mixtures on utility. Note that we do not use the term $a_r x_3$, because $x_1 + x_2 + x_3 = 1$. The next two terms pick up any effect of a combination of the mixture beyond their single effects on the utility. Finally, the last part expresses the influence of the two context variables in terms of interactions with all other variables of the model.

10.4   ILLUSTRATION

We illustrate the suggested approach based on artificial data using energy conservation strategy as an example. Table 10.2 shows the rating data. As explained in the experimental design, there are four context profiles. For example, in context (profile) 1 (late autumn or winter and heavy luggage when traveling), the first seven ratings involve the amount of €25, the next seven ratings from row 8 to 14 relate to the amount of €40, and the last seven ratings from row 15 to 21 relate to €55. A similar pattern can be recognized for

Table 10.3   Results of OLS regression

Variable	Coefficient	*t*-statistic	Variable	Coefficient	*t*-statistic
a	0.4113	2.9064	w1x2	−2.7226	−0.9575
a2	−0.0052	−3.0381	w1x3	−3.2226	−1.1333
ax1	0.0521	1.0765	w1x1x2	−1.5114	−0.6058
ax2	0.0354	0.7320	w1x1x3	−0.5114	−0.2050
x1	−5.9675	−2.0986	w1x2x3	3.8636	1.5486
x2	−3.5509	−1.2488	w2a	0.0210	0.1486
x3	−2.8842	−1.0143	w2a2	−0.0002	−0.0921
x1x2	1.3977	0.5602	w2ax1	0.0062	0.1292
x1x3	−0.8523	−0.3416	w2ax2	0.0187	0.3875
x2x3	7.0227	2.8148	w2x1	−1.4953	−0.5259
w1a	0.1516	1.0711	w2x2	−0.7453	−0.2621
w1a2	−0.0017	−1.0127	w2x3	−0.7453	−0.2621
w1ax1	−0.0063	−0.1292	w2x1x2	−2.3523	−0.9428
w1ax2	0.0062	0.1292	w2x1x3	−0.1023	−0.0410
w1x1	−2.3059	−0.8109	w2x2x3	1.7727	0.7105

Note: Context variables *w* were coded as: late autumn or winter as −1, other seasons 1; taking heavy luggage as −1, no heavy luggage 1. Adjusted *R*-square: 0.859.

the other three contexts. Using the hypothetical ratings given in Table 10A.1 in the appendix, OLS regression analysis can be used to estimate the utility function. Results are shown in Table 10.3. The adjusted *R*-squared value of 0.859 indicates that the estimated model performs quite well.

The coefficients reflect the contribution of the corresponding variable to the utility (preference rating). The positive sign for the amount variable suggests that utility increases with an increase in the amount of savings, suggesting that respondents would be willing on average to save to compensate for increasing energy bills. Examining the estimated parameters of the mixtures and their interaction in this hypothetical illustration, the sign and value associated with the parameters indicate which saving option people prefer more. The signs of w_2 represent the influence of context variables. For example, the positive sign of the estimated coefficient for w_1a (late autumn or winter) indicates that respondents are less willing to save on energy in late autumn or winter than in other seasons. Remember that $w_1 = -1$. Similarly, the positive sign of the estimated coefficient for w_2a (traveling with heavy luggage) suggests that people are less willing to save energy when traveling with heavy luggage. In addition, the change in coefficients for the mixtures and their interactions with different context conditions suggest which option is especially preferred or disliked in different contexts.

Figure 10.2 shows the quadratic relationship between $U(E)$ and context.

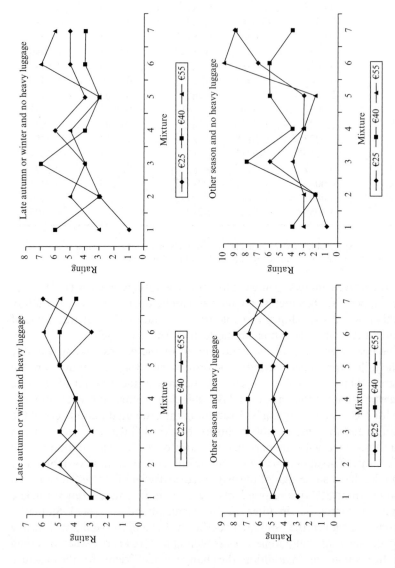

Figure 10.2 Relation between U(E) *and context*

It shows that there is less sensitivity in willingness to save energy consumption when it is late autumn or winter and/or when consumers need to carry heavy luggage when traveling. When the context situation changes, preference shifts from one mixture to another. For example, in the cold season when people do not need to travel with heavy luggage, they prefer the third mixture, but in warm seasons when they have to travel with heavy luggage, their preference shifts from saving only at home to a combination of an energy-efficient car and saving energy at home. Consequently, their preference for the amount to save will also change.

10.5   SUMMARY AND CONCLUSIONS

In this chapter, we discussed the principles of designing mixture–amount experiments and proposed an extended context-dependent mixture–amount model. This modeling approach may be potentially relevant for those cases, where we wish to model consumer response to policies for which no historical data (actual choices in real markets) exist, budget constraints are deemed important in the analysis, and utilities may be context dependent. An example illustrated the approach. While the present approach considered preference ratings, the approach can be extended to choice data. The construction of the design in this case becomes slightly more complicated. We plan to collect data along these lines and report the results in future publications. In the meantime, the approach may be relevant to other constrained choices.

NOTE

*   The research leading to these results has received funding from the European Research Council under the European Community's Seventh Framework Programme (FP7/2007–2013) / ERC grant agreement no. 230517 (U4IA project). The views and opinions expressed in this publication represent those of the authors only. The ERC and European Community are not liable for any use that may be made of the information in this publication.

REFERENCES

Arentze. T., Hofman, F. and Timmermans, H.J.P., 2004. 'Predicting multi-faced activity–travel adjustment strategies in response to possible congestion pricing scenarios using an internet based stated adaptation experiment', *Transport Policy* **11**, 31–41.

Berkhout, P.H.G., Muskens, J.C.W. and Velthuijsen, J., 2000. 'Defining the rebound effect', *Energy Policy* **28**, 425–32.

Caussade, S., Ortuzar, J., Rizzi, L. and Hensher, D.A., 2005. 'Assessing the influence of design dimensions on stated choice experiment estimates', *Transportation Research B* **39**, 621–40.

Cornell, J.A., 1973. 'Experiments with mixtures: a review', *Technometrics* **15**, 437–55.

Doherty, S.T. and Miller, D.J., 2000. 'A computerized household activity scheduling survey', *Transportation* **27**, 75–97.

Doherty, S.T., Lee-Gosselin, M., Burns, K. and Andrey, J., 2002. 'Household activity rescheduling in response to automobile reduction scenarios', *Transportation Research Board* **1807**, 174–81.

Gardner, G.T. and Stern, P.C., 2002. *Environmental Problems and Human Behavior*, Boston, MA: Pearson.

Hensher, D.A., 1994. 'Stated preference analysis of travel choices: the state of practice', *Transportation* **21**, 107–33.

Hess, S., Axhausen, K.W. and Polak, J.W., 2006. 'Distributional assumptions in mixed logit models', Proceedings of the 85th Annual Meeting of the Transportation Research Board, Washington, DC, January 22–26.

Lee-Gosselin, M.E.H., 1989. 'In-depth research on lifestyle and household car use under future conditions in Canada', in: International Association for Travel Behaviour Research, *Travel Behaviour Research*, Aldershot: Avebury, pp. 102–18.

Louviere, J., Hensher, D.A., Swait, J.D. and Adamowicz, W., 2000. *Stated Choice Methods: Analysis and applications*, Cambridge and New York: Cambridge University Press.

Oppewal, H. and Timmermans, H.J.P., 1991. 'Context effects and decompositional choice modeling', *Journal of Regional Science* **70**, 113–31.

Phifer, S.P., Neveu, A.J. and Hartgen, D.T., 1980. 'Family reactions to energy constraints', *Transportation Research Record* **765**, 12–16.

Raghavarao, D. and Padgett, L.V., 2005. *Block Designs: Analysis, Combinatorics and Applications*, Singapore: World Scientific Publications.

Raghavarao, D. and Wiley, J. B., 2009. 'Conjoint measurement with constraints on attribute levels: a mixture–amount model approach', *International Statistical Review* **77**, 167–78.

Van der Waerden, P., Borgers, A., Timmermans, H.J.P. and Berenos, M., 2006. 'Order effects in stated choice experiments: a study of transport mode choice decisions', Proceedings of the 85th Annual Meeting of the Transportation Research Board, Washington, DC, January 22–26.

APPENDIX 10A

Table 10A.1   List of ratings for mixture–amount combinations in four different contexts

Profile	Rating	Buy energy-efficient car	Use more energy-efficient transport modes	Buy energy-efficient installations and/or use less energy at home	Energy saving amount
Profile 1 (Late autumn or winter and heavy luggage)					
1	2	25.00	0.00	0.00	25
2	6	0.00	25.00	0.00	25
3	4	0.00	0.00	25.00	25
4	4	16.67	8.33	0.00	25
5	5	0.00	16.67	8.33	25
6	3	8.33	0.00	16.67	25
7	6	8.33	8.33	8.33	25
8	3	40.00	0.00	0.00	40
9	3	0.00	40.00	0.00	40
10	5	0.00	0.00	40.00	40
11	4	26.67	13.33	0.00	40
12	5	0.00	26.67	13.33	40
13	5	13.33	0.00	26.67	40
14	4	13.33	13.33	13.33	40
15	3	55.00	0.00	0.00	55
16	5	0.00	55.00	0.00	55
17	3	0.00	0.00	55.00	55
18	4	36.67	18.33	0.00	55
19	5	0.00	36.67	18.33	55
20	6	18.33	0.00	36.67	55
21	5	18.33	18.33	18.33	55
Profile 2 (Late autumn or winter and no heavy luggage)					
1	1	25.00	0.00	0.00	25
2	3	0.00	25.00	0.00	25
3	4	0.00	0.00	25.00	25
4	6	16.67	8.33	0.00	25
5	4	0.00	16.67	8.33	25
6	5	8.33	0.00	16.67	25
7	5	8.33	8.33	8.33	25
8	6	40.00	0.00	0.00	40
9	3	0.00	40.00	0.00	40
10	7	0.00	0.00	40.00	40
11	4	26.67	13.33	0.00	40
12	3	0.00	26.67	13.33	40
13	4	13.33	0.00	26.67	40

Table 10A.1 (continued)

Profile	Rating	Buy energy-efficient car	Use more energy-efficient transport modes	Buy energy-efficient installations and/or use less energy at home	Energy saving amount
Profile 2 (Late autumn or winter and no heavy luggage)					
14	4	13.33	13.33	13.33	40
15	3	55.00	0.00	0.00	55
16	5	0.00	55.00	0.00	55
17	4	0.00	0.00	55.00	55
18	5	36.67	18.33	0.00	55
19	3	0.00	36.67	18.33	55
20	7	18.33	0.00	36.67	55
21	6	18.33	18.33	18.33	55
Profile 3 (Other season and heavy luggage)					
1	3	25.00	0.00	0.00	25
2	4	0.00	25.00	0.00	25
3	5	0.00	0.00	25.00	25
4	5	16.67	8.33	0.00	25
5	5	0.00	16.67	8.33	25
6	4	8.33	0.00	16.67	25
7	7	8.33	8.33	8.33	25
8	5	40.00	0.00	0.00	40
9	4	0.00	40.00	0.00	40
10	7	0.00	0.00	40.00	40
11	7	26.67	13.33	0.00	40
12	6	0.00	26.67	13.33	40
13	8	13.33	0.00	26.67	40
14	5	13.33	13.33	13.33	40
15	5	55.00	0.00	0.00	55
16	6	0.00	55.00	0.00	55
17	4	0.00	0.00	55.00	55
18	5	36.67	18.33	0.00	55
19	4	0.00	36.67	18.33	55
20	7	18.33	0.00	36.67	55
21	6	18.33	18.33	18.33	55
Profile 4 (Other season and no heavy luggage)					
1	1	25.00	0.00	0.00	25
2	2	0.00	25.00	0.00	25
3	6	0.00	0.00	25.00	25
4	3	16.67	8.33	0.00	25
5	3	0.00	16.67	8.33	25
6	7	8.33	0.00	16.67	25
7	9	8.33	8.33	8.33	25
8	4	40.00	0.00	0.00	40

Table 10A.1   (continued)

Profile	Rating	Buy energy-efficient car	Use more energy-efficient transport modes	Buy energy-efficient installations and/or use less energy at home	Energy saving amount
Profile 4 (Other season and no heavy luggage)					
9	2	0.00	40.00	0.00	40
10	8	0.00	0.00	40.00	40
11	4	26.67	13.33	0.00	40
12	6	0.00	26.67	13.33	40
13	6	13.33	0.00	26.67	40
14	4	13.33	13.33	13.33	40
15	3	55.00	0.00	0.00	55
16	3	0.00	55.00	0.00	55
17	4	0.00	0.00	55.00	55
18	3	36.67	18.33	0.00	55
19	2	0.00	36.67	18.33	55
20	10	18.33	0.00	36.67	55
21	9	18.33	18.33	18.33	55

11. Smart governance and the management of sustainable mobility: an illustration of the application of policy integration and transition management in the Port of Rotterdam

Harry Geerlings and Bart Kuipers

11.1 INTRODUCTION

Transport has many positive characteristics both for the individual user and for society as a whole. This explains why the transport sector, for more then a century now, has experienced an unprecedented growth. At the same time, transport has undesired side-effects. The almost unlimited demand for transport leads to congestion, and at the same time there are other serious concerns related to emissions (at the regional, national and the global levels), safety, health issues, and resource management. These concerns are encompassed in the concept of sustainability and sustainable mobility.

Governments and other stakeholders are generally aware that policy measures are needed to find a balance between accessibility and sustainability. This is an enormous challenge, and the question arises: how can this be materialised? The challenge is often presented as the need for policy integration and a transition towards a sustainable transport system and new governance initiatives, such as transition management.

The sometimes seemingly opposing goals of accessibility and sustainability are also coming together in the Port of Rotterdam. The port invests in the development of new port capacity, the 'Second Maasvlakte' – an extension of the port including large-scale container infrastructure. A major problem related to this port extension is the accessibility of the Second Maasvlakte and the effects on the quality of life in the surrounding urban areas. Despite a powerful modal shift policy aimed at transferring cargo from truck to barge and rail, it is expected that cargo flows by road will increase significantly. Because of the negative effects related to this growth, a new governance approach is needed. This chapter presents an innovative governance approach to meeting the goals of sustainability, accessibility and acceptability in the Port of Rotterdam area, based on the theoretical concept of the governance of complex systems.

11.2 THE DEMAND FOR SUSTAINABLE TRANSPORT

The concern for the environmental burden caused by human action has been noted for many years and is reflected in numerous reports and policy documents (see, for instance, Meadows et al., 1970). The discussion first gained momentum by the introduction of the concept of sustainable development in the 1980s. One of the first references to the term 'sustainable development' appeared in UNCED's 1980 World Conservation Strategy. Later, in 1987, the World Commission for Environment and Development (WCED, 1987, p. 15) described the concept of sustainable development more extensively in their report 'Our Common Future' (the Brundtland Report). In this report, sustainable development is defined as: 'a development that meets the needs of the present without compromising the ability of future generations to meet their own needs'. It is interpreted by Geerlings et al. (2009a, p. 405) as 'a process of change in which the exploitation of resources, the direction of investment, the orientation of technical development, and institutional change are all in harmony and enhance both current and future potential to meet human needs and aspirations'.

As a result, the thinking about sustainable development in relation to technological development also received considerable attention. On the international level, the discussion then received a new impetus from the Rio Summit organised by the United Nations Conference on Environment and Development (UNCED) 1992, where the action plan Agenda 21 (United Nations, 1992) was adopted in which 'sustainable development' was chosen as the leading principle for future development.

However, as yet there is, no universally accepted definition of sustainability, sustainable development, or sustainable transport. The Brundtland report interprets sustainable development as a process of change in which the exploitation of resources, the direction of investments, the orientation of technical development, and institutional change are all in harmony, and enhance both current and future potential to meet human needs and aspirations. In the WCED report (1987) on sustainable development, three interrelated systems are identified: the ecological system (the exploitation of resources); the economic system (investments and technological development); and the socio-cultural system (institutional change). These systems are interrelated and these interrelations can be expressed as functions. Two of these are the production function and the regeneration function. The three interrelated systems are also presented as the triple-P approach, which refers to the balance between planet (the ecological system), profit (the economic system) and people (the socio-cultural system). In policy making this is a commonly used terminology.

Sustainable development distinguishes several, sometimes seemingly opposing, goals, which make it very difficult to find synergy between these different goals. Especially in matters where finding the right balance between ecological and economic aspects is concerned, development in harmony with sustainability will be more difficult to put into operation. It is one of those concepts which 'inevitably involve endless disputes about their proper uses on the part of their users', and 'to engage in such disputes is itself to engage in politics' (Lukes, 2002, p.45). In other words, the concept of sustainable development implies that it is subjective and dynamic with different degrees of freedom.

Sustainability is sometimes defined narrowly. Some studies of sustainability focus on long-term resource depletion and air pollution problems, on the grounds that they represent the greatest risk and are prone to being neglected by conventional planning (TRB, 1997). Other studies dealing with sustainable transport, stress the need to find a balance between accessibility and sustainability (Geerlings et al., 2009b).

Given the serious impact of transport, there is growing interest in the concepts of sustainability and sustainable transport. Transport systems exist to provide social and economic connections, and people quickly tend to take up the opportunities offered by increased mobility. But sustainability is increasingly being defined more broadly to include the range of issues listed in Table 11.1.

Table 11.1   Sustainability issues

Economic (profit)	Environmental (planet)	Social (people)
Affordability	Pollution prevention	Equity
Resource efficiency	Climate protection	Human health
Cost internalisation	Biodiversity	Education
Trade and business activity	Precautionary action	Community
Employment	Avoidance of irreversibility	Quality of life
Productivity	Habitat preservation	Public participation
Tax burden	Aesthetics	

Source: TRB (2008).

It is also important to stress that the concept of sustainable mobility is not a static situation that can be described in the sustainability issues as presented above. The concept of sustainability has to be achieved over time, and is part of a process (temporal aspects) which also manifests on a spatial scale (spatial aspects). The concept of sustainability is being translated and applied in many different sectors, such as agriculture, production processes and energy conservation. It is also being applied in the transport sector. Sustainable transport, according to a report by the Transportation Research Board (TRB, 2008), is a transport system which:

1.   allows the basic access and development needs of people to be met safely and is consistent with human and ecosystem health, and promotes equity within and between successive generations;
2.   is affordable, operates fairly and efficiently, offers a choice of transport mode and supports a competitive economy, as well as balanced regional development; and
3.   limits emissions and waste, and uses resources at the level of generation or development, while minimising the impact on the use of land and the generation of noise.

But in the development of the transport sector and all its external effects, this optimum situation rarely occurs (Banister, 2008). This is largely due to the characteristics of the external effects. The negative external effects of motorised transport are quite substantial in significant ways. In terms of timescales, some are instantaneous (for example, noise), some are pervasive (for example, hydrocarbons), some are permanent (for example, visual intrusion), and others are cumulative (for example, CO_2). Spatially, there is a clear distinction between those adverse effects that have a direct impact at the place where they are generated (for example, emissions of lead) and those which are transported through the air on a continental or even a global scale (CO_2). Some of the impacts are associated with direct physical effects and can easily be measured (SO_2); others, particularly those affecting public health and the quality of urban life, are more subtle, and less susceptible to objective measurement and so on.

From a societal perspective there is, for instance, a tension between improving accessibility and the increase of emissions or between economic growth and increasing congestion. It is expected that the environmental interest will increase in importance, and will have implications for the transport sector.

11.3   THE GOVERNANCE REFLEX

11.3.1   The Traditional Approach

Traditional, transport planning aims to improve mobility, especially with respect to the usage of vehicles, but may fail to adequately consider the wider or long-term impacts (Geerlings and Van Meijeren, 2008). This is also reflected in policy-making experiences in modern times. The ideology of a welfare state was generally accepted.

There was also a new spirit within political science, where governments were encouraged to claim a central role in society to provide guidance for these new prospects. Therefore, a new policy steering paradigm was developed. This paradigm, which we now consider to be the 'classical steering paradigm' in political science, identifies the relationship between the policy maker and the public as the central object of study.

After all the expectations raised by new management tools and the government policies developed in the 1950s, 1960s and 1970s, the results actually achieved were disappointing. The failures of government policies were reflected in new types of problems, such as economic recessions, unemployment and environmental problems. It appeared that the execution of each policy measure had its own dynamics. Consequently, policies were less effective than expected, the effects of policies were addressed to the wrong group, and the production of procedures and legislation took more time than was expected. There are various explanations for the failure of government policies: first, the problems confronting society became increasingly complex; second, an increasing number of actors became involved in the decision process ('administrative pressure'); and third, there was an increasing interdependence between (related) policy areas.

As a result, a debate took place on the role of the central rationale and central directing role of government in society. The conclusion was that the classical steering paradigm was not capable of implementing effective policies of central governments (In't Veld, 1989). It became accepted opinion that these failures have led to a strong decline in the legitimacy of governments and governmental agencies, on both the international and the national levels; hierarchically organised governments created bureaucracies, were less efficient, and were mainly focused on their own interests.

These developments are also recognisable in the transport sector, which is a complex system that depends on multiple actors and factors, including the pattern of human settlements and consumption, the organisation of production, and the availability of infrastructures. This means that decision making in the transport sector is often a complex issue. Any intervention to make the transport system more sustainable must be based on a long-term vision concerning the goals of sustainable mobility for people and goods, not least because policies of a structural character take a long time to be implemented successfully. Recently we have observed the need to address new and very complicated policy challenges, such as global warming, and to transform transport into real sustainable transport. It is now time for a new policy paradigm that focuses on a transition management in the transport industry.

11.3.2   The Need for an Integrative Action Perspective

Due to the complexity of policy making, there is an increasing demand for policy integration. This is also the case when it comes to the ambition to realise a sustainable transport system, where seemingly contrasting issues such as economic growth and the related negative external effects, increasing emissions for example, have to be solved (the balance between the three Ps). Policy integration in the context of sustainability has been on the agenda since the1980s, particularly since UNCED 1992. The concept gained in importance when the EU launched a series of environmental action programmes, and in the inclusion and strengthening of the integration requirement in successive amendments to the EC Treaty. The literature on policy integration comes from general studies in policy science, organisational science and political studies, and is not specific to the integration of land-use, transport and environment policies.

Within the literature concerning the theory on policy integration, various concepts can be identified (for a more detailed review, see Geerlings and Stead, 2003). These include 'coherent policy making', 'cross-cutting policy-making', 'policy coordination' and 'holistic government', also known as 'joined-up policy' or 'joined-up government'. While some authors see policy coordination as more or less the same as integrated policy making, others regard them as quite separate and distinct. The OECD, for example, observes that policy integration is quite distinct from and more sophisticated than policy coordination in two ways: (i) the level of interaction; and (ii) the output (OECD, 1996). Stead et al. (2004) distinguish between a number of distinct terms and suggest a hierarchy of these terms (Figure 11.1):

1. *policy cooperation*, at the lowest level, which simply implies dialogue and information;
2. *policy coordination, policy coherence* and *policy consistency* – all quite similar, implying cooperation plus transparency and some attempt to avoid policy conflicts (but not necessarily by making use of similar goals); and
3. *policy integration* and *joined-up policy* – includes dialogue and

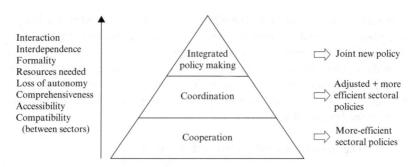

Source: Stead and Geerlings (2005, p. 445).

Figure 11.1   Different levels of policy cooperation and integration

information (as in policy cooperation), transparency and avoidance of policy conflicts (as in policy coordination, policy coherence and policy consistency) but also includes joint working, attempts to create synergies between policies (win – win situations) and the use of the same goals to formulate policy.

This need for integration is also recognisable in the transport sector. As stated above, the transport sector is a complex system that depends on multiple actors and factors, including the pattern of human settlements and consumption, the organisation of production, and the availability of infrastructure. This means that decision making in the transport sector is often a complex issue. Any intervention to make the transport system more sustainable must be based on a long-term vision concerning the goals of sustainable mobility for people and goods, not least because policies of a structural character take a long time to be successfully implemented. We can observe, partly because of the need to address new and very compli-cated policy challenges such as global warming and to transform transport into real sustainable transport that is now time for a new policy paradigm that focuses on a transition management. For instance, in the Netherlands we have recently witnessed an increasing focus on integrated policy making with respect to spatial, environmental and transport policies. Programmes such as 'Nota Ruimte en Mobiliteit' (2006–07) (Ministerie voor Verkeer en Waterstaat en Ministerie voor Volksgezondheid en Milieuhygiëne VROM, 2008), 'Mooi Nederland' (from 2008 onwards) (Ministerie voor Volksgezondheid en Milieuhygiëne, 2008) and the Zuidvleugelprojecten 'Stedenbaan' (from 2006 onwards) (Bestuurlijk Overleg MIRT, 2006; Programmabureau Stedenbaan Zuidvleugel, 2008) and 'Deltapoort' (also from 2006 onwards) (Programmabureau Deltapoort Zuidvleugel, 2008) underline the need for an integrated approach of the different challenges in spatial policy making. In mobility policy making we also see the traces of this approach. It was in 2008 when the Elverding Commission (Commissie Elverding, 2008) advocated the creation of a spatial structure plan as the basis for decisions about mobility and infrastructure. And the traditional MIT survey (MIT: Multi-annual program Infrastructure and Transport), a survey dedicated to planning priorities in infrastructure investment, has since become the MIRT, to illustrate the need for integrating spatial interests (the R stands for *ruimte* = space). The transition from MIT to MIRT is in fact an illustration of the search for a new integrative action perspective. This illustrates that there is awareness among governments and other stakeholders that new approaches and policy measures are needed.

11.4 THE APPLICATION OF NEW LEADING PRINCIPLES IN TRANSPORT

11.4.1 The Emerging Concept of Transition Management

New principles of policy making for the transport sector that need to be introduced should be based on a set of priorities which are in balance with the importance to facilitate transport, but which also specify enhanced criteria from the point of view of sustainable development. The priority is prevention, modal shift, optimisation and facilitation.

The pyramid shown in Figure 11.2 (known as a priority ladder) presents options and types of transport that could identify policies to alleviate

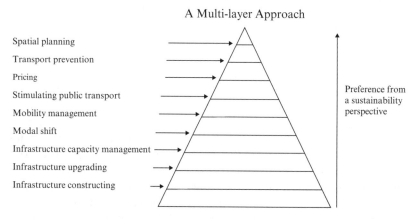

Figure 11.2   Priority pyramid for the development of sustainable transport policies

transport problems. The fact that transport growth cannot proceed at the same speed as the expansion of the required infrastructure shows that coping with the increased demand of transport by infrastructure construction (bottom of the pyramid) does not comply with sustainability perspectives. In fact, it often leads to more congestion. On the other hand, integrating transport and spatial planning may result in a more sustainable outcome with, for example, reduced travel demand and an increase in non-motorised transport.

In the field of transport, there is a general awareness among governments and other stakeholders that new approaches and policy measures are needed to find a balance between accessibility and sustainability. Evolving within the framework of policy making, one of these new approaches is 'transition management'.

Transition studies refers to a field of research that focuses on 'transitions', generally defined as non-linear processes of social change in which a societal system is structurally transformed (Avelino, 2011). A 'sustainability transition' generally refers to a 'radical transformation towards a sustainable society as a response to a number of persistent problems confronting contemporary modern societies' (Grin et al., 2010, p. 57). One of the central premises in transition studies is that persistent problems are symptoms of unsustainable societies, and that dealing with these persistent problems in order to enable more sustainable systems, requires transitions and system innovations. Transition research has its intellectual roots in innovation studies as found in social studies of technology (Geels, 2005).

The new approach of transition management seems to evolve in a natural way from the existing process-oriented perspectives and the dynamics of integrated system innovation. Transition management is defined by Rotmans (2003, p. 22) as 'a management strategy for public decision makers and private actors that deals with the question how and to what extent complex societal transformation processes can be directed in a certain desirable direction'.

The theoretical concept of transitions refers to a transformation process in which society changes in a fundamental way over a generation or more. Transitions can best be understood as gradual transformation processes as a result of simultaneous developments in different societal domains and the combined action of macro-, meso- and micro-level developments (Rotmans, 2003). Transition management can also be described as a governance model for sustainable development, as a specific policy discourse and as a field of academic research. Transition management differs from classical management or innovation management in that it is not so much concerned with achieving predefined results, but rather with orienting development towards sustainability goals, while acknowledging that the exact outcomes of this development are unknown. Transition management is a governance approach which *makes the future more clearly manifest in current decisions*, by adopting longer timeframes, exploring alternative trajectories, and opening avenues for system innovation (as well as system improvement). The basic premise of transition management in both theory and practice, is that sustainable development requires transitions: non-linear processes of social change in which a societal system is structurally transformed. In order to describe processes of change in these complex societal systems, different levels in time and (functional) aggregation are distinguished, resulting in the 'multi-phase', 'multi-level' frameworks applied in transition analysis (Rotmans, 2005; Rotmans and Loorbach, 2009). The multi-level framework is a central concept in transition studies: it distinguishes between different levels of functional aggregation; the multi-level framework serves to analyse a transition process as an interaction through time, between 'landscape' (macro), 'regimes' (meso), and 'niches' (micro).

This complex system perspective, and the multi-level and multi-phase frameworks in transition studies, form the theoretical basis of transition management.

An important hypothesis in transition theory is that fundamental change occurs only if developments at the macro, meso and micro levels reinforce one another, and if developments within different domains come together at a particular scale level. A transition then is the result of a mixture of long-term, slow developments and short-term, rapid developments. This is illustrated in Figure 11.3, where the classical linear approach and the

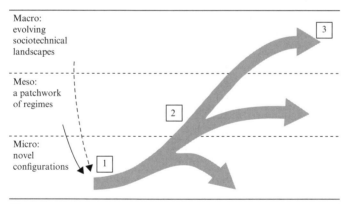

Key
1 Novelty, shaped by existing regime.
2 Evolves, is taken up, may modify regime.
3 Landscape is transformed.

Source: Geerlings et al. (2012).

Figure 11.3   The multi-level model of innovation and transformation

evolutionary way of thinking are combined and integrated in the concept of transition management.

Transition management aims to foster learning about system innovations and to bring together many actors (technologists, designers, governments, business and citizens) to work on sustainability transitions, taking on board criticism of sociologists that ecological modernisation is often too much supply and technology oriented and that it neglects issues of lifestyle and values. It is a model for working towards systemic change and innovation (Weterings et al., 1997).

11.4.2   The Meaning of Transition Management for Sustainable Transport

The concept of transition management is being applied in various sectors, such as energy, agriculture and water management. The transport sector is also suitable in this regard. It is generally accepted that the physical infrastructure is a relatively stable environment where change is difficult to achieve (for example, cities, road infrastructures). But the situation in relation to transport is becoming more and more challenging. The continuous growth of transport worldwide has created problems such as the emission of CO_2, noise, congestion, and a strong dependency on energy supply. It is clear that sustainable solutions need to be found for these transport problems, and that technology in relation to transition management might be a promising approach: a significant environmental amelioration can be gained from the implementation of new technologies. These prospects are in line with the revaluation of the role of technology in society that is presently taking place. We observe a certain fascination with technology, which is seen as key to a number of different problems (for example, introducing filters, alternative fuels). From this perspective, technological innovations are considered to be the motor for economic welfare. This opinion is expressed particularly in the transport sector. Indeed, it is indisputable that technological development has made possible the more-efficient use of energy, materials and capital that, in turn, has led to higher productivity and, as a direct effect, more transport in the world.

Rotmans (2003) states that a significant improvement of the factors contributing to the transport problem is simply not attainable with present technological insights and policy structures. Measures to tackle these problems often lack widespread support or fail to achieve true solutions. Rotmans believes that, the transport system seems to be locked-in, and is not developing in a sustainable direction. He thinks that this is caused by a lack of sustainability objectives, and innovation on the system level. In this context, Rotmans calls for a change in thinking, leading to new perspectives, with far-reaching measures and integrated solutions based on the new theory of transition management. Some authors (ibid.; Grin et al., 2010) present the concept of transition management as an innovative approach to overcome barriers from the past. They advocate finding solutions for the system as a whole, instead of for parts of the system. Therefore, top-down governance needs to be partly abandoned in favour of user demands and market developments. Thus, a transition path is not chosen, but rather created, and possible breakthrough solutions have to be generated rather than designed, with technology playing a role.

This approach of transition management sounds ambitious, but the practical implications still remain somewhat unspecific. Past transport policies are described as ineffective, but a thorough analysis has not been made, and appealing alternatives are lacking. Specific expertise in the technological aspects of the transport sector is needed in order to understand its underlying processes and mechanisms. However, the impression has been created that transition management is a methodology that consists of a toolbox applicable in every sector, in every situation, and at any moment. The case studies indicate that the approach is somewhat descriptive, not analytical and hardly *ex ante* oriented (applicable). In advocating a 'radical' approach and ideas, the different scholars do not acknowledge the achievements achieved in the past.

11.5 THE APPLICATION OF TRANSITION MANAGEMENT IN TRANSPORT

11.5.1 Transition Management in Dutch Transport Policy Making

The transition management model has gained much attention from policy makers, managers and other practitioners in the last few years, particularly in the Netherlands. In 2001 the concepts of 'transition' and 'transition management' were introduced in the 4th Dutch National Environmental Policy Plan, presented as 'a strategy to deal with environmental degradation by stimulating sustainable development as a specific aim of policy making'. Moreover, in 2003 the Dutch government decided to grant subsidies from natural gas revenues to 'strengthen the Dutch knowledge economy in its innovative and societal needs', by improving the 'knowledge infrastructure' in fields that have a specific societal relevance. Thirty-seven research programmes were funded through these gas revenues, totalling €800 million. Transition management was (partly) applied in some of these programmes, many of which were studied, evaluated and monitored by transition management researchers (Avelino, 2011; Bressers, 2011).

The 'transition to sustainable mobility' was one of the four 'necessary transitions' mentioned in the 4th Dutch National Environmental Policy Plan in 2001. Subsequently, 'transition to sustainable mobility' emerged as a catchphrase that has increasingly been used throughout the Netherlands. In addition to the research community involved in transition studies and transition management, a variety of policy makers, business representatives, and NGO representatives have referred to this 'transition to sustainable mobility' in both written and spoken word. One can distinguish between four main settings in which the concept of transition (management) appeared in relation to sustainable mobility: (i) national mobility policy, (ii) transition research networks on sustainable mobility, (iii) the Dutch 'energy transition', and (iv) the innovation programme *Transumo* (Avelino et al., 2012). A good overview of how the concept of transition (management) was applied in these four settings is given by Avelino (2011) and Avelino and Rotmans (2009).

A particular case of note here concerns the Transumo programme. Transumo (TRAansition to SUstainable MObility) is one of the 37 innovation programmes subsidised by the natural gas revenues. Its main ambition was 'to accelerate/encourage the transition to sustainable mobility' by establishing a new knowledge infrastructure (Kemp and Rotmans, 2009, p. 96; Avelino et al., 2012, p. 47). To this end it facilitated over 250 organisations from public, private and knowledge sectors to collaborate in applied research projects on sustainable transport. The programme was started in 2004 and finalised at the end of 2009. It had a turnover of €60 million, of which 50 per cent was provided by Transumo through government subsidy, and the other 50 per cent by project participants. The tripartite 'co-financing' structure, as regulated in the subsidy conditions, required that if Transumo provided a certain amount of money to a coalition to conduct a project, then the coalition was required to also invest the same amount of money in the project. Transumo implemented its transformative ambition through the development and dissemination of 'trans- and interdisciplinary' knowledge, through conferences, meetings, workshops, websites and numerous publications (articles, books, reports, brochures, websites and so on). The tripartite structure was supposed to form coalitions (between researchers, business representatives and government officials) that would ultimately 'own' the knowledge and then develop and implement it further, even if Transumo ceased to exist (Avelino, 2011).

11.5.2 The Transumo A15 Experiment in the Rotterdam Port Area

The Rotterdam Port area (Figure 11.4) is an area of major economic importance for the Netherlands (about 5 per cent of the national employment,

Source: Port of Rotterdam (2008).

Figure 11.4   Impression of the 'Second Maasvlakte'

and about 10 per cent of the GDP is generated in this region). Rotterdam is Europe's largest logistic and industrial hub (Port of Rotterdam, 2008). 'Maasvlakte', the name of the port and industrial zone, was built on reclaimed land in the vicinity of the Port of Rotterdam. It was developed because more space was needed in the Europoort – the complex of ports and industrial areas that was created in 1957 between the city of Rotterdam and the North Sea. The port is thus growing, and from an economic perspective it is seen as important that the continued growth of the port is facilitated. However, its handling capacity is bounded by the transport capacity of the available infrastructure. In the port there are five major transport modalities: road, rail, coastal and inland shipping and pipeline. Most freight is transported by road, but increasing congestion extends travel time considerably. This not only increases the transport costs of transporters and shippers, but also has a negative impact on the international competition position of the port.

As well as longer travel time and congestion, there are also impacts on the regional environment. Air pollution and noise put pressure on the quality of life in the region. In the neighbourhood of the A15 motorway, which runs from the Maasvlakte eastwards, there are several urban areas that suffer from pollution and noise. In the short term, between 2010 and 2015 a large-scale road expansion from two to three lanes is planned for the busiest parts of the highway (Geerlings et al., 2009b). However, this

extra capacity will only be a temporary solution. The ongoing expansion
of the road capacity with additional lanes is not considered a sustainable
solution in the long run: in the light of the expected growth in transport it
will enhance capacity only temporarily. Furthermore, traffic is expected to
increase further, as the government has decided to invest in an expansion
of the port area.

This enlargement of 400 km^2, Maasvlakte 2, is being achieved by
reclaiming new land from the sea. This additional area will provide
increased growth possibilities for the port, and hence, increased transport. Furthermore, the extra infrastructure will probably attract latent
transport (ibid.), which means that more sustainable solutions are needed.
There are many possible different solutions, such as the modal shift policy
(for example, more rail transport and inland shipping), increasing the
efficiency of existing infrastructure, the introduction of new technology,
logistical innovations, organisational innovations, and better cooperation.
The combined issues at play in the port area lead to a high degree of complexity in the decision-making processes and complicate the determination of future directions. Some actors have to make decisions under great
uncertainty, while others are also making strategic decisions and choices
(Ostrom, 1990, p. 210). The port is thus a good example of an area with
complex problems (or 'wicked' problems) (see, for instance, Rittel and
Webber, 1973, Rotmans, 2003).

11.5.3 Empirical Findings

The consortium of participants in the A15 project together explored and
discussed many possible solutions, some of which were analysed in more
detail. The results of this work were presented in 'reports and deliverables'
in which the project results and visualisations were formalised on paper.
By then, the project management had gained some confidence in the
trajectory, and the results, which had been presented under the three
keywords – Dynamic, Sustainable, and Daring – were welcomed. The
results were quite remarkable and organised along the lines of integration (as presented in Figure 11.1), policy priorities (Figure 11.2) and the
principles of transition management (Figure 11.3). In summary these are
presented in Figure 11.5.

One of the general observations in the A15 project relates to the exces-
sive use of transition terminology. The project documents (proposals,
plans and reports) were littered with the terms 'sustainability', 'transition
management', 'system innovation' and 'transition to sustainable mobility'.
During the actual meetings, however, these phrases were used much less,
and sometimes not at all. Transumo provided a format in which project

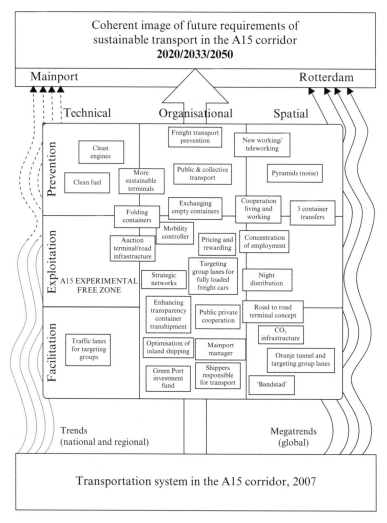

Coherent image of future requirements of
sustainable transport in the A15 corridor
2020/2033/2050

Mainport   Rotterdam

Technical   Organisational   Spatial

Prevention

Clean engines

Clean fuel

More sustainable terminals

Freight transport prevention

New working/ teleworking

Public & collective transport

Pyramids (noise)

Exploitation

A15 EXPERIMENTAL FREE ZONE

Folding containers

Auction terminal/road infrastructure

Mobility controller

Exchanging empty containers

Strategic networks

Enhancing transparency container transhipment

Pricing and rewarding

Targeting group lanes for fully loaded freight cars

Public private cooperation

Cooperation living and working

Concentration of employment

Night distribution

Road to road terminal concept

3 container transfers

Facilitation

Traffic lanes for targeting groups

Optimisation of inland shipping

Green Port investment fund

Mainport manager

Shippers responsible for transport

CO_2 infrastructure

Oranje tunnel and targeting group lanes

'Bandstad'

Trends (national and regional)

Megatrends (global)

Transportation system in the A15 corridor, 2007

Source: Geerlings et al. (2009b).

Figure 11.5 Scheme of the innovation impulse (D16) of the Transumo project

documents had to be delivered (Lohuis et al., 2008). The participants had to specify how their project would contribute, or had contributed, to the transition to sustainable mobility, which system innovations were involved, and how transition management was applied. 'Sustainability' was defined in terms of 'people, planet and profit'. In the meetings, the competitive position of the Dutch transport sector and the economic value of logistics were treated as a given by most project participants, because of the economic importance of the Rotterdam Port. It is interesting to observe how the Transumo A15 project also dealt with sustainability and transition management in the context of the theoretical notions that were presented in the previous sections on the meaning of sustainability, effective policy making and the theory of transition management. The observations of the next two subsections are based on Avelino's PhD thesis, which she completed in 2011 with the distinction cum laude (Avelino, 2011).

Retaining the principle of sustainability

In order to comply with the 'people–planet–profit balance', participants emphasised the 'side-effects' of economic optimisation that are indirectly beneficial for the planet and people. 'Increasing efficiency' and 'combining freight loads' primarily leads to cost reduction and the speeding up of traffic flows (good for profit). However, it also leads to 'less transport' (in terms of fewer kilometres), and therefore also to 'less noise' (that is, good for people), and 'fewer emissions' (that is, good for the planet). In this way the goals of accessibility and economic optimisation were framed in terms of sustainability. However, the concept of sustainability was also used in a more profound manner, and went beyond strategic framing.

The ostensible paradox between accessibility and sustainability

The Transumo A15 project started with a strong focus on economic performance and the importance of accessibility for the competitive position of the Port of Rotterdam. Through the introduction of transition management, another discussion on sustainability was triggered which went beyond the issue of economic performance. Interestingly, the concepts of 'accessibility' and 'sustainability' were often posed as opposites in meetings, and participants had a tendency to categorise one another in terms of 'those that cared more about accessibility' and 'those that cared more about sustainability' (Bressers et al., 2012, p. 97). A participant in the project stated that there were many discussions in the steering group on the goal of the project, and the concession they found was to frame accessibility as a 'goal' and sustainability as a 'condition'. The members of the steering group argued that conditions were actually more important than goals, for 'a goal is flexible, while conditions are hard' (Avelino, 2011, p. 55).

At the start of the project it was agreed that accessibility and sustainability would receive equal attention in the research, but soon the priority was accessibility within the boundaries of environmental conditions. At the end of the project it was evident that the restriction was unnecessary, because it was expected that environmental conditions would, in the long term, no longer create a problem. A conclusion that emerges from the project is that there is no reason to make sustainability secondary to accessibility, but that a proactive sustainability policy can be set up to which transport developments can be adapted. As such it was a new insight that 'accessibility' and 'sustainability' did not contradict each other and that sustainability was not just about legally imposed environmental restrictions. In this sense, the A15 project challenged government and business actors in the A15 region to take up sustainability as an ambition and opportunity, rather than confining it to environmental restrictions that 'threaten' the economic position of the port (Avelino, 2011).

The importance of policy integration

As in the case of sustainable development, there is widespread consensus at all levels of policy making that a balance between accessibility and sustainability was needed. But despite frequent recent claims of policy integration, little has changed in terms of policy-making processes or implementation. Organisational structures, while important, are no guarantee of policy integration. Furthermore, no single measures or techniques can bring about policy integration alone. Different approaches may result in similar levels of policy integration. And similar approaches in different settings may have different effects in terms of policy integration. Finally, it is important to stress that, while policy integration is of key importance for sustainable development, policy integration is not an end in itself. Policy integration is just one means by which decisions can be made more sustainable: it is equally important that implementation is consistent with integrated policy if outcomes are to be more sustainable.

Openness for innovative solutions

The participants in the A15 project explored and discussed many possible solutions to deal with the problems in the A15 region. Suggested solutions ranged from dynamic traffic management, night distribution, innovative public transport, inland terminals for short-haul sea shipping to new infrastructural works. The combined package of these measures applied to road, rail and water. Although the initial result looked promising, in the process of being formulated in a 'deliverable' formal, it appeared that this 'package of solutions' was not innovative enough and that there was a lack of strategies on *how* to implement these solutions. Consequently a second round was initiated aiming to give more attention to environmental aspects and innovation. The results of this new trajectory were presented as Deliverable D15 (Kuipers et al., 2007) under the three keywords: Dynamic, Sustainable, and Daring. Even though the results were not optimal, it became clear that they could provide a substantial contribution. The concept of sustainability became more and more accepted as a challenge that could be overcome.

At the same time, during the second round a parallel trajectory was initiated. This was called the 'transition trajectory' or innovation impulse'. The starting point for the innovation impulse was that it was deemed necessary to realise (higher) ambitions in the project, which had not been realised in the first phase. More innovative measures were found to be both possible and necessary. This alternative trajectory gave an innovation impulse to the project, by using the expertise and creativity of 'outsiders'. The results of the innovation impulse were collected and presented in project deliverable D16 (Avelino et al., 2007) and became a source of inspiration for the vested project participants: achieving sustainable transport became a common challenge (Avelino, 2011).

Adapting to the dynamic social context
A project that deals with transitions and sustainability is inherently dealing with normative and subjective notions that are contested, long term, dynamic and dependent on the context in which they are applied. During the period that this project was running (2006–09), a broader trend manifested itself, namely an increasing interest in the phenomenon of climate change. Initially the representatives of the business community were not willing to address the issue of greenhouse effects. But this perception changed when the abstract notion of climate change was translated into new, more concrete issues and business opportunities such as a bio-based economy, electric vehicles and so on. For policy makers it meant that sustainability could lead to concrete actions and that the concept became more embedded at national and regional levels. For the A15 project, this was an unexpected development that supported those participants who argued that sustainability should be considered as being at least as important as accessibility.

11.5.4   Lessons Learned from the Application of Transition Management

Transition management as a source of inspiration
During the meetings the participants had to specify how their project would contribute, or had contributed, to the transition to sustainable mobility, which system innovations were involved, and how transition management was applied. Although the A15 project could not afford to apply a fully fledged transition management process with the use of a 'transition arena', room was made for an 'alternative transition trajectory', that is, (i), (ii) . . . (a), (b), which resulted in the 'innovation impulse' that consisted of two

sessions. This innovation impulse was inspired by transition management, as far as possible given the time constraints (Avelino et al., 2011).

Transition management as a structure for the processes

With regard to the regular trajectory of the A15 project, there was a clear application of some of the more fundamental, underlying principles of transition management. The first principle was the advocacy for a pro-active attitude by new governance networks and regional coalitions, involving different sectors (business, local government, research) – rather than solely relying on government to solve public sector problems. The second principle was an inter- and transdisciplinary approach, and in a combination of qualitative and quantitative research to identify the problems at hand. The third principle could be found in the acknowledgement of uncertainty and complexity with regard to future developments, and the resulting recommendation to be prepared for an uncertain future through adaptive strategies that combined 'flexible and dynamic measures', for example, not to let the accessibility of the port be entirely dependent on the construction of specific infrastructure such as the A4 road, but to experiment with a variety of alternative measures (for example, road pricing, transport avoidance, mobility management, infrastructure for other modalities and so on).

Flexible project architecture

It was clear from the beginning that to give sustainability and accessibility an equal value in the project, a well-defined and flexible project design was necessary. The researchers in the consortium (who were mainly academics and specialised consultants) were responsible for collecting the data and analysing it by means of document reviews, statistics, traffic modelling, interviewing, and collecting, analysing and applying quantitative data (with regard to traffic and environmental effects in the A15 region) in traffic models and scenarios. But there were also 'open' meetings, to which 'outsiders' were invited to identify possible solutions in close cooperation with the 250 stakeholders in order to deal with the problems and make recommendations based on these possible solutions. These open meetings provided a forum in which the 'insiders' presented their vision for the future, project results and 'deliverables', and the 'outsiders' were asked to react, comment, discuss and provide input with regard to a specific theme (Bressers et al., 2012, p. 110). Furthermore, the A15 project was flexible in the sense that the process architecture was continuously reconsidered and adapted depending on new developments and needs. After each round, the process and results so far were evaluated, and a new set of activities were initiated (Avelino, 2011). The alternative trajectory/innovation impulse, and the thematic working groups, were not planned beforehand, but incorporated into the ongoing process, in interaction with new actors involved in the project. The outcomes of these new activities were integrated with ongoing activities and synthesised in final reports.

Recognising the challenges

In the final publications and meetings of the Transumo programme, the A15 project was characterised by outsiders and participants as a unique project with an interesting consortium, providing substantive results and an innovative process approach inspired by transition management. A remaining question is to what extent the project will contribute to a transition to a sustainable region, where a dynamic port and a future-proof industrial complex become a natural part of the region. In a concluding report, the participants of the A15 project identified three main barriers for a transition to a sustainable region. First, it is very difficult to achieve breakthroughs; even if certain innovative solutions are embraced enthusiastically by stakeholders, it remains difficult to upscale and mainstream them. Second, many important stakeholders seem to be captured in locked-in visions of port and business development. Related to this, it is difficult to find leaders of change in such a context (the so-called 'frontrunners' in transition management). Third, there are a number of participants who are happy to fulfil the minimum requirements, rather than striving for maximum results. This leads to a situation in which some parties are satisfied with an 'as good as' outcome, instead of aspiring to one that is 'better than'.

11.6   SYNTHESIS AND CONCLUSIONS

In the field of transport, there is a general awareness that new approaches are needed to find a balance between accessibility and sustainability. The need for a more sustainable transport sector is relevant on different levels such as local, regional, continental and global, but the spatial–temporal characteristics of the impacts differ very strongly. The challenge is to develop a proactive and *ex ante* methodology that addresses the economic (people), environmental (planet), and social (people) objectives in one coherent strategy. At the same time, it is necessary to recognise the need for cooperation and interaction between the government and private firms to fulfil the changing needs of society. The methodology to develop a sound sustainable transport policy should be based on developing targets for the longer term. In this chapter we advocate the need for governments to come up with new and integrated policy principles; and we introduce the concept of transition management theory. In the same context, the authors advocate the application of new guiding policy principles before policy initiatives are taken.

There is at present much discussion on policy making. The current mobility policy is mainly formulated by means of the traditional 'government' approach, including a certain optimism in the effects of technology. The sense of urgency of this mobility policy is driven primarily through specific decisive priorities: a clear national direction and a strong local execution. At the same time, there seems to be emerging slowly, but quite clearly, a need for a new governance approach: this is illustrated in the call for connecting different levels of spatial scale, involving civil society organisations, businesses and citizens, and maintaining relations at the European level.

A few general observations should be made on the conclusions. First, the theory provides a wide range of different definitions of transition management and sustainable mobility. This is not unusual. A review of literature in the field quickly reveals a similar situation of different terms and concepts being used. Second, the contributions illustrate a range of different theoretical and empirical approaches that are being used to investigate transition management and sustainable mobility. Again, this can also be seen in the literature more generally. Third, this chapter illustrates the variety of issues and challenges that transition management needs to address if real progress is to be made towards more sustainable transport patterns. On one hand, the diversity of definitions, approaches and issues provides a richness of subject material on the topic. On the other, this diversity makes the identification of overarching conclusions a great challenge. The A15 project, the issue under research in this chapter, illustrated that it is possible to apply the full model of the transition arena in practice. It is shown that a coherent and well-structured process of transition management can ultimately lead to a wide variety and a richness of results, that include consideration of public engagement, public acceptability issues, behavioural change, opinion shaping, and time and monetary constraints.

It is our conviction that the concept of transition management will create a common basis for understanding the complexities related to the new challenges currently facing the transport sector. When the necessary conditions are fulfilled, this concept of transition management can contribute to a process of change that might lead to a more sustainable transport system.

REFERENCES

Avelino, F., 2011. 'Power in transition: empowering discourses on sustainability transitions', PhD thesis, Erasmus University Rotterdam, Rotterdam.

Avelino, F., Bressers, N., Geerlings, H., Lohuis, J., Bouma, I., Vonk Noordegraaf, D.M. and Soeterbroek, F., 2007. 'Deliverable D16-Uitkomsten van de innovatie-impuls', Erasmus University Rotterdam, Rotterdam.

Avelino, F., Bressers, N. and Kemp, R., 2012. 'Transition management as new policy making for sustainable mobility', in Geerlings et al. (eds).

Avelino, F. and Rotmans, J., 2009. 'Power in transition: an interdisciplinary framework to study power in relation to structural change', *European Journal of Social Theory* **12**, 543–69.

Banister, D., 2008. 'The sustainable mobility paradigm', *Transport Policy* **15**, 73–80.

Bestuurlijk Overleg MIRT, 2006. *Gebiedsagenda Zuidvleugel / Zuid-Holland Een wereldregio*, Den Haag: Rijk en de Zuidvleugelpartners.

Bressers, N.E.W., 2011. 'Co-creating innovation: a systemic learning evaluation of knowledge and innovation programmes', PhD thesis, Erasmus University Rotterdam, Rotterdam.

Commissie Elverding, 2008. 'Sneller en Beter. Advies Commissie Versnelling Infrastructurele besluiten', Den Haag.

Geels, F., 2005. *Technological Transitions and System Innovations: A Co-evolutionary and Socio-Technical Analysis*, Cheltenham, UK and Northampton, MA, USA: Edward Elgar.

Geerlings, H., Lohuis, J., Wiegmans, B. and Willemsen, A., 2009a. 'A renaissance in understanding technology dynamics? The emerging concept of transition management', *Transportation Planning and Technology* **32**, 401–22.

Geerlings, H. and Stead, D., 2003. 'The integration of land use planning, transport and environment in European policy and research', *Transport Policy* **10**, 179–96.

Geerlings, H., Stead, D. and Shiftan, Y. (eds), 2012. *Transition towards Sustainable Mobility: The Role of Instruments, Individuals and Institutions*, London: Ashgate.

Geerlings, H., and van Meijeren, M., 2008. 'The dominance of the Lisbon agreement as a barrier for an environmentally oriented transport policy in Europe: the gap between theory and implementation in policy integration', *European Transport – Trasporti Europei* **39**, 14–32.

Geerlings, H., van Meijeren, J. and Soeterbroek, F., with Huybregts, R., Kuipers, B., Kul, H., Smaal, M. and Vonk Noordegraaf, D., 2009b. 'Deliverable D25: Synthese: resultaten en aanbevelingen van 3 jaar studie', Erasmus University Rotterdam, Rotterdam.

Grin, J., Rotmans, J. and Schot, J., 2010. *Transitions to Sustainable Development: New Directions in the Long Term Transformative Change*, New York: Routledge.

In 't Veld, R.J., 1989. *De verguisde staat*, Den Haag: Vuga Uitgeverij.

Kemp, R. and Rotmans, J., 2009. 'Transitioning policy: co-production of a new strategic framework for energy innovation policy in the Netherlands', *Policy Sciences* **42**, 303–22.

Kuipers, B., van Rooijen, T. and Vonk Noordegraaf, D.M., 2007. 'Deliverable D15 Uitwerking Maatregelenpakket 2: 3D "Duurzaam, dynamisch en gedurfd"', Erasmus Universiteit Rotterdam, Rotterdam/Delft.

Lohuis, J., Bouma, I., Avelino, F., Bressers, N., Vonk Noordegraaf, D., Soeterbroek, F. and Geerlings, H., 2008. 'Deliverable 16 Uitkomsten van de innovatie-impuls', Erasmus University Rotterdam, Rotterdam.

Lukes, S., 2002. 'Power: a radical view', in: Haugaard, M. (ed.), *Power: A Reader*, Manchester: Manchester University Press, pp. 35–58.

Meadows, D., Meadows, D.L. and Randers, J., 1991. *Beyond the Limits. Confronting Global Collapse: Envisioning a Sustainable Future*, London: Earthscan.

Ministerie voor Verkeer en Waterstaat en Ministerie voor Volksgezondheid en Milieuhygiëne VROM, 2008. 'Nota Ruimte en Mobiliteit', Ministerie van V&W en VROM, Den Haag.

Ministerie voor Volksgezondheid en Milieuhygiëne, 2008. 'Mooi Nederland', Rapport, Ministerie van VROM, Den Haag.

Organisation of Economic Co-operation and Development (OECD), 1996. *Building Policy Coherence: Tools and Tensions*, Paris: OECD.

Ostrom, E., 1990. *Governing the Commons: The Evolution of Institutions for Collective Action*, Cambridge: Cambridge University Press.

Port of Rotterdam, 2008. 'MER-Maasvlakte 2', Port of Rotterdam, Rotterdam.

Programmabureau Deltapoort Zuidvleugel, 2008. 'Zuidvleugelprojecten Ruimtelijke ambities Deltapoort 2020', Den Haag.

Programmabureau Stedenbaan Zuidvleugel, 2008. 'Zuidvleugelprojecten Stedenbaan Ruimtelijke ambitie stedenbaan 2020', Den Haag.

Rittel, H.W.J. and Webber, M.M., 1973. 'Dilemmas in a general theory of planning', *Policy Sciences* **4**, 155–69.

Rotmans, J., 2003. *Transitiemanagement: sleutel voor een duurzame samenleving*, Assen: Van Gorcum.

Rotmans, J., 2005. 'Societal Innovation: between dream and reality lies complexity', Inaugural Address, Erasmus Research Institute of Management, Erasmus University Rotterdam, Rotterdam.

Rotmans, J. and Loorbach, D., 2009. 'Complexity and transition management', *Journal of Industrial Ecology* **13**, 184–96.

Stead, D. and Geerlings, H., 2005. 'Integrating transport, land use planning and environment policy in Denmark, Germany and England: from theory to practice', *Innovation* **18**, 443–53.

Stead, D., Geerlings, H. and Meijers, E., 2004. *Integrating Transport, Land Use Planning and Environment Policy in Denmark, Germany and England: From Theory to Practice*, Delft: Delft University Press.

Transportation Research Board (TRB), 1997. 'A Guidebook for Forecasting Freight Transport Demand', NCHRP Report 388, Transportation Research Board Washington, DC.

Transportation Research Board (TRB), 2008. 'Sustainable Transportation Indicators: A Recommended Research Program for Developing Sustainable Transportation Indicators', Data Report ADD40, Transportation Research Board, Washington, DC.

United Nations, 1992. *Report of the United Nations Conference on Environment and Development, Rio de Janeiro, 3–14 June 1992. Volume I: Resolutions Adopted by the Conference*, New York: United Nations.

Weterings R., Kuijper, J., Smeets, E., Annokkée, G.J. and Minne, B., 1997. '81 mogelijkheden: Technologie voor duurzame ontwikkeling' (81 possibilities: Technology for sustainable development), TNO report for the Ministerie van Volksgezondheid, Ruimtelijke Ordening en Milieuhygiëne (VROM), Delft.

World Commission on Environment and Development (WCED), 1987. *Our Common Future*, Oxford: Oxford University Press.

12. Stakeholder bias in multi-actor multi-criteria transportation evaluation: issues and solutions

Cathy Macharis and Peter Nijkamp*

12.1 INTRODUCTION

Evaluating and deciding on transport projects is often the background for much debate, controversy and disagreement. Transport project plans can range from infrastructural projects to implementation projects of road pricing or the choice between different transport technologies. Since different points of view have to be brought together – usually from the perspective of sustainable development – distinct evaluation aspects have to be taken into account simultaneously and able to cope with difficult valuations. Furthermore, there are planning issues where several levels of public policy may be involved (local, provincial, regional, state, or European). Decision making in the transport sector normally comprises a number of stakeholders (such as freight forwarders, investors, citizens, industry and so on) who have a vested interest in the ultimate decision. Failure to take these interests into account may lead to a neglect of the evaluation study by policy makers or even to countervailing reactions by the stakeholders (Walker, 2000).

Against this background, Multi-Actor Multi-Criteria Analysis (MAMCA) is a suitable tool for the evaluation of transport projects (Macharis, 2000; Macharis et al., 2009). It allows us to incorporate explicitly the aims and views of the actors involved, and to structure the manifold dimensions of transport projects. Such dimensions may relate to costs, accessibility, safety, human health, geographical isolation, social equity, and the like. As no monetisation is necessary, the valuation of sustainability aspects is less troublesome and hence better incorporated within the analysis. However, the inclusion of multiple stakeholders within the assessment process leads clearly to a complex evaluation procedure. Four types of actors are involved in this procedure, namely the stakeholders, the decision maker, the experts, and the analyst. According to Freeman

(1984, p. 46) a stakeholder is 'any individual or group of individuals that can influence or are influenced by the achievement of the organization's objectives'. Or, as Banville et al. (1998, p. 17) put it: 'stakeholders are those people who have a vested interest in a problem by affecting it or/and being affected by it'. As they have a vested interest in the problem and its solution, it is conceivable that they will try to influence the outcome of the process. Strategic bias – in the context of group decision models – occurs when individuals provide specific preference information to a group decision model which most likely will improve their own results and not necessarily those of the group (Hajkowicz, 2012). The decision maker is the one who makes the final decision or choice. This actor can be the government, for example, or a private investor. At the same time a decision maker can also be a stakeholder, which implies that the analyst should try to keep this decision maker at a reasonable distance in the procedure so as not to influence the procedure in one or another direction. The experts are the persons who will be consulted for the evaluation of the different scenarios on specific criteria, according to their specific expertise. If the evaluation scale is well explained, no bias should be expected from this group of actors. The analyst is the person who guides these different actors through the procedure and who should avoid possible biases.

In this study, the authors aim to analyse whether it is possible to take account of bias in a MAMCA model. This exploration will be structured along three main axes: the choice of the actors (will the inclusion or exclusion of certain stakeholders change the outcome?), the choice of the criteria of each actor, and the choice of the weights of these criteria by the actors. Finally, possible solutions in order to avoid strategic bias in MAMCA will be put forward. Before doing so, a concise overview of issues related to multi-criteria group decision making (MGDM) will be offered (Section 12.2), followed by a literature review on bias within group decision support systems (Section 12.3). MAMCA will be explained in Section 12.4, while possible sources of bias will be analysed in Section 12.5. In Section 12.6, strategies for coping with bias will be addressed, and concluding remarks will be offered in Section 12.7.

12.2 MULTI-CRITERIA GROUP DECISION MAKING (MGDM)

The combination of stakeholder involvement and multi-criteria decision analysis (MCDA) has shown a dynamic evolution over the years. Starting from the convincing plea of Banville et al. (1998) for introducing the concept of stakeholders in multi-criteria analysis, various applications can be found where stakeholders are taken into account in the evaluation process, which is often nowadays referred to as 'group decision making' (GDM). The goal of GDM is to achieve a consensus between different stakeholders involved in the decision-making process (Leyva-López, 2010). In the past, many GDM systems have been developed that include MCDA to support a group decision-making problem (for an overview, see Álvarez-Carrillo et al., 2010). They are often called 'multi-criteria group decision making' (MGDM). The difference between these methods is mainly based on the manner in which the information is brought together. One may talk about input- or output-level aggregation, as Leyva-López and Fernández-González (2003) do. But one can also distinguish between models with the same value tree for all stakeholders (or decision makers) and those with different value trees for each stakeholder (De Brucker and Macharis, 2010). The same value tree corresponds mainly to an input-level aggregation where the group is asked to agree on a common set of criteria, weights, and remaining parameters. If several individual value trees can exist and are only aggregated in the end, then we talk about output-level aggregation. In the evaluation of transport projects it is important to distinguish between different points of view, and hence different value trees and output-level aggregation are most appropriate. Another important classification is between the methods mainly developed for tackling business/organisational decision problems on the one hand and social choice problems on the other. The evaluation of complex transport projects can normally be seen as a societal issue. Social multi-criteria analysis, as defined by Munda (2004), addresses decision problems from the perspective of society as a whole and hence, can be positioned in the domain of public choice. MAMCA can be classified as a social multi-criteria method in which several individual value trees can be used. This is in contrast to other evaluation methods which are located in the organisational domain, and if they are within the group of social multi-criteria analysis, they use one common value tree for the whole group.

12.3 STAKEHOLDER BIAS IN GROUP DECISION PROCESSES

If no formal evaluation procedure is used, biases can occur due to cognitive, perceptual, and motivational reasons. A cognitive bias occurs due to the restrictions of our short-term memory to store and correctly process everything (Reyna et al., 2003). Perceptual bias can take the form of a self-perception bias, if individuals fail to analyse their motivations in multi-person and multi-objective group decision making. Also in risky decisions, a loss aversion bias might occur, which may lead to inferior choices (Mercer, 2005). An example of a motivational bias is a positive confirmation bias. In this kind of bias, the decision makers select a preferred option early in the decision process and seek to gather all kinds of information that supports this choice and discard all the information that suggests that other options might be better (Jones and Sugden, 2001; Fischer et al., 2008). This kind of bias can also be seen in the distinction in types of decision makers. Baumeister and Newman (1994) distinguish between an intuitive scientist who is open and objective and an intuitive lawyer who is using a kind of motivational bias in order to defend his/her choice. Hamilton (2003) showed that participants might suggest inferior alternatives and ideas in order to influence the other group members to support their idea. Even worse, they might misrepresent facts in order to influence the group decision (Steinel and De Dreu, 2004). Also, group dynamics can play a role: isolates will not be taken into account in the decision (Thomas-Hunt et al., 2003). Next, the size of the group and the status of a decision maker will play a role in a group dynamics: if the group becomes larger than five or if the group members are not sure about their opinion, the high-status decision will exert more influence on the group (Baumann and Bonner, 2004; Ohtsubo and Masuchi, 2004). For a further overview of biases and heuristics related to human judgement and decision making, see Gilovich et al. (2002).

Several authors have claimed that formal methods can avoid many of these pitfalls. Regan et al. (2006) state that formal methods such as consensus convergence modelling have the advantage of being transparent, reproducible, and resistant to manipulation and the vagaries of member status and group size. Furthermore, De Sanctis and Galuppe (1987) argued many years ago that thanks to technology for group decisions more equality is possible, as it discourages dominance by an individual member.

However, also in the context of formal methods, dishonesty is possible. Ramanathan and Ganesh (1994) state that in the available literature on social choice there is no method to tackle dishonesty, and this dishonesty has first to be uncovered. In addition, within this literature, the Arrow impossibility theorem states that essentially no constitution exists for group decision making such that the group can be assured that in every possible circumstance it satisfies some basic principles of rationality, unanimity, and Pareto optimality and independence of irrelevant alternatives without there being an explicit or implicit dictator (French, 2007). French extended this argument by showing that any constitution is susceptible to manipulation through strategic voting, dishonest revelation of preferences or agenda rigging.

Also when a multi-criteria approach is used in an MGDM context, there is evidence that strategic bias can occur. This is usually done through the determination of the weights attached to policy criteria. Decision makers will manipulate criterion weights in order to favour their desired outcome (Hajkowicz, 2012). Bennet (2005) calls this 'rent seeking behaviour'. Condon et al. (2003) showed that within an AHP (Analytic Hierarchy Process) approach (see Saaty, 1988), people can conceal true agendas or try to distort their pairwise comparisons. In the group AHP, when using one value tree for the whole group, a geometric mean is mostly used for bringing together the individual points of view. Group members can specify extreme entries in the matrix such as 9 or 1/9 in order to manipulate the ultimate outcome. However, by displaying clusters of decision makers as well as outliers, at some point these extreme values will be uncovered. Jacobi and Hobbs (2007) even propose a model to de-bias the results of weight elicitation. Hajkowicz (2012) also performed a test to uncover strategic bias in the determination of the weights. This test can be applied if one criteria set is used for the whole group. Clearly, if decision makers have to give weights to each other and to themselves, it is also possible that they will award high values to themselves.

Another important source of bias and errors is the so-called 'splitting bias', in which the structure of the value tree affects the weights (Hamalainen and Alaja, 2008). In a splitting bias, decomposing an objective into multiple attributes leads to a higher overall weight for that objective when compared to a direct assessment of the objective's relative importance (Jacobi and Hobbs, 2007). Other experiments have also shown the evidence of biases occurring with the use of value trees. Borcherding and von Winterfeldt (1988), for example, demonstrated that weights for an objective tend to be higher when the objective is presented at a higher level in a value tree, while Stillwell et al. (1987) claim that hierarchically assessed weights tend to have a larger variance than weights assessed in a non-hierarchical way.

The great advantage of formal methods is that, when transparent, decision makers will have to defend and reveal their criteria weights and discuss them with the entire group and possibly with the public (Hajkowicz, 2012). So, the idea is that, although it is not possible to avoid dishonesty in the short run, it will be discovered in the long run and at that point it can be corrected (Ramanathan and Ganesh, 1994). Consequently, it is very important to make the process as transparent as possible. Decision support and choice methods ultimately rest upon people's values, and the aim of the analyst is to combine them with factual data in order to inform and support people's decisions (Hajkowicz, 2012). In the next section we shall show how this is done in the MAMCA methodology.

12.4   THE MAMCA APPROACH

MAMCA allows us to evaluate different alternatives (policy measures, scenarios, technologies and so on) for the objectives of the various stakeholders that are involved. Unlike a conventional multi-criteria analysis where alternatives are evaluated on several criteria, the MAMCA methodology explicitly includes the points of view of the different stakeholders.

The methodology consists of seven steps (see Figure 12.1). The first step is the definition of the problem and the identification of the alternatives. These alternatives can take different forms according to the problem situation; they can compromise different technological solutions, different policy measures, long-term strategic options, and so on. Next, the relevant stakeholders are identified (step 2). Stakeholders are people who have an interest, financial or otherwise, in the consequences of any decisions taken. Third, the key objectives of the stakeholders are identified and given a relative importance or priority by the stakeholders themselves (weights) (step 3). These first three steps are done interactively and in a circular way. Fourth, for each criterion, one or more indicators are constructed (for example, direct quantitative indicators such as money spent, number of lives saved, reductions in CO_2 emissions achieved and so on or scores on an ordinal indicator such as high/medium/low for criteria with values that are difficult to express in quantitative terms, and so on.) (step 4). The measurement method for each indicator is also made explicit (for instance, willingness to pay, quantitative scores based on macroscopic computer simulation, and so on). This permits us to measure each alternative's performance in terms of its contribution to the objectives of specific stakeholder groups. Steps 1 to 4 can be considered as mainly analytical, and they precede the 'overall analysis', which takes into account the objectives of all stakeholder groups simultaneously and is more 'synthetic' in nature. The fifth step is the construction of the evaluation matrix. The alternatives are further described and translated into scenarios which also describe the contexts in which the policy options will be implemented. For example, when evaluating different advanced driver assistance systems such as intelligent speed adaptation, advanced cruise control, and so on the scenarios contain information on the type of road on which these systems will be used (rural/ urban), the volume of cars that are equipped with these systems (penetration rate), and so on. The different scenarios are then scored on the objectives of each stakeholder group by experts. An MCDA is performed for each stakeholder. Already a comparison of the values and results of each individual MCDA can be performed in order to identify systematic differences in value judgements. The different points of view are then brought together in a multi-actor context. This MAMCA yields a ranking of the

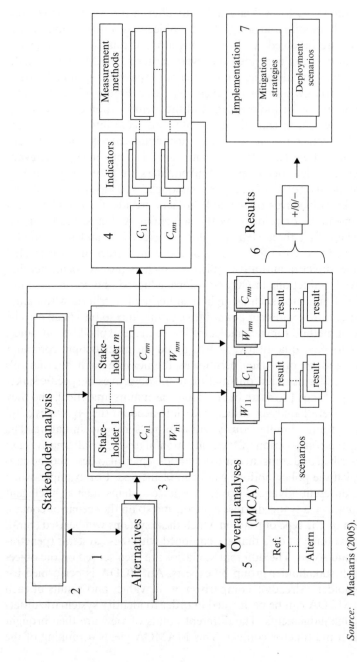

Source: Macharis (2005).

Figure 12.1 The MAMCA methodology

various alternatives and reveals their strengths and weaknesses (step 6). The last stage of the methodology (step 7) includes the actual implementation. Based on the insights of the analysis, an implementation path can be developed, taking into account the wishes of the different actors.

More important than the ranking, this multi-criteria analysis reveals the critical stakeholders and their criteria. MAMCA provides a comparison of different strategic alternatives, and supports the decision maker in making his/her final decision by pointing out for each stakeholder which elements have a clearly positive or a clearly negative impact on his or her objectives. We shall now offer a few illustrations.

In Figure 12.2, an example is given of a multi-actor approach in AHP. The figure (which can be found in the expert choice software as a sensitivity graph called 'performance'), shows directly who finds which alternative the most preferred option. In Figure 12.2 the intersection of the horizontal alternative line graphs with the vertical objective lines shows the priority of the alternative for the given actor, as can be read from the right axis, Alt%. The priority that each stakeholder attaches to the alternatives is obtained by his/her individual multi-criteria analysis in which the evaluations are based on the objectives of that specific stakeholder group. The weight of the actor is represented by the height of his/her bar, which can be read from the left axis, Obj%. So the rectangles at the bottom represent these weights. On the right-hand side, the axis 'OVERALL' shows the final scores of the scenarios by computing the weighted averages of the scores on the different actors multiplied by their weights (sometimes set equal for all stakeholders). This provides a final ranking of the scenarios. However, the aim of MAMCA is to provide insight into what is important for each stakeholder and not just to sum up these different points of view and come to a final decision. So this last axis, with the overall result, should always be interpreted with care.

MAMCA can also be performed with other MCDA methods such as the PROMETHEE method (Macharis et al., 1998, and illustrated in Macharis, 2000). In this chapter, however, we concentrate on the possible biases that can occur when using it with the AHP method.

12.5   STAKEHOLDER BIAS WITHIN MAMCA

As shown in the above literature overview on biases, methodologies that are transparent allow us sooner or later to uncover strategic bias. The MAMCA methodology is especially transparent and allows a clear overview of every step of the methodology. Another strong point is that the evaluation itself is done by experts and not by stakeholders

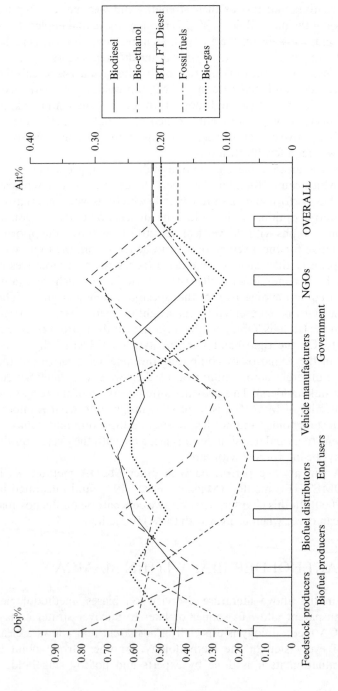

Source: Biofuel example in Turecksin et al. (2010).

Figure 12.2   Multi-actor approach in AHP

themselves (although for some more intangible criteria such as prestige, for example, the stakeholder might be consulted by the experts). However, in MAMCA, care should be taken that bias is avoided in critical steps of the methodology. For example in the first step, namely the definition of the problem and the choice of alternatives, there might be a discussion on what the problem really is. Here it is very important to work in an iterative and circular way with steps 2 and 3, so that the stakeholders are also able to propose new alternatives. A feedback loop at the end of the analysis towards step one will also enable us to integrate ideas on compensating measures as a result of the complete process. Another important issue is the input of the experts, as they also might be biased. In this chapter we concentrate on the possible bias in the steps of the choice of the stakeholders, the choice of the criteria, or the choice of the weights of the stakeholders. We shall now examine these steps in more detail and indicate how bias could take place and be addressed.

12.5.1 Choice of Stakeholders

The choice of stakeholders and how to cluster them into groups is a delicate process. A stakeholder can be defined as an actor in the range of people who are likely to use a system or be influenced either directly or indirectly by its use (Macharis and Stevens, 2003). In other words, stakeholders have an interest, financial or otherwise, in the consequences of any decisions taken. An in-depth understanding of each stakeholder group's objectives is critical in order to assess different choice alternatives appropriately. Stakeholder analysis should be viewed as an aid to clearly identify the range of stakeholders that should be consulted and whose views should be taken into account in the evaluation process. In the scientific literature, various methods are described in order to compile an appropriate list of stakeholders. Munda (2004) claims that by an analysis of historical, legislative and administrative documents, complemented with in-depth interviews with locals and other interested parties, a map can be drawn up of the most important social actors. In Banville et al. (1998) one can find some formal methods to identify stakeholders: the seven procedures of Mason and Mitroff (1981), the identification of potential reasons for people to mobilise around any aspect of the problem (Weiner and Brown, 1986), the distinction between external stakeholders, corporate and organisational stakeholders (Savage et al., 1991), and Martin's (1985) classification into seven components: family, friends, fellow-travellers, fence sitters, foes, fools and fanatics. Only the second method is not explicitly developed for organisational decision contexts. When using MAMCA, the approach of Weiner and Brown (1986) and/or Munda (2004) seems to offer a good start. Next, in the context of transportation planning, one should clearly define the (physical) border of the transport problem. How far does the project impact extend? This clarifies which policy level (commune, province, region, country, European, worldwide) should be included as a governmental actor. In some cases, it is possible that several levels have to explicitly be taken into account (such as in the case of the Oosterweel decision where the Flemish government had other objectives than the city of Antwerp (Macharis and Januarius, 2010))[1]. Clearly, it is also important to find out whether there are demand and supply sides in the problem at stake. For example, when evaluating driver assistance systems, we need to incorporate the manufacturers on the one and the users on the other (Macharis et al., 2004). One can also take a supply-chain perspective, as in a study on biofuel, where all actors from the supply side were included (the agricultural sector, biofuel convertors, fuel distributors, end users, car manufacturers, government and NGOs, and North–South organisations) (Turcksin and Macharis, 2009). Once certain stakeholders are identified, they can be asked who, according to them, should also be involved. So, although there are no strict rules on who to include (Banville et al., 1998), it is important to ensure that all actors who could be affected or can affect are in the list of stakeholder groups. Even if they cannot organise themselves, or if one cannot elicit weights from the criteria, they will be included and taken into account, since it would be problematic to leave unorganised groups out of the analysis. Munda (2004) gives the example of people living in a rainforest. Should they be forgotten because they might have no official representatives? Or because it is not possible to organise a survey among them? Thus, Munda claims that they should be incorporated as important stakeholders.

Usually, stakeholder groups will be involved and not single stakeholders. The supply side of driver assistance systems, for example, will encompass different car manufacturers and manufacturers of the systems themselves. In the case of biofuels, feedstock producers are not represented by the agricultural sector or biomass-based industry alone, but also by the wood sector, waste processors, and traders. A good criterion to ascertain if a stakeholder belongs to a certain stakeholder group is whether the same objectives appear in their criteria tree. Within a certain stakeholder group, we expect the group to be homogeneous in the sense that they largely agree on the same judgement criteria. Possibly, the priorities and weights might differ a bit, but the same criteria tree is used within the stakeholder group. The homogeneity of the group is important, as the weights given by the different members of a stakeholder group will be aggregated by the geometric mean (when AHP is used) or an average. If the weights given by the stakeholders within a stakeholder group differ markedly, a sensitivity analysis should be performed in step 6.

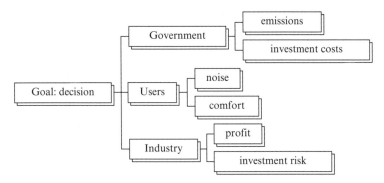

Figure 12.3   Example of group fragmentation

In this choice of stakeholder groups the analyst plays an important role. Outlier analysis can be used to check the homogeneity of the stakeholder groups that were formed. A bias that can occur is group fragmentation. If a group splits into two, they would get a double weight, at least if the corresponding criteria are mutually correlated and if every stakeholder group receives an equal weight. This means that their opinion would weigh more on the ultimate outcome. The example in Figure 12.3 shows this very clearly. The example is quite simple: there are three alternatives, three stakeholder groups involved (for example, government, users and industry), and every stakeholder has two criteria.

If a new stakeholder group (for example, a different type of industry, for example, Industry 2) enters the model (see Figures 12.3 and 12.4), the preferred alternative is that of the aggregate industry group (see Figures 12.5 and 12.6).

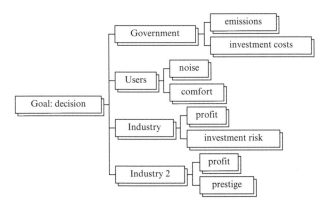

Figure 12.4   Example of entry of new stakeholder

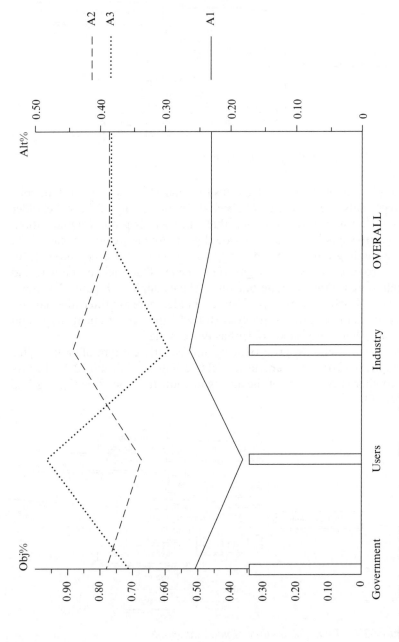

Figure 12.5   Multi-actor view of Example 1

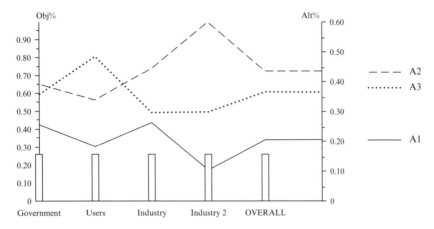

Figure 12.6   Multi-actor view of Example 2

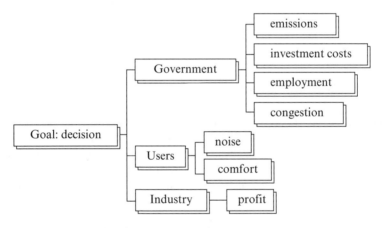

Figure 12.7   Example of composition of criteria

12.5.2   Choice of Criteria

If a stakeholder has only one or a few criteria, his/her point of view might be more extreme and again weigh more heavily in the final decision. In our example (Figure 12.7), for the government, four criteria are now used hypothetically, whereas the industry has only one left, namely profit.

Indeed, what can be seen is that the latter point of view counts more in the final decision. Within social decision contexts, this is something to be aware of, as often the pressure or lobby groups have only a few objectives,

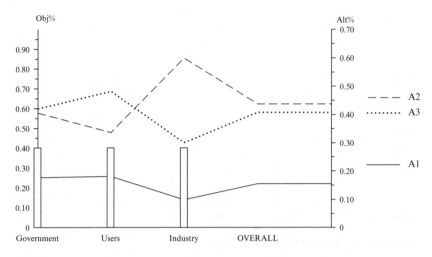

Figure 12.8   Multi-actor view of composition of criteria

whereas governments tend to have several, as they represent democratic interests (Figure 12.8).

12.5.3   Choice of Criteria Weights by Actors

The choice of the weights of these criteria is mainly the same as the problem stated above. If all weights are given to a single criterion, this will lead to more extreme results. If the weights are evenly distributed, more moderated choices will be the result. The analyst can check the weights of the criteria to see if these correspond to the real priorities of the stakeholders.

12.6   HOW TO COPE WITH STAKEHOLDER BIAS?

In order to avoid stakeholder bias, the process should stay transparent. As described above, some pitfalls can be avoided by checking some critical elements:

1.   Are the stakeholder groups chosen in a correct way and is there no double counting due to a splitting up of stakeholder groups that essentially belong together?
2.   Is there an asymmetry in the number of criteria over the different stakeholders?

3. Are the weights chosen by the stakeholders for their criteria corresponding to their real priorities?

Checking these elements is a delicate process to be undertaken with caution. Essentially, the MAMCA methodology aims to elicit the objectives and priorities of the stakeholder groups. The evaluation and checking should not result in accusing stakeholders of being dishonest or reacting in a strategically biased way. The objectives and corresponding weights should be discussed openly with the whole group and also extreme preference values may be discussed. Clearly, if these extreme values correspond to the real preferences of the stakeholders, these should be kept. The decision maker might have to give weights to the different stakeholder groups, and in that sense check which solution on average is most preferred.

A careful checking, however, may also lead to the conclusion that in a particular case symmetry is not guaranteed and that it is not clear whether the presence of a distinct stakeholder group will not result in double counting. In that case, the weighted average as used in the AHP method is not a good way to aggregate the individual scores into a global one.

The most prudent way in that situation is to not aggregate the points of view of the actors at all. For each stakeholder, an individual MCDA would have to be performed and analysed, and then the results can be shown to the decision makers. Figure 12.9 offers an example of the results on which further discussions can be based.

A first pre-selection of alternatives can be made according to the rankings made by the different stakeholders. If an alternative is not in the top two alternatives of one of the stakeholders, this alternative can normally be disregarded. In Figure 12.9 (Example 2), alternative A1 is not in the top of what the different stakeholders would like. This alternative can thus be disregarded. The remaining alternatives can then be further analysed.

By keeping the stakeholders separated and by using sensitivity analyses to analyse the individual MCDAs, strategic bias behaviour from the stakeholders can easily be uncovered. It will anyway not influence the ranking in the end result, but only their own individual ranking of alternatives. If this result is based on the priorities they have, this is important information for the decision makers. A splitting up of stakeholders would be of no help in that case and the number of criteria that each individual stakeholder considers will have no influence on the end result.

A step further might be to use the distinct rankings for each stakeholder to come to a common ranking, by using, for example, the Borda count method (see, for example, Hajkowicz and Higgins, 2008), which takes the sum of the ranks to come to arrive at an aggregate rank. In the above

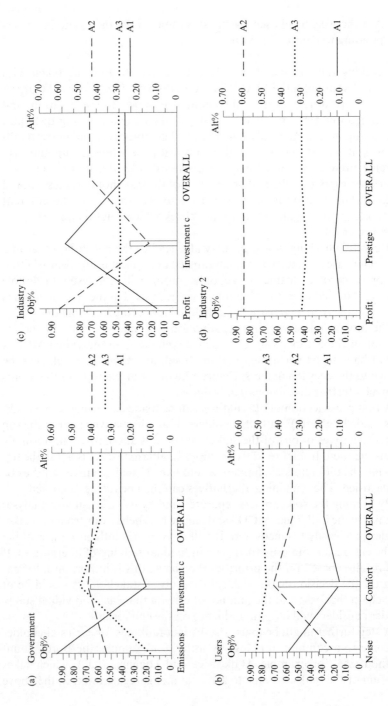

Figure 12.9 Individual points of view of Example 2

Table 12.1 Ranking of the alternatives with the Borda count method

	Rank gov	Rank users	Rank industry	Rank industry 2	Aggregate rank
A2	1	2	1	1	5
A3	2	1	2	2	7

example this would give (after elimination of the dominated alternative A1) the results shown in Table 12.1.

A2 might then be regarded as the alternative that would most likely lead to a consensus or a good modus vivendi. This allows us to resolve the difficulty of asymmetry in the criteria. However, it does not completely resolve the problem of the choice of the stakeholders. Double counting might still be possible, for example, by increasing the number of intercorrelated criteria. Clearly, although the method proposed here is already more transparent, it can only be a partial element in the consensus discussion.

12.7 CONCLUSIONS

The MAMCA methodology helps us to take into account the viewpoints of different stakeholders. In the field of transport and mobility, this is an essential condition for a balanced socioeconomic evaluation method, as it is a crucial factor in implementing decisions in this field. Including the essential stakeholders in the analysis enables us to find a modus operandi and support for the option to be chosen. It also allows us to find compensating measures for the stakeholders that are 'losing' by the decision. A feedback loop to step 1 can integrate these insights into new or adjusted alternatives.

A more participatory process, however, also creates the risk of stakeholder bias. In this chapter we showed the possible pitfalls within the MAMCA methodology. A first focus of attention is the choice of stakeholders. If a group is split into two, their opinion would weigh more in the final ranking. So a careful selection and categorisation of the stakeholders should be adopted (following the definition of what makes up a stakeholder group). Second, the choice of the criteria and more precisely the number of criteria and the weights attached to them can also influence the final outcome. Extreme positions will weigh more in the final ranking. A check may be needed to ascertain whether these extreme values correspond to the real preferences.

Transparency is in all cases key to avoiding (strategic) bias. The multi-actor ranking might hide some elements such as an unequal number of criteria by the stakeholders or a splitting up of the stakeholders. In order to avoid this and to enhance transparency, it seems good practice not to stress the achievement of an overall global end result, but to keep the results of the individual stakeholders separated and to start the discussion from there.

NOTES

* The authors would like to thank Michel Beuthe and Rob Konings for their constructive remarks on an earlier version of the chapter.
1. While the Flemish government has more general objectives on congestion and emissions for the region as a whole, for the citizens of Antwerp the emissions (certainly the PM emissions) have a direct impact on their welfare.

REFERENCES

Álvarez-Carillo, P.A., Duarte, A. and Leyva-López, J.C., 2010. 'A group multi-criteria decision support system for ranking a finite set of alternatives', paper presented at the EURO XXIV conference, Lisbon, July 11–14.

Banville, C., Landry, M., Martel, J.M. and Boulaire, C., 1998. 'A stakeholder approach to MCDA', *System Research* **15**, 15–32.

Baumann, M.R. and Bonner, B.L., 2004. 'The effects of variability and expectations on utilization of member expertise and group performance', *Organizational Behavior and Human Decision Processes* **93**, 89–101.

Baumeister, R.F. and Newman, L.S., 1944. 'How stories make sense of personal experiences: motives that shape autobiographical narratives' *Personality and Social Psychology Bulletin* **20**, 676–90.

Bennett, J., 2005. 'Australasian environmental economics: contributions, conflicts and "cop-outs"'. *Australian Journal of Agricultural and Resource Economics* **49**, 243–61.

Borcherding, K. and von Winterfeldt, D., 1988. 'The effect of varying value trees on multiattribute evaluations', *Acta Psychologica* **68**, 153–70.

Condon, E., Golden, B. and Wasil, E., 2003. 'Visualizing group decisions in the analytic hierarchy process', *Computers and Operations Research* **30**, 1435–45.

De Brucker, K. and Macharis, C., 2010. 'Multi-Actor Multi-Criteria Analysis (MAMCA) as a means to cope with societal complexity', paper presented at the EURO XXIV conference, Lisbon, July 11–14.

De Sanctis, G. and Gallupe, R.B., 1987. 'A foundation for the study of group decision support systems', *Management Science* **33**, 589–605.

Fischer, P., Jonas, E., Frey, D. and Kastenmüller, A., 2008. 'Selective exposure and decision framing: the impact of gain and loss framing on confirmatory information search after decisions', *Journal of Experimental Social Psychology* **44**, 312–20.

Freeman, R.E., 1984. *Strategic Management: A Stakeholder Approach*, Boston, MA: Pitman.

French, S., 2007. 'Web-enabled strategic GDSS, e-democracy and Arrow's theorem: a Bayesian perspective', *Decision Support Systems* **43**, 1476–84.

Gilovich, T., Griffin, D.W. and Kahneman, D., 2002. *The Psychology of Intuitive Judgment: Heuristic and Biases*, Cambridge: Cambridge University Press.

Hajkowicz, S., 2012. 'For the greater good? A test for strategic bias in group environmental decisions', *Group Decision and Negotiations* **21**, 331–44.

Hajkowicz, S. and Higgins, A., 2008. 'A comparison of multiple criteria analysis techniques for water resource management', *European Journal of Operational Research* **184**, 255–65.

Hamalainen, R.P. and Alaja, S., 2008. 'The threat of weighting biases in environmental decision analysis', *Ecological Economics* **68**, 556–69.

Hamilton, R.W., 2003. 'Why do people suggest what they do not want? Using context effects to influence others' choices', Journal of Consumer Research **29**, 429–506.

Jacobi, S.K. and Hobbs, B.F., 2007. 'Quantifying and mitigating the splitting bias and other value tree induced weighting biases', *Decision Analysis* **4**, 194–210.

Jones, M. and Sugden, R., 2001. 'Positive confirmation bias in the acquisition of information', *Theory and Decision* **50**, 59–99.

Leyva-López, J.C., 2010. 'A consensus model for group decision support based on valued outranking relations', paper presented at the EURO XXIV conference, Lisbon, July 11–14.

Leyva-López, J. and Fernández-González, E., 2003. 'A new method for group decision support based on ELECTRE III methodology', *European Journal of Operational Research* **148**, 14–27.

Macharis, C., 2000. 'Strategische modellering voor intermodale terminals: socio-economische evaluatie van de locatie van binnenvaart/weg terminals in Vlaanderen', Vrije Universiteit Brussel, Brussels.

Macharis, C., 2005. 'The importance of stakeholder analysis in freight transport', *Quarterly Journal of Transport Law, Economics and Engineering* **8**, 114–26.

Macharis, C., Brans, J.P. and Mareschal, B., 1998. 'The GDSS Promethee procedure', *Journal of Decision Systems* **7**, 283–307.

Macharis, C., De Witte, A. and Ampe, J., 2009. 'The Multi-Actor, Multi-Criteria Analysis methodology (MAMCA) for the evaluation of transport projects: theory and practice', *Journal of Advanced Transportation* **43**,183–202.

Macharis, C. and Januarius, B., 2010. 'The Multi-Actor Multi-Criteria Analysis (MAMCA) for the evaluation of difficult transport projects: the case of the Oosterweel connection', paper presented at the 12th WCTR conferences, Lisbon, July 11–15.

Macharis, C., and Stevens, A., 2003. 'The strategic assessment of driver assistance systems: a multi-criteria approach', paper presented at the 7th Nectar conference 'A New Millennium. Are Things the Same?', Umeå, Sweden, 13–15 June.

Macharis, C., Verbeke, A. and De Brucker, K., 2004. 'The strategic evaluation of new technologies through multi-criteria analysis: the advisors case', in: Bekiaris, E. and Nakanishi, Y. (eds), *Economic Impacts of Intelligent Transport Systems, Innovations and Case Studies*, Amsterdam: Elsevier.

Martin, A.P., 1985. 'The first order of business: testing the validity of the objectives', Professional Development Institute, Ottawa.

Mason, R.O. and Mitroff, I.I., 1981. *Challenging Strategic Planning Assumptions: Theory, Cases and Techniques*, New York: Wiley.

Mercer, J., 2005. 'Prospect theory and political science', *Annual Review of Political Science* **8**, 1–21.

Munda, G., 2004. 'Social Multi-Criteria Evaluation (SMCE): methodological foundations and operational consequences', *European Journal of Operational Research* **158**, 662–77.

Ohtsubo, Y. and Masuchi, A., 2004. 'Effects of status difference and group size in group decision making', *Group Processes and Intergroup Relations* **7**, 161–72.

Ramanathan, R. and Ganesh, L.S., 1994. 'Group preference aggregation methods employed in AHP: an evaluation and an intrinsic process for deriving members' weightages', *European Journal of Operational Research* **79**, 249–65.

Regan, H., Colyvan, M. and Markovchick-Nicholls, L., 2006. 'A formal model for consensus and negotiation in environmental management', *Journal of Environmental Management* **80**, 167–76.

Reyna, V.F., Lloyd, F.J. and Brainerd, C.J., 2003. 'Memory, development, and rationality: an integrative theory of judgment and decision-making', in: Schneider, S. and Shanteau, J. (eds), *Emerging Perspectives on Judgment and Decision Research*, New York: Cambridge University Press, pp. 201–45.

Saaty T.L., 1988. *The Analytic Hierarchy Process*, New York: McGraw-Hill.

Savage, G.T., Nix, T.W., Whitehead, C.J. and Blair, J.D., 1991. 'Strategies for assessing and managing organizational stakeholders', *Academy of Management Executive* **5**, 61–75.

Steinel, W. and De Dreu, C.K.W., 2004. 'Social motives and strategic misrepresentation in social decision making', *Journal of Personality and Social Psychology* **86**, 419–34.

Stillwell, W.G., von Winterfeldt, D. and John, R.S., 1987. 'Comparing hierarchical and non-hierarchical weighting methods for eliciting multiattribute value models', *Management Science* **33**, 442–50.

Thomas-Hunt, N.C., Ogden, T.Y. and Neale, M.A., 2003. 'Who's really sharing? Effects of social and expert status on knowledge exchange within groups', *Management Science* **49**, 464–77.

Turcksin, L. and Macharis, C., 2009. *Proceedings of the BIVEC-GIBET Transport Research Day 2009*, Brussels: VUB University Press.

Turcksin, L., Macharis, C., Lebeau, K., Boureima, F., Van Mierlo, J., Bram, S., De Ruyck, J., Mertens, L., Jossart, J.-M., Gorissen, L. and Pelkmans, L., 2010. 'A Multi-Actor Multi-Criteria Analysis to assess the stakeholder support for different biofuel options: the case of Belgium', *Journal of Transport Energy* **39**, 200–214.

Walker, W.E., 2000. 'Policy analysis: a systematic approach to supporting policy-making in the public sector', *Journal of Multi-criteria Decision Analysis* **9**, 11–27.

Weiner, E. and Brown, A., 1986. 'Stakeholder analysis for effective issues management', *Planning Review* May, 27–31.

Index